WOMEN IN GOVERNANCE IN TRIPURA

About the Author

Dr. Bhola Nath Ghosh is currently a lecturer of Sociological Research Unit, Indian Statistical Institute, Kolkata. He is the author of *Rural Leadership and Development* (1996), as well as *Rural Women Leadership* (2002), co-editor and co-author of *Issues on Empowerment of Women* (2004) and *Tribal Farmer and New Agricultural Technology* (2005), Co-editor of *Women Speak* (2008).

His areas of interests are *Rural Development and Gender Issues.*

Dr. Ghosh has completed a course on Monitoring, Evaluation and Project Analysis at Norwich University, England.

WOMEN IN GOVERNANCE IN TRIPURA

Bhola Nath Ghosh

CONCEPT PUBLISHING COMPANY, NEW DELHI-110059

Cataloging in Publication Data—DK
Courtesy: D.K. Agencies (P) Ltd. <docinfo@dkagencies.com>

Ghosh, Bhola Nath, 1954-
Women in governance in Tripura / Bhola Nath Ghosh.
p. cm.
Includes bibliographical references (p.)
Includes index.
ISBN 13: 9788180695193
ISBN 10: 8180695190

1. Panchayat—India—Tripura. 2. Women in politics—India—Tripura. 3. Women in politics—India—Tripura—Charts, diagrams, etc. 4. Rural women—India—Tripura—Social conditions. 5. Rural women—India—Tripura—Economic conditions. I. Title.

DDC 320.840 820 954 15 22

ISBN-13: 978-81-8069-519-3
ISBN-10: 81-8069-519-0

First Published 2008

Published and Printed by
Ashok Kumar Mittal
Concept Publishing Company
A/15-16, Commercial Block, Mohan Garden
New Delhi-110059 (INDIA)

Phones : 25351460, 25351794
Fax : 091-11-25357103
Email : publishing@conceptpub.com

Foreword

This book is a commendable painstaking effort to assess women's participation in Panchayati Raj Institution in Tripura. The author, Dr. Bholanath Ghosh, has come all the way from Kolkata to Tripura to undertake this study on the role and achievements of women participating in decision-making institutions at the local level during the period 1994-1998. The study is the outcome of eulogistic work and it is the first of its kind for Tripura which has revealed a lot of facts relating to the issue of political empowerment of women in the State. No word is sufficient to congratulate the author for accomplishing such an important study on empowerment of women through Panchayati Raj Institution in Tripura.

The distinctive approach and methodology adopted by the author have enabled him to capture the socio-economic profile of the women members of six Gram Panchayats in two Districts of Tripura which is very important for analyzing their performances and achievements in Panchayati Raj Institution. His study shows how energetic attempts of the members made the Panchayati Raj Institution in rural areas under survey vibrant and lively. The gradual politicizations of the women members through various socio-political and developmental activities are other important findings of the present study.

The 73rd Constitution Amendment Act provided the much-needed opportunity for women in Tripura to actively participate in the decision making process of their locality through the political right that was conferred on them through the Central Act. Tripura had made great strides towards women's political empowerment since 1994. In this new era of Panchyati Raj, there are now more than 1900 women elected representatives to the three tiers of Panchayat in Tripura who give more meaning for democratic representation as they become spokespersons of the local community. Among its many penetrating observations, the study shows how Panchayati Raj Institution has helped to change local government beyond simply increasing the numerical presence of women in Tripura. The study also shows how women's political empowerment in Tripura through the Constitutional Amendment has shattered myths, like belief that they are passive and disinterested in political institutions, women are only proxy-members.

The awareness of women through their involvement in democratic movement and social work in the State has got a tradition in Tripura and this tradition is intensified when women were allowed to lead Panchayats. Through statistics, the author has shown that the numbers of women representatives in local self-government have increased over the period under his study. The present study also shows, the participating women in Gram Panchayats of Tripura are not only corruption free but also showing increasing interest towards literacy, education and knowledge to enrich them in particular and society at large. Majority of women members are aware about the fact that the strength comes not only from their numbers but also from their knowledge, information and skill. Thus women see training as very important part of their empowerment. The author expresses his confidence on the capabilities of women representatives by indicating that there is no lack of dynamism or leadership qualities among rural women of Tripura.

The author has identified the problems faced by the women involved in local self-government along with his valuable recommendations from grassroots study which may help the researchers, administrators, planners and policy makers. In this book the author has come out with many thoughtful suggestions where he has asserted for the need for providing other supportive and enabling conditions to the women members without which empowerment of women through Panchayati Raj is not possible in this deeply patriarchal and unequal socio-economic system. The writer has evinced committed interest in the empowerment of women through their participation in decision making institutions at all levels.

One welcome feature of the book is the lucid style of expression even as it deals with complicated issues relating to women's added responsibility of managing Panchayat along with their reproductive activities. This will make it useful and interesting to both social scientists and general readers. I am sure the book will commend itself to a wide cross-section of readers.

Agartala,
Tripura West
2nd April, 2007

Dr. Tapati Chakravarti
Chairperson
Tripura Commission for Women

Preface

The book is an outcome of curiosity. Curiosity convinced me to investigate and uncover what was the objective situation for women panchayat members; their socio-economic background, nature of panchayat participation, problems they confront and their performances.

The book is basically a report of a fact-finding mission on women panchayat members of two districts in Tripura.

The main inference of the study indicates that women's political participation is somewhat less than their participation in different walks of life. The masses of the rural women, who represent the majority of women in our country, spend most of time in the grim struggle for survival. They have little time left for political activities. Generally, women's participation in politics and social work was rare especially in the rural areas. Women participated in the freedom struggle, different democratic struggles and class struggles, but their number was very small especially because of their social status in the patriarchal society. They would remain confined within the households and concentrate on making their own personal homes. They would not be able to look after others in the society or think of issues, which were not directly related to their family welfare. Furthermore, their status in society, their levels of literacy and awareness of their legal rights as well as their limited knowledge of the procedures of Panchayati Raj Institution account for their low participation. Due to long drawn movements by women for equal status with men, there was change in the constitution in order that their participation in political and social activities get legal sanction, our enquiry starts from this point, namely, after reservation of seats for them in Self-Government bodies. There has been a considerable change in the situation due to enactment of 73rd Amendment to the Constitution of India in 1992.

With the passage of 73rd Amendment Act, 1992 India is at a crucial juncture in the evaluation of Panchayati Raj Institution. It has the potentiality to usher in new era in the participatory process and decentralized polity as it has conceptualized panchayats as 'Institution of Self-government'. Rural people have been entrusted upon to decide by themselves their felt needs. The Panchayat Acts of State Government of Tripura has been amended to incorporate the stipulations of the Central Act. Included in this Amendment was the reservation of seats, at all the tiers, for SC's and ST's as well as for women. One-third of the total members in each tier of the Panchayats would be reserved for women. The 1993 election, in Tripura, was held on the basis of this reservation. Though the women participated in the elected Panchayat in Tripura before 1993, their number was far less compared to the participation of men. From 1993 onwards participation of women became more, at least 33 per cent due to reservation, in the self-government bodies.

The study was made possible by research grant provided by Social Sciences Division of Indian Statistical Institute, Kolkata. I am grateful to my Institute and the Divisional Committee of Scientific Workers in Social Sciences for rendering material support for this study.

In undertaking and completing the field study I must acknowledge and indebtedness and gratitude to Honourable and respected Chief Minister of Tripura, Sri Manik Sarkar Sir, and Dr. Panchali Sarkar, for their inspiration and suggestions.

I express my gratitude to Prof. Manoranjan Pal of Indian Statistical Institute, Kolkata, Prof. Malabika Dasgupta, Department of Analytical and Applied Economics, Tripura University, Tripura, Dr. Utpal De, Reader, Department of Economics, North Eastern Hill University, Shillong, Meghalaya, who enriched this study with their valuable suggestions and comments. I also thank to Joyita Roy Chowdhury, Project Assistant at Indian Statistical Institute, Kolkata.

I thank the B.D.O. of the Dukli Block of West Tripura district, the B.D.O. of Kankraban Block of South Tripura district, Pradhans (Chair persons) and members of the Gram Panchayats of West and South Tripura districts and all respondents who provided all information.

I would like to thank Ms. Rebeka and Md. Salim, Tripura, for helping me in the collection of field-data.

I thank all the colleagues of Sociological Research Unit at Indian Statistical Institute for their understanding and kindness.

I am grateful to all villagers who provided hospitality and mental support, as we know most of the areas including our sampled villages in Tripura have a problem of insurgency. So, without help of villagers, it was almost impossible to conduct the study and without whose cooperation I would not have written a line. So, various individuals and officials of different Government departments and organizations in Tripura were kind enough to extend their co-operation to this humble endeavour. I am grateful to all of them.

Kolkata

Bhola Nath Ghosh

Contents

1

Background

Institutionalization of Panchayati Raj

'One of the tasks of nation building and development', writes Milton J. Esman 'is to bring members of the National Community into a network of relationship and institution which enable them to participate actively in decisions affecting their individual and their group welfare'[1]. While this is true for all nations, it has posed a considerable problem to the developing nations. This principle that members of the national community should have an opportunity to participate actively in decisions affecting their lives is accepted by most of the persons charged with the responsibility of shaping the destinies of these new nations. Various countries have, therefore, started experimenting with different types of politico-administrative institutions which would provide opportunities to people to take part in nation-building; the nature, character, and scope of such institutions vary depending upon the attitudes of their national elites and level of development of the country concerned. However, their capacities for mobilizing the effective participation of rural material and human resources have been dependent on the governmental process and structures.[2]

Our concern is only one aspect (Local Government) of Rural Development.

Panchayati Raj in Tripura has progressed a long way from its traditional to present day structure. Prior to independence the erstwhile princely state, Tripura, had an informal Panchayat system in both hills and plains. At that time the *Gaon Buras* or village chiefs, the ruler of villages, ruled under the guidance of the king. The system was very simple. The village chiefs had much power. They would tackle crimes and litigations chiefly by means of oath and ordeals. The justice was quick, visible and cheap. Each year a village council of any tribe consisting of four or five male members was formed through selection by the villagers in a meeting held at the beginning of the year. Over all village councils of every tribe had its own tribal council. Among the Bengalees, in every village a few members of elderly persons, having qualities of head and heart formed Panchayat. In any matter concerning the village, their decision was final. With the beginning of political turmoil during the first quarter of the 20th century, the village councils or Panchayats began to lose their power and with the out-break of the Second World War the system collapsed.

After independence efforts were made to revive and form a uniform structure of Panchayats in the state. For this, the Uttar Pradesh Panchayati Raj Act (Act XXVI of 1947) was extended to Tripura in 1959 and the statutory Gaon Panchayat was formed in 1962. In the Act, there was no provision for Panchayat at the block or district level. The village Panchayat had two wings, one was administrative wing called, Gaon Panchayat and the other was Nyaya Panchayat; the judicial wing. Gaon Panchayat was responsible for administrative and developmental functions. According to the Act, their duties were of two types, the mandatory and discretionary. The obligatory functions were the establishment, maintenance and supervision of public roads, ponds, wells, tanks, market, control of flood, epidemics, welfare of children and women and the development of agriculture, commerce and industry. The discretionary functions include the establishment of and maintenance of live stocks, improvement of public health etc. The Nyaya Panchayat was responsible for the establishment of justice. They could manage minor civil and criminal cases.

The Panchayat members were elected by Gram Sabha, consisting of adult residents of a village or of a group of contiguous villages. They were selected by way of counting and comparing the number of hands raised in favour of each candidate in a meeting of Gram Sabha, held on a ground. The strength of Gram Panchayat would vary from 9 to 13 on the basis of population. There was a provision of reservation of seats for the scheduled castes and tribes. The term of office of the Panchayat was five years. Nyaya Panchayat was constituted of some elected members from Gram Panchayat. Though there was no provision of block Panchayat, there was a Block Development Committee consisting of Gram Panchayat Prodhans and district Panchayat Officer. But the committee had basically no function or official duty.

In 1978, an Amendment took place and secret ballot system for the election of Gram Panchayat was introduced. Political parties were permitted to participate openly in election. From then Prodhans were elected directly. The function and power of the Panchayat were more or less as before. However, on account of political high-handedness, corruption, financial crunches, and illicit relation between political leaders and bureaucrats, the working of Panchayats was not satisfactory. The Nyaya Panchayats willingly or unwillingly would take some undesirable decisions and thus create problems. To remove these difficulties, in 1983, another Amendment took place and Tripura Panchayat Act, 1983 came into force in 1984. The Panchayati Raj Institutions started functioning on an increasing scale. They were assigned more tasks and thus sphere of work enhanced. The Nyaya Panchayat was abolished. From then onward the elected members from among them elects the Panchayat Pradhan. Political instability stopped the rural development process and was one of the major causes for the malfunctioning of the Panchayats. The Left front came to the power and started giving emphasis on democratic process at the village level. They gave much importance to Panchayat system and in accordance with the provision of 73rd Amendment Act, Tripura Panchayat Act, 1993 was passed. Accordingly, a 3-tier Panchayat system was formed all over Tripura. In the new Act, there are provisions of Panchayat not only at village level but also at block and district level. In the Act, much power has been given to the Panchayat and their responsibility has been increased remarkably.

Now different government developmental schemes are

being implemented through Panchayats. The Panchayats are given much financial assistance for different programmes. Now the Panchayat can impose tax on certain items within its limit and raise funds. Each year 'Pradhan' of a Panchayat within a stipulated time, as may be prescribed by the Panchayat Samiti, is to prepare a budget of income and expenditure for the following year and after passing in the Gram Panchayat meeting, place it before Panchayat Samiti for its approval. Similarly, the Panchayat Samiti and Zilla Parishad have to submit their budget to Zilla Parishad and State Government respectively.

Since the Panchayati Raj bodies are charged with the responsibility of rural development programmes in addition to traditional civic functions, they tend to have special relation with State Government, which is concerned with planned development.

The institutionalization of the ideal of Panchayati Raj, as units of self-government, has undergone several phases of development prior to the 73rd Constitutional Amendment. Participation of women in this process remained nominal and almost ineffective. Limited nominations and cooption of women since the year 1958 (following the recommendation of the Balwantrai Mehta Committee Report) may have ensured the physical presence of some women in the PRIs. However, such steps did not promote any scope for a perceptible impact. Women's groups and others to be the most logical first step towards women's effective political participation and gender equality gradually realized the imperative for an ensured presence of a "critical minority". The 73rd Amendment has fulfilled this lacuna and a million women are expected to be part of the three-tier power structure at the grassroots. Who are these women? How effective is their presence? Have they been able to make a breakthrough in the power structure in real terms? How are they facilitating the process of empowerment and social transformation envisaged for the PRIs and of women through them? Will a qualitative shift in power relations leading ultimately to equal sharing of power be brought about?

A micro level assessment of the situation was attempted through a survey of the elected women of Dukli Block and Kankraban Block in West Tripura and South Tripura districts in Tripura. The study was undertaken in two parts. A set of questions was used to identify the women panchayat members' socio-demographic background, the election process and their preparedness for the new role, the patterns of decision-making, support structures and the women panchayat members' views on development issues including economic needs, health needs etc., as well as their perception of the social and political issues. Further assessment was done in the second part of the study through a variety of communication techniques such as camps, small cluster meetings, observation etc.

Based on the 'directive principles' of Constitution of India, the Balawantrai Mehta Committee appointed by Government of India recommended democratic decentralization of administration. The Committee recommended that the development of rural society would necessitate self-governance bodies, because the rural societies cannot be changed from above. In the national plan, the necessities of rural societies are seldom reflected. So, the elected representatives of the people should be entrusted with the task of development administration. On the basis of this recommendation the process of evolution of Panchayati Raj started in Tripura as well as in other states of India. The Tripura Panchayat Act, 1957 and Zilla Parishad Act, 1963 enabled institution of Gram and Anchal Panchayats as well as Zilla Parishads. The Tripura Panchayat Act, 1973 enveloped both the Acts of 1957 and 1963 and took the shape of a comprehensive Act in which there was provision of three-tier system of Gram Panchayat at Anchal level, Panchayat Samiti in block level and Zilla Parishad at district level. There was election of all the three tiers of Panchayats on the basis of Adult franchise in Tripura. Different political parties participated in this election process. All these were done on the basis of 1973 Act.

In the meantime, there was a great change in the situation due to passing of 73rd Amendment to the Constitution of India in 1992, which is a landmark in the history of the evolution of the Panchayati Raj. The Amendment clearly laid out that

Panchayat is a self-Government institution that would be statutory and the State Government cannot dissolve this before the expiry of its terms resorting to legislation.

A state level Election Commission would conduct the entire election process right from listing of Voters, organizing voting and declaration of the result. Moreover, there would be a Finance Commission in each state in every five years, which would go into the economic conditions of the Panchayat bodies and recommend necessary actions for procurement of resources.

Included in this amendment was the reservation of seats at all the tiers for SC and ST as well as for women. One-third of the total members in each of the tiers of Panchayats would be reserved for women. The 1993 election in Tripura was held on the basis of this reservation as aforesaid. It, therefore, enabled the women to participate in the self-government bodies in greater strength. We do not however say that women participated in the Panchayats for the first time in 1993 but they were only a few in previous elections. From 1993, women became more numerous in the self-government bodies and were inducted into active political and social work. In this process the question of rural women leadership came to the forefront which initiated a systematic inquiry into the process of evolution of rural women leadership. In short, this is the background of the present study.

NOTES

1. Milton J. Esman, 'Politics of Development Administration', in *Approach to Development: Politics, Administration and Change*, (ed.), John D. Montgomery and William J. Siffin, New York, McGraw Hill, 1966, p. 63.
2. See Nicolas Luyks, 'Rural Governing Institutions,' in *Institutions in Agriculture Development*, (ed.), Melvin G. Blasé, Iowa State University Press, Ames, Iowa, 1971, p. 192.

2

Objectives

Generally women's participation in politics and social work was rare especially in the rural areas, except of course some noble and glorious exceptions. Women participated in the freedom struggle, different democratic struggles and class struggles, but their number was very small especially because of their social status in the patriarchal society. They would remain confined within the households and concentrate on making their own personal homes. They would not be able to look after others in the society or think of issues, which were not directly related to their family welfare. Due to long drawn movements by women for equal status with men, there was change in the Constitution in order that their participation in political and social activities get a legal sanction our enquiry starts from this point, namely, after reservation of seats for them in self-government bodies. The objectives of this study are as follows.

To find out:

(a) Whether election of women to Panchayat bodies made any remarkable change in the status of women in the rural areas and if so, how it was?
(b) How could the women members were motivated and/ or inducted into politics as well as in Gram Panchayat elections?
(c) What are the difficulties they might be facing for devoting time outside family? In other words, the contradiction of their role-playing in management of households and management of social affairs.

(d) Whether they are being able to perform their role in this new situation and the problem and prospects of such participation in social and political affairs?
(e) Whether there has been some sense of achievement in different works of women members in Panchayats?
(f) Whether the women members in Gram Panchayats are now able to make decision independently?

The research questions addressed are as follows:

1. What is the social, economic and cultural status of women who have been promoted as representative of the people?
2. What are their levels of awareness about socio-political situation and their exposure to outside world?
3. What problems they might be facing in their new roles from within and without their families?
4. What could they do with their uplifted status for her own, for her family and for the women and the society as a whole?
5. Do they like being placed in the administrative position and what prospects they expect out these?
6. Does their changed status alienate them from fellow women-folks, male-folks and their relations?
7. What are the difficulties they are facing which should be removed in order that they could discharge their duties as representative of the people as well as administrator?

Since we would be studying the phenomenon as and when it is happening, we would be able to get an insight into the process of politicization of the women. Moreover, the documentation would be an important aspect of the study.

Social thinkers, political administrators, planners as well as social activists would be able to get a clue from this documentation which would enable them to formulate legal and administrative policy for furtherance of the interest of women, who constitute around half of the population of the country.

3

Methodology

Because of limited resource and time of an individual researcher, the study was undertaken in two districts of Tripura covering a few Gram Panchayats, which is the lowest tier of Panchayat. The women elected to these bodies are all rural.

Standard sociological and anthropological methods of studying social phenomena have been followed in the study.

We have taken a census of all the members of Gram Panchayat under our study and ascertain their socio-economic and cultural status through a pre-ordained, pre-tested schedule.

In order to understand the process of induction and motivation, their problems in discharging the duties entrusted to them, the prospects of taking initiative and improving the qualities of leadership, we would undertake case studies for women leaders of different socio-economic and cultural status. We would formulate attitudinal questions to take stock of the suggestions made by them, their evaluation of themselves as well as others' evaluation about them.

So, canvassing of standardized schedule, questionnaire, and case studies would be the main method of collecting information.

For the present study, we have followed the method of survey research for which several field research techniques have been adopted.

The schedules were finalized after pre-testing. The researcher himself conducted the interviews and the data collected from this source was supplemented and tested by some other methods.

Non-Participant Observation

Because of the previous contact and stay in Agartala in Tripura, the researcher had substantial opportunity to observe the various aspects of social and political life of the panchayat members especially of women living in different parts of Tripura. Moreover, by observing them in meetings of Panchayats, paying informal visits to the houses of women and attending their informal gatherings, more information could be gathered. Insight was developed when the researcher had to participate actively in their informal decision-making process many a time because of his close knowledge of the area and familiarities with the Panchayat members especially of women of these areas.

Informal Discussions

Apart from the schedule and observation techniques, the researcher collected information through informal conversations. By staying for some time at the houses of women and developing good relations with them, the researcher had sufficient opportunity to have free and frank conversations sometimes individually and sometimes in-groups. This technique proved to be very effective in understanding their attitude towards existing social and political system. This also helped in understanding the political dynamics of the area under study and some 'inner stories' about the leaders.

Other Sources of Information

To understand the administrative aspects of Survey Report, the District Gazetteers, the Census Handbook and Economic and Statistical Analysis, as well as Government circulars issued from time to time were also consulted. Some of the information was also collected with the help of Block and Panchayat Officials.

At many places, it was necessary to rely upon the information supplied by Block Officials and the local knowledgeable person. However, cross-checking was made as far as possible to avoid incorrect and biased information.

To understand the social and political process of areas under study, it was thought to have been proper to use a combination of field study techniques, instead of replying upon a single method. Moreover, it is also very difficult to get a real insight into the problem by administering a well-prepared questionnaire alone. They always apprehend that if they say something against the powerful section of the society, they may be unduly harassed. As such, due emphasis was given on observation technique, case history and informal discussion. By staying with them for a long period, a close association was developed with the concern people. By this way more information was gathered.

As stated above, the researcher had the previous acquaintance with the people of study areas. However, at the time of field study, the elders of their families formally introduced him to the respondents. For establishing good rapport and administering the schedule he had to stay the whole day with them for months along. At the initial stage, stay for fifteen days, purpose of the study was explained to the respondents and informal contacts were established with them and data about the situation was collected.

To avoid the official touch to the interview, the time and place of interview was arranged according to respondent's convenience. The place of interview generally used to the houses of respondents and in rare cases the houses of their leaders. In some cases interviews were also arranged at the site of their work. Only a few respondents who were not easily approachable, were formally notified. In spite of all these precautions, some of them became too conscious and spoke in a guarded manner. However, after a few days, most of them became free and frank in expressing their views. The fieldwork process took about six months.

Along with interview, the techniques of observation and informal conversation were followed. The areas of the respondents were frequently visited, their community meetings were attended and informal discussions were also arranged at the places of interviews. To give a friendly touch to the entire fieldwork, the researcher frequently shared breakfast, teas and a glass of water with the respondents. As a researcher, I believe, it was necessary to observe their behaviour, habits, and attitudes to get actual facts collected. The researcher used to maintain a personal diary and used to write his observations and personal impressions of the respondent Panchayat members especially women such interactions. This technique proved to be quite useful in gaining insight into their attitude.

Time Schedule

Though the interview and collection of primary data were completed within six months, another one month was spent for follow up to bridge data gap, if any. Moreover scrutiny, transcription, tabulation and analysis of data took some time.

Limitations of the Study

This study was confined to six Gram Panchayats in two districts, which cannot be claimed as the true representative picture of rural leadership in Tripura. It is, therefore, necessary to test the relevance of my findings in other geographical area and Gram Panchayats, so that one can make any kind of generalization of leadership pattern and their activities.

Even then this exercise attempts to capture the diversities and typology of leadership functions in Gram Panchayats.

The analysis and exposition of the study are almost solely based on the responses of the sampled respondents. All interpretations and conclusions revolve around the findings from this state. Given the cultural, economic and political condition of the state, any extrapolation for other areas as has to be made cautiously.

Above all, due to two other factors such as communication and insurgency in the particular areas prohibited us to conduct the study with greater freedom.

4

Literature Review

We tried to explore the literature review for this study. To identify the problems of women and development not much work has yet been done in Tripura.

However, a book entitled *A Corpus of Tripura* was written by J. Gan. Chaudhury (1990), dealing with social conditions of Tripuri Women. Their economic condition was also touched upon. Girijan and Tripuri Women's situation was discussed in the book. According to him, Tripuri women's status is somewhere between that of Arunta Women of East Africa and the Iroquois Women of upper New York. Both men and women have equal opportunity for divorce. The Tripuri women are assiduous but they participate in taking decision on major issues.

A report of "Tripuri Commission for Women" and "Tripura University" dwelt on the status of women in Tripura. This discussed the characteristics (demographic, health and nutritional) of women. Besides, educational position was also discussed in the context of their work assignment. In addition, decision-making at home and in the public sphere has been given due attention. A chapter also made to include women work and status. In addition, decision-making at home and in the public sphere by women was also discussed in the report. The report discusses the vulnerability of women and tried to understand the acuteness and severity of their problem.

An attempt is being made to present the major findings of some materials available either in the form of book or dissertation or articles, which are somewhat related to our study.

Dennis Jack[1], in 'Socialization to Politics' tried to provide the "Major Problems of Political Socialization", which helps the researchers, who approached this research area for the first time and lacks a consistent overall picture, to fit together many bits and pieces of the literature in a consistent manner. After discussing the different agencies of political socialization, the author has tried to measure the impact of these variables on the respondents (i.e. students).

Mishra tried to study the process of political socialization and the impact it has on the social system in a north Indian village (Bihar village). In the introductory chapter the author has tried to provide a theoretical framework of political socialization, which is based on the studies made on this topic in some western countries. The author has tried to measure the impact of these variables on the respondents of the area under study. The author has finally tried to depict the process of change, which are occurring in the said village as a result of the process of socialization (Mishra, 1980)[2].

Imtiaz Ahmed[3] in his article "Women in Politics" points out that the real obstacle to equality in the political sphere lies in the division of spheres between men and women though legal provisions have not substantially allowed this. Inder Jeet Kaur[4] has found that women are no more behind men in the different spheres of life including politics. B.R. Nanda[5] observed that family influence plays an important role in shaping the participatory attitude of the women in politics.

B.R. Nanda[6] draws attention to the factor of family influence playing an important role in shaping the participant's attitude of the women, whether the atmosphere at home was nationalistic, and women also imbibed it.

Rao[7] pointed out that there were many prejudices about rural women, viz. they do not use their mind on political issues; they do according to the will and pleasure of their men-folk etc. She found this opinion as false. The women of Chickmaglur were found conscious of their voting right and they knew as to whom they should vote. They showed keen interest in political matters and took part in political meetings. Contrary to the findings of Rao, Khan[8] found that the rural women of Karnataka reported that their discussion for voting in favour of a candidate depended upon the advice of their husband or male members of their family. Norms of traditional society press them to obey their husband or other male members of their family. Khan also found that majority of women (Sixty-four per cent) did not favour equality in political activities, only fifteen per cent women were in favour of political activities and twenty-one per cent women were neutral (Khan, 1982).

Among the terms used in the Social demography literature are not only "Status of Women" (e.g., Dixon[9], 1978), but also "female autonomy" (Dyson[31] and Moorc, 1983), "Patriarchy" (Cain *et al.*[11], 1979), "rigidity of the Sex Stratification System" (Safilos-Rothschild[12], 1989), "women's rights" (Dixon[13], 1975) and "men's situational advantage" (Caldwell[14], 1981). All of these terms refer, its part, to some aspect of gender inequality. For example, implicit in most definitions of the status of women is a comparison with the status of men. Similarly, "female autonomy", usually refers to the extent to which women are free of men's control; "Male dominance", to the extent to which they are not free from such control; "patriarchy", also to the extent to which men control women; "women rights", to the rights of women as compared to these of men; and "situational advantage", to men's advantage as compared to women's.

According to Atul Kohli[15], "The new Panchayat in West Bengal represent a break from the past political patterns in rural India. The Panchayat in West Bengal or in most parts of India have seldom been free of domination by landlords or rich peasants...this is beginning to change in West Bengal. The CPM is carving out a pattern of political organization in rural West Bengal, rare in India, namely that of involving a penetration of the countryside without depending on the larger landowners, G.K. Lieten's[16] study shows that a new type of leadership has come to dominate the stage of lower levels in the system of political devolution. Poor peasants, agricultural labourers, and therefore, also the scheduled castes and tribes have very much come to the forefront on account of the composition of CPI(M) panels. Chattopadhyay & Sen[17] also bring out this feature of the West Bengal Panchayati Raj system.

The study on 'Panchayat and Rural Development' also

confirms the hypothesis that the Panchayat in West Bengal have a pro-poor orientation in respect of selection of beneficiaries under the different schemes. The data show that the beneficiaries have come mostly from the weaker and poorer sections of the society, and we have got mostly from the weaker and poorer section of the society, and we have got no evidence which proves that the rural rich are influencing the decision-making processes in Panchayat. The findings of the study stand in sharp contrast to the findings of a smaller study done by Prodosh Nath[18]. Nath who had studied the social background of the Panchayat leadership of Purulia in 1980, had found that the representation of marginal farmer families in the Panchayats under study was 2.8 per cent and that of small farmers, 15 per cent and the rest 82.2 per cent came from the richer section of the village community.

Neil Webster[19] had found the role of Panchayat in making use of NREP (National Rural Employment Programme) and RLEGP (Rural Landless Employment Guarantee Programme) funds remarkable as these programmes were used to assist genuinely deprived section of the rural population. Madhura Swaminathan[20] showed that whereas access to IRDP in Tamil Nadu remained restricted to friends and protégé of the local landlords with considerable leakage, in West Bengal, in terms of caste, gender and assets (land) the degree of leakage of non-target groups is remarkably low. The relatively low degree of leakage in West Bengal can be attributed to the active participation of the Panchayat Samiti and the Gram Sabha in the process of selection of beneficiaries. In Tamil Nadu there was hardly any democratic participation in the process of selection of beneficiaries.

David Ziblati (1965)[21] in an article showed how extra-curricular activities play an active role in socializing the high school students of America. It has been analyzed that extra-curricular activities are supposed to teach the attributes of good citizenship. The study found no direct relationship between participation in high school extra-curricular activities and attitude towards politics. The teenagers that participated feel more integrated into the formal high school status system. The feeling of integration is associated with social thrust. The more socially trusting teenager have a more positive attitude towards politics. The teen agers have a more positive attitude towards politics. The teen agers from working class background participate least, but are more likely to see the informal status system as open. It has been inferred that these students were insulated by a belief in equality of opportunity from a direct awareness of how the status system actually operates.

Jagodzinski Wolfgany (1975)[22] in his article analyses two assumptions of the classical socialization model which are central to certain theories of values and values change and which have played an important role in political sociology for some time. (i) Value orientations are acquired in the early stage of the life cycle; (ii) they structure political attitude and determine political behaviour, indirectly or directly. It has been analysed that value orientations, therefore, must mediate between the indicators of socialization influences, on the one, and political attitude and behaviour, on the other.

The kind of socialization necessary for able participation of women in Panchayat and other political activities must have some relevance to value orientation.

Literature Survey of Panchayat Members

My previous study was an empirical study on the subject[23]. The study was confined to three Gram Panchayats in the district of Birbhum and three in the district of Midnapore. The study brings out the women members are capable not only in identifying the problem areas in their locality but also of playing active role in pursuing the programme. Women are free to move from one village to another without being accompanied by the male members. The honour of the women panchayat members in the society has been augmented. They have become conscious of their legal rights. They are attaching more importance to the protection of the rights of the women either in property related or in matrimonial cases. They are organizing meeting to make women aware of the legal rights and encouraging them to claim their rights. Women have also become conscious about the protection of the environment. The problem identified by the women respondents include financial dependence on their male folk who often exploit this weakness lack of attitudinal change in all spheres of life and the like.

Manoshi Roy profiles a woman GP *Pradhan* in Bankura in 1996.[24] Chayya Patra, who was nominated by the CPI (M), became Pradhan at the age of 22. She was encouraged and supported by her family. She has been relieved of many of her household responsibilities. In child care she receives adequate help from the female members of the family.

As a woman Pradhan she feels that she has additional responsibility to ensure that social justice is done to the women of fifty-six villages in all spheres of their lives. She perceives herself to be duty-bound to respond to women's critical needs of literacy, legal rights, health, wage equality etc. As a result of her being woman Pradhan many women specific issues are discussed in their GP meeting. Many a time women in distress approached her with their peculiar difficulties which would not have been possible had there been a male Pradhan.

Manoshi has reported that Chayya's position has been acknowledged by the community at large. She has, however, confessed that she does not have a free reign over everything in the GP because her party regulates her activities and endeavours. This is quite expected in a party-based panchayat system as in West Bengal.

Institute for Socio-Economic Development, Bhubaneswar, did a study on the political empowerment of women through panchayats[25]. The study shows that the younger generation (18-30 years, 52 per cent) followed by the middle age group (31-50 years with 46 per cent) have greater presence in the PRIs in West Bengal.

Married women have come forward in the state to participate in the grassroots democracy, as most respondents are married. More educated women (88%) have come forward to join these institutions in the state. Only more than one-fourth of the respondents depend on agriculture (92%).

In respect of political awareness and performance in panchayats the study observes that almost one-fourth of the respondents have prior experience in politics through their involvement in movements such as farmers' movement and women's movement in the state. Almost three-fourth of the respondents had no prior knowledge on PRIs which shows that most of them are new entrants into the system. All the respondents in this study are politically affiliated where elections to the PRI are party based. CPI(M) (64.5%) has strong presence in the local government followed by All India Trinamool Congress (17.3%). BJP and Jharkhand parties have very negligible presence in PRIs of the state. The respondents have greater involvement in the grassroots democracy through regular attendance of meetings of PRIs and ability to communicate in such meetings. Opinions of almost two-third of the respondents are taken seriously in the meetings whereas opinions of the rest that mostly belong to the lowest positions are not taken seriously. The respondents with higher positions are members of various standing committees with the responsibilities of supervision of development programmes. Except being involved in the routine works of local government, the respondents are not involved in social/gender issues that women comfortably present.

More than three-fifth of the respondents get co-operation from bureaucracy in their functioning. Most of the respondents know about powers and functions of Gram Sansad as well as Gram Sabha and attend their meetings regularly, which indicates their greater involvement in the grassroots democracy.

Lieten studied women's participation in Memari block in the district of Bardhaman. He found that most of the women participated in public life before getting elected. They have been nominated by the party in consultation with the Mahila Samiti. They are by and large in their twenties. Most of them come from the poor families, are agricultural labourers themselves and usually do not have much educational accomplishment.

Lieten also studied women members in the Ramnagar block in the district of Midnapur (East). The team interviewed 20 members all of whom have confirmed the picture of improving educational achievement. Most of them studied up to class VIII some were wives or daughters and some were teachers.

The other study on the all-women panchayat done by Asim Mukhopadhyay in 1995 attempts to present a profile of the members to access the performance of the panchayats[6]. Of the 13 members, nine are less than 28 years old. There are 7 scheduled tribe members and two members from scheduled castes. In regard to their educational qualifications, only one is at the under-graduate level, two have passed the secondary examination and three have crossed the secondary level. From the analysis of data about their occupational background it is found that eight had farm lands, one is a dress maker, one works as a cook and one as a primary school teacher, one is a housewife, one is still a student. All the members belong to peasant families and four of the member households still depend on agriculture.

All the SC and ST members are alert, articulate, inquisitive and determined. They do not have any significant academic background. Except for two they do not have much political experience and none had ever served in any panchayat.

The performance of the GP is remarkable. The IRDP loans were given to 53 persons. The panchayat has leased out ponds to mobilize resources. It has arranged all infrastructural facilities, to start training-cum-production centres of reading made garments for the economic empowerment of the women. It has played a leading role in the literacy campaign.

Mukhopadhyay has identified some failures too. It has failed to create social forests at 12 sites. The DWCRA project on basket making at Phulbani has not made much headway. The entire business is controlled by a Tamluk-based Marwari. It was expected that panchayat would set up a non-profiteering body to control the business but in vain.

Another study on the subject done by this author along with Chandan Datta in 1999 in the district of Birbhum sought to collect data about the socio-economic and political background of the women members in GPs, to tap the role perceptions of the members and to identify the problems they face while playing their roles[27]. The sample included 108 members out them there were 8 chairpersons, 16 vice-chairpersons. The data indicated that almost all the members were newcomers. The study showed that most of them were young. One-third of the office bearers belong to the age-group 18-39. A little more than 50 per cent of them are married, thus having family commitments which, as they have reported, do not stand in the way of their work. Only 11 per cent of them are illiterate. While 50 per cent of them do not have any lands, the rest have small lands. One-third of them, are engaged in household activities and one-fourth are connected with agricultural work. The financial dependence of the women on the male members is very high. One-third of them has been in politics for at least five years. Their perception about the role of the panchayats, in general and their role in women's development in particular is confused. Only a few of them are aware about the 73rd Amendment of the Constitution. Nearly 90 per cent of them attend meeting and nobody has reported about gender discrimination. More than 50 per cent of them have reported that they do not have any idea about the West Bengal Panchayat Act. The problems identified by them relate to the lack of information about the schemes, every-increasing demands of the people and growing dependence of the people on the Panchayats.

Joshi-Adhikari Institute of Social Studies did an empirical study in 1998[28]. The study districts included Midnapur, Murshidabad and North 24-Parganas. These Panchayat Samitis were taken up for field investigation. The purpose of the study was to assess the impact of women empowerment. The findings demonstrate that women are playing their roles properly. It has been found that 75 per cent of the constituents approach women functionaries with their problems, the rest make their way to panchayats through political parties and other channels. The incidence of attendance of women in panchayat meetings and proposal initiated by them is high. The same has been the case with regard to women involvement in major programmes of the panchayats such as Development of Women and Children in Rural Areas (DWCRA).

The study has, however, noticed marginalization of women in some panchayats. Interestingly, this is not due to gender discrimination but rivalry among the political parties. This is matter of concern, and this issue needs to be addressed properly by political parties.

The research has convincingly brought out that empowerment has exposed the mobilizing potential of women panchayat functionaries. The village women now come to the panchayat office and place their problems before the women functionaries. They find themselves comfortable in interacting with them.

The field study observes a positive change of attitude in respect of women's role in society. There is no longer any strong objection to their coming out of the domestic boundaries and also taking part in politics.

The study, however, ends up with a word of warning. It has been argued that the gains of empowerment are to a considerable extent neutralized by the discouraging trends towards dowry, torture and violence against women and discrimination between male and female children. There is a slow recognition of women's problems. One Pradhan regretted the role of the police administration.

Dilip Ghosh did an interesting work on the placement of women as heads of offices in different tiers of panchayat bodies in 1993 when reservation of seats for the women was made for the first time[29]. He examines this issue taking into account the proportion of women in the bodies under study. The findings bring out a disappointing picture. In Zilla Parishad, there was no Sabhadhipati although in percentage terms the share was 33.28. In Panchayat Samiti, women representatives accounted for 33.65 per cent but only 0.25 per cent of them headed these bodies. At the Gram Panchayat level 5.7 per cent of the Pradhans were women.

Aurabinda Ghosh collected data to find out representation of women in the different standing committees and their assignments in 1997[30]. incidentally, the PS works through standing committees headed by *karmadhyakshyas*. However, all the PSs in West Bengal except those in South 24-Parganas, Malda and Siliguri Mahukuma Parishad were taken up. The district-wise representations of the *karmadhyakshyas* clearly indicate that women as *karmadhyakshyas* are only 16.55 per cent, although their strength was to the extent of 33.65 per cent. It reflects gender bias. While finding out the assignments given to the women it has been noticed that women have been assigned such works as health, education, relief, social work and the like. They were not given such functions as lands, forest, irrigation, and agriculture. According to the scholar, there is a clear divide between the welfare functions and development functions. Women's role has been confined to the welfare domain.

There are two studies on the all-women panchayat. Earlier there was one all-women panchayat in Midnapur district. After the election in 1988 one more such panchayat has been added and it is located in the same district. The winds of change are sweeping the panchayat[31]. Nobody dies of hunger. The socio-economic scene has undergone a basic change. There are 14 primary schools and one high school. Out of 12,560 population of the panchayat only 1350 have remained illiterate due to old age and poor eyesight. School dropout is 10 per cent. Assets of the panchayat include 300 acres of forest area and 32 acres of mango groove. Mango groove fetches one and half lakh rupees yearly. Panchayat earns about 30,000 to 35,000 yearly from fishery. It gets about Rs. 5 lakh as toll from the wooden bridge.

In 1933 PR elections they ultimately stood for elections and were sponsored by parties. We have been appraised that when the constituencies became reserved, parties had to search for women candidates, not capable candidates as such. At the beginning local level party leaders searched for required number of women candidates from the inner circle of their family women. Because of unwillingness and unavailability of required number of women candidates from among themselves, party leaders shifted searchlight to families of general party members. Because of compulsion of reserved seats, political parties in most cases persuaded male family party members or supporters to seek and secure consent of their women.[32] Though male family members motivated most women members to stand for the hustings, the initiative of parties was no less significant. Those women who finally stood for the PR elections might have attended party meetings or cast vote for the respective party candidates but they were not definitely considered for public posts in earlier times. But for the reservation those women would not have been members of panchayat and parties would not have brought them to political institutions.

The parties almost unilaterally selected the candidatures of women respondents, though husband or in-laws informed party leaders about their readiness. Only 6 per cent women tried to contest election by own effort. In fact it entails that they spontaneously volunteered to be at the fray and parties later back them up. It should not be taken to mean that anybody contested independently. In view of party based elections almost all candidates including women have invariably to embrace party support and it is vindicated by the responses of women respondents.

Because of traditional values, segregation of society along sex lines women in rural India have no other alternative role 'than that of wife and mother[33] where family is the hearth and heaven and anything beyond it tends to be despised. Women's predominant role as wife and mother has the direct bearing on limiting assumption of other roles[34]. Duverger (1955: 129) is still convincing in arguing that men are the medium between women and political world.

If women are handicapped by the role of wife and mother, any additional role assignment would surely upset the delicate balance in sex based division of labour. It is no doubt true that by now women have joined in various socio-economic and political activities. But almost everywhere they are caught in a dilemma of role adjustment. Rather than role redefinition, role expansion is more visible for women. The data of Bhoite (1987: 17-18) proved that genesis of role conflict for women lies in unchanging role expansion in families and its magnitude can only be lessened if there is corresponding change in family structure and value. Against this backdrop it is worth examining whether public roles are at variance with domestic roles for women panchayat members.

NOTES

1. Dennis Jack, *Socialization to Politics*, p. 503, 1973.
2. Mishra, S.N. *Political Socialization in Rural India*, Inter-India Publications, p. 153, 1980.
3. Ahmed, Imtiaz, Women in politics in Devaki Jain's (ed), *Indian Women*, New Delhi: Publication Division Ministry of Information and Broadcasting, Government of India,
4. Kaur, Inderjeet, *Status of Hindu Women*, Allahabad: Chugh Publication: 1963.
5. Nanda, B.R., *Indian Women: From Purdha to Modernity*, New Delhi: Vikas Publishing House: 1976.
6. Basu, Aparna, The Role of Women in the Indian Struggle for Freedom, in B.R. Nanda (ed.), *Indian Women: From Purdha to Modernity*, New Delhi, Vikas Publishing House, 1976.
7. Rao, N.J. Usha, *Women in Developing Society*, New Delhi: Ashis Publications, 1983.
8. Khan, Mumtaz Ali, *Status of Rural Women in India*, New Delhi: Uppal Publishing House, 1982.
9. Dixon, Ruth B., *Rural Women at Work: Strategies for Development in South Asia*, Battimore: John Hopkins University Press, 1978.
10. Dyson,, Tim and Mick Moore, On kinship structure, female autonomy, and demographic behaviour in India, in *Population and Development Review*, 9 (March), pp. 35-60, 1996.
11. Cain, Mcad, Syeda Rokeya Khanam and Shamsun Nahar, Class, Patriarchy, and Women's work in Bangladesh, in *Population and Development Review*, 5 September, pp. 405-438, 1979.
12. Safilos-Roths Child, Constantina, Female Power, autonomy and demographic change in the third world, pp. 117-132 in R. Anker, M. Buvinic and N.H. Youssef, (eds.) *Women's Roles and Population Trends in the Third World*, London: CromHelm, 1982.
13. Dixon, Ruth B., Women's Rights and Fertility. Reports on Population/Family Planning, No.17 (January), 1975.
14. Caldwell, John C. The Mechanisms of Demography Change in Historical Perspective, *Population Study*, 35 (March): pp. 5-27, 1981.
15. Atul Kohli, Parliamentary Communism and Agrarian Reform Evidence from India's West Bengal, Asian Survey, 1983, p. 794.
16. G.K. Lieten, 'Panchayat Leaders in West Bengal District', *Economic and Political Weekly*, October 1, p. 2075, 1988.

17. Basudev Chattopadhyay and Prantosh Sen, Who Controls Rural West Bengal? A Case Study of Gram Panchayat Members of Murshidabad District', *Socialist Perspective*, Vol. 19, No. 4, 1999.
18. Prodosh Nath, 'Panchayat and Rural Development', *Society and Change*, October-December, 1982.
19. Neil Webster, Panchayati Raj and Decentralization of Development Planning in West Bengal, Calcutta, K.P. Bagchi, p. 131, 1992.
20. Madhura Swaminathan, Village Level Implementation of IRDP: Comparison of West Bengal and Tamil Nadu, *Economic and Political Weekly*, Vol. XXX, No. 13, pp. 17-27, 1992.
21. David Ziblati, *High School Extra-curricular Activities and Political Socialization*, 361, 30-32. The Annals of American Academy of Political and Social Sciences, 1965.
22. Jagodzinski Wolfgany, Social Structure, Value Orientation and Party Commitment, the problem of socialization model, *Zeritschrift for Sociology* 10, 2 April, 81, pp. 170-191, 1988.
23. Asim Mukhopadhyay, 'Kultikri: West Bengal's only All Women Gram Panchayat', *Economic and Political Weekly*, June 3, 1995.
24. Prabhat Datta and Chandan Datta, *Women Panchayat Members in West Bengal* (unpublished), Participatory Research in Asia, New Delhi, 1999.
25. Bhola Nath Ghosh, 'Women Leadership in Gram Panchayat: Prospects and Constraints', *Socialist Perspective*, June-September, Kolkata, 1999.
26. Manoshi Roy, 'A Woman Panchayat Pradhan in Bankura: A Profile' *Uma Prachar*, February, Bangalore, 1996.
27. Institute for Socio-Economic Development, Bhubaneswar. (unpublished), 2000.
28. Satyabrata Datta *et al.*, *Impact of Women Empowerment: A Pilot Study of West Bengal Panchayat* (unpublished), Joshi-Adhikari Institute, Kolkata, 1998.
29. Dilip Ghosh, 'Women Panchayat Members as Heads of Offices: A Study in West Bengal', *Journal of Rural Development*, October-December, 1995.
30. Aurabinda Ghosh, Inside-Outside Dichotomy in Panchayati Raj Institutions in West Bengal, *The Administrator*, October-December, 1997.
31. *Panchayat Update*, June, 2001.
32. Mitra, apprehended that most of the women candidates in West Bengal assumed office virtually by default as women were

selected from where male of the families could make it for women's reservation. 'Changing Role of Women in Bengal Panchayats'. *Down to Earth*. Vol. 2(4), p.22, 1993.

33. D'Souza, Alfred (ed.). *Women in Contemporary India* Manohar, New Delhi, 1995.
34. Lipset, S.M., *Political Man*. Doubleday. New York, p. 92, 1980.

5

Area of Study

Tripura was a princely State whose dynasty of tribal kings stretches back to antiquity. After rule by Khilji dynasty was established in Bengal in 1240, Tripura became a tributary State to the rulers of Bengal. Later, the East India Company extracted a tribute on the accession of every new prince, sending him a deed of acknowledgement and robe of honour in return. After 1857, there was no treaty between the British government and the rulers of Hill Tipperah (as the British then called Tripura) but the Rajas paid a succession duty to the Government (Hunter, 1873 : 461).

After India became independent, on 15 October 1949, the Regent Maharani of Tripura acceded to the Indian Union as a 'C' category State. Tripura became a Union Territory in November 1956. A popularly elected ministry was formed in Tripura in July 1963 and since then the State has had a government elected on the basis of Universal Adult Franchise. Later, after passing of Northeast Areas (Reorganization) Act on 30th December 1971, Tripura attained full-fledged statehood on the 21st January, 1972. It is situated between latitudes 22°56′ and 24°32′ north, and longitude 91°09′ and 92°20′ east. It is the third smallest State in the country and covers an area of 10,491.69 sq. km. Tripura is a land-locked State, surrounded by Bangladesh on its north, south and west. The length of its international Border is 856 km, while it shares a 53 km-long border with Assam and a 109 km-long border with Mizoram.

The partition of India in 1947 was a defining event in the history of Tripura, and had an enduring effect on the process of social and economic development in the State. The partition was perhaps the largest movement of evicted people in modern history. The partition had a dramatic effect on both the economy and the Demography of the state. The partition resulted in a huge infrastructural and economic setback for Tripura. The partition thus aggravated the geo-political isolation of Tripura and indeed, of entire North Eastern region.

The state is situated in thc southwest extreme corner of the north-eastern region spread over an area of 10, 492 sq. km. About 70 per cent of the total area of the state are hilly, leaving very little area cultivable. About 60 per cent of the total area of the state are classified as forest under the ambit of the Forest Conservation Act. Despite being geographically the smallest state of the north-eastern region, it is the second most populous state in the region following Assam. The present population is 31,99,203 (Census of 2001).

Natural gas deposits are among the most important features of Tripura's natural resource base. Natural gas has been struck in Baramura Hills and in Rokhia in South District and natural gas-based thermal power plants have been set up at both places. The hills of Tripura have red laterite soil which is porous and lacks essential mineral salts, so the irrigation and fertilizers are needed to make it suitable for cultivation. It have alluvial soil. However, the alluvial soil is sandy, lacks the capacity for water retention, and in humus and essential nutrients.

With historical transformation, the demographic composition of the state underwent significant changes. Till independence it was a tribal majority state (approximately 56 per cent in 1921 and about 51 per cent in 1931 and 1941). Subsequently, Tribal; was reduced to minority owing to the influx of people across the border. The present composition of the population is about 31 per cent tribal, 16 per cent SC, about 30 per cent OBC and the rest are others (Census Report, 2001, Provisional Population Totals).

Table 1: Area and population of Tripura, by district, 2001

District	*Area (in sq. km.)*	*Share of Total Area %*	*Population*	*Share of Total Population (%)*
West Tripura	2,996.8	28.6	15,32,982	47.9
South Tripura	3,051.5	29.1	7,67,440	24.0
Dhalai	2,348.1	22.4	3,07,868	9.6
North Tripura	2,095.3	19.9	5,90,913	18.5
Tripur State	10,491.7	100.0	3,199,203	100.0

The State is divided into four districts, namely, West Tripura, South Tripura, Dhalai (formed in 1995), and North Tripura. Agartala, the capital, is in West Tripura.

Agartala was the capital of Tripura since the time of Maharaja Krishna Manikya (1760-83) who had shifted the capital from Udaipur to this place.

Ujjayann Palace is situated in the heart of Agartala town. The palace has recently been acquired by the State government and now houses the legislative Assembly, besides a few Government offices.

Agartala became the capital of the State during the time of Maharaja Krishnakishore Manikya (1830-50). It has remained since then the seat of the State headquarters. Maharaja Birendra Kishore Manikya (1909-23) who was a good artist and is said to have prepared himself the plan of the Palace built Kunjaban Palace of Agartala.

Rabindranath Tagore during his seventh and last visit to Agartala in 1926 stayed in the eastern apartment of this Palace. One could get a distant view of the Baramura Hills on the eastern horizon from the round (*gol*) verandah, attached to this eastern part. This verandah has been the "mute witness of many a dear moments" when the poet composed a few popular songs (all incorporated in the Vaikali series).

Selection of Districts, Blocks and Gram Panchayats

In consideration of individual capability to undertake the study, three Gram Panchayats from each of the districts of West Tripura and South Tripura were undertaken. It was natural for me to be tempted to take up the Mirza Gram Panchayat under Kankraban Block, under South Tripura, which was an all women affair in the previous election. 'All the members of this Panchayat were women' was the merit of this selection. Kankraban Block is situated nearer to Udaipur town.

Besides Mirza Gram Panchayat, we chose another two Gram Panchayats, namely, Purba Mirza and Dakshin Mirza under the same block.

In West Tripura, we took three Panchayats under Dukli Block adjacent to Agartala, the state-capital which again is district head-quarters of the Tripura. Dukli is connected with Agartala by metal road. The Gram Panchayats are Dukli, Rajlakshminagar and Paschim Pratappur under the same block.

Not all the Gram Panchayat studied are homogeneous in nature. There are economic, social as well as cultural variations besides ethnic variations among them. It should be mentioned that all the Panchayats are predominantly agricultural and all of them are rural under any definition.

Dukli block is one among the 19 blocks in West Tripura district. Still it is predominantly an agricultural area, split up into two kinds, namely low-lying double cropped area and another an undulating, dry and mono-cropped area.

Dukli Gram Panchayat is one of 12 Gram Panchayats under Dukli block. It is composed of '28 moujas' and total population is 11,265, out of the population males are 6230 and females are 5035.

Rajlakshminagar Gram Panchayat is composed of 29 'moujas' of which one is uninhabited and total population is 11270—male 6028 and female 5242.

Paschim Pratappur Gram Panchayat is composed of 25 'maujas' and total population is 6320—male 5321 and female 2799.

Kankraban is a block under Udaipur sub-division of South Tripura district and situated by the side of the metal road between Mirza, a brisk commercial centre and Udaipur. A very few private buses ply between the two towns.

There are 10-Gram Panchayats under the Kankraban block, out of these we have chosen Mirza, Purba Mirza and Dakshin Mirza. All the Gram Panchayats are under Kankraban Panchayat Samiti, which is composed of 29 'moujas' and out of which two uninhabited moujas are there in each of these three-Gram Panchayats.

In all villages of six-Gram Panchayats under West Tripura and South Tripura districts, residential areas are divided along caste lines. Each of the caste groups resides in separate hamlet within the villages. In predominantly tribal villages the residential pattern is according to ethnic origin. The non-tribal live in separate hamlets.

All these six Panchayats are being given equal emphasis, but there are ethnic variations among them. It is needless to mention that the economics of all the Panchayats are predominantly agricultural.

MAP 1: NORTHEAST REGION

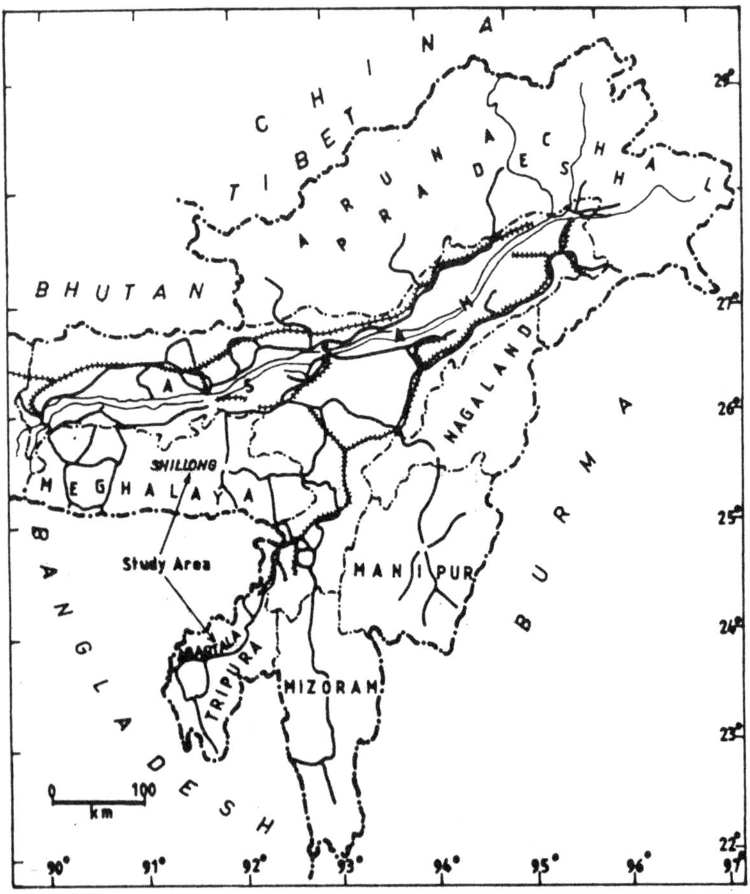

MAP 2: TRIPURA

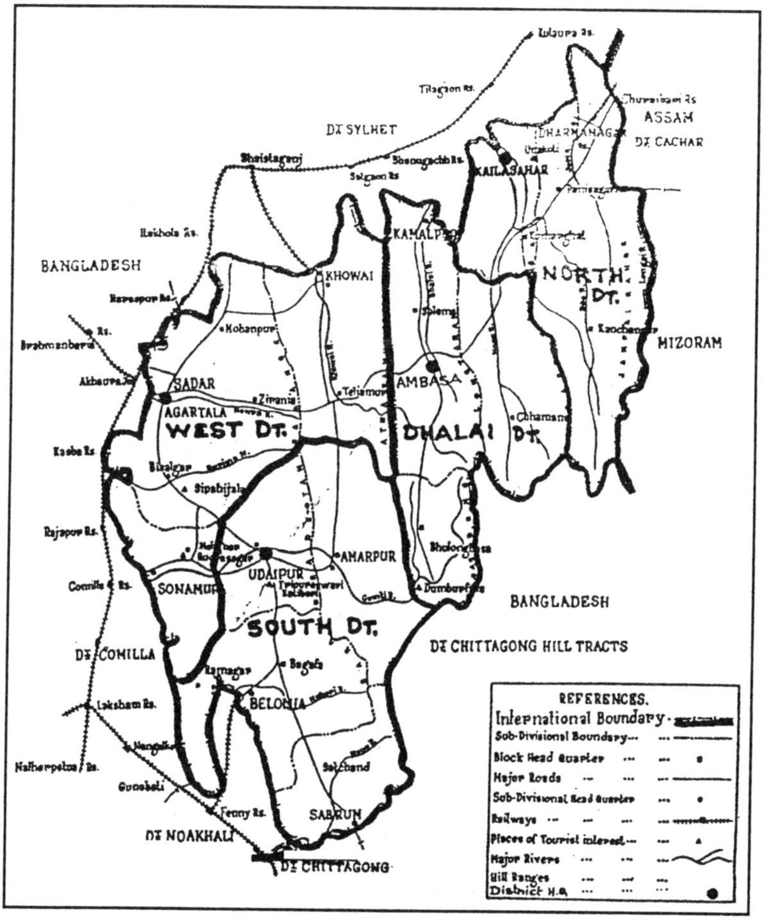

MAP 3: TRIPURA WITH GRAM PANCHAYAT SAMPLE

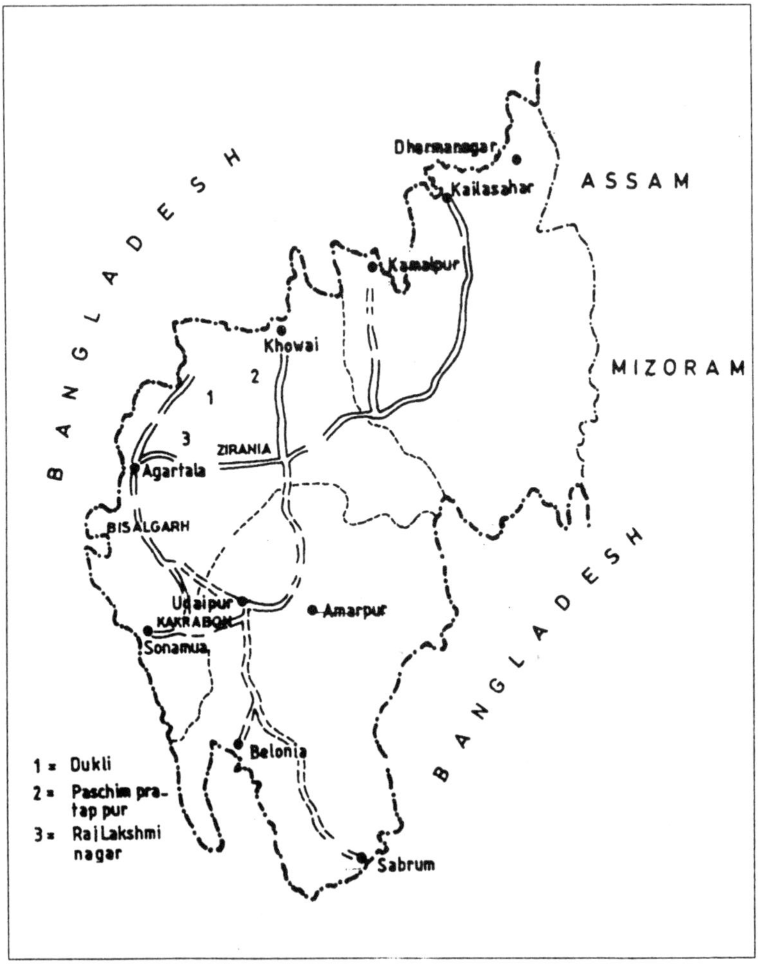

MAP 4: MIRZA GRAM PANCHAYAT

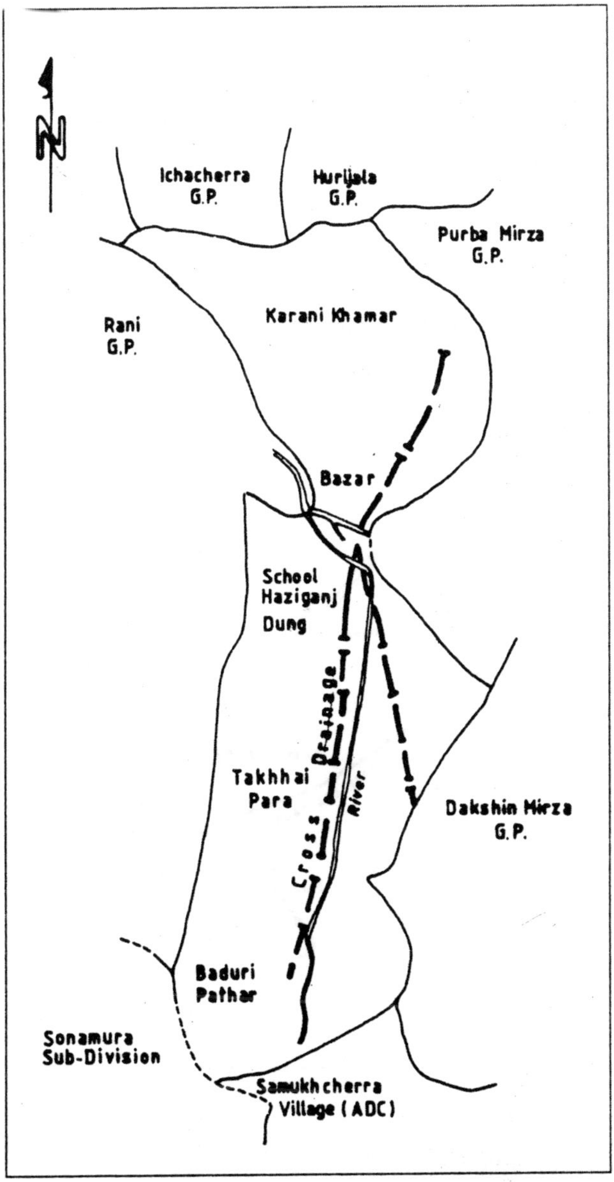

Map 5: Daskhin Mirza Gram Panchayat

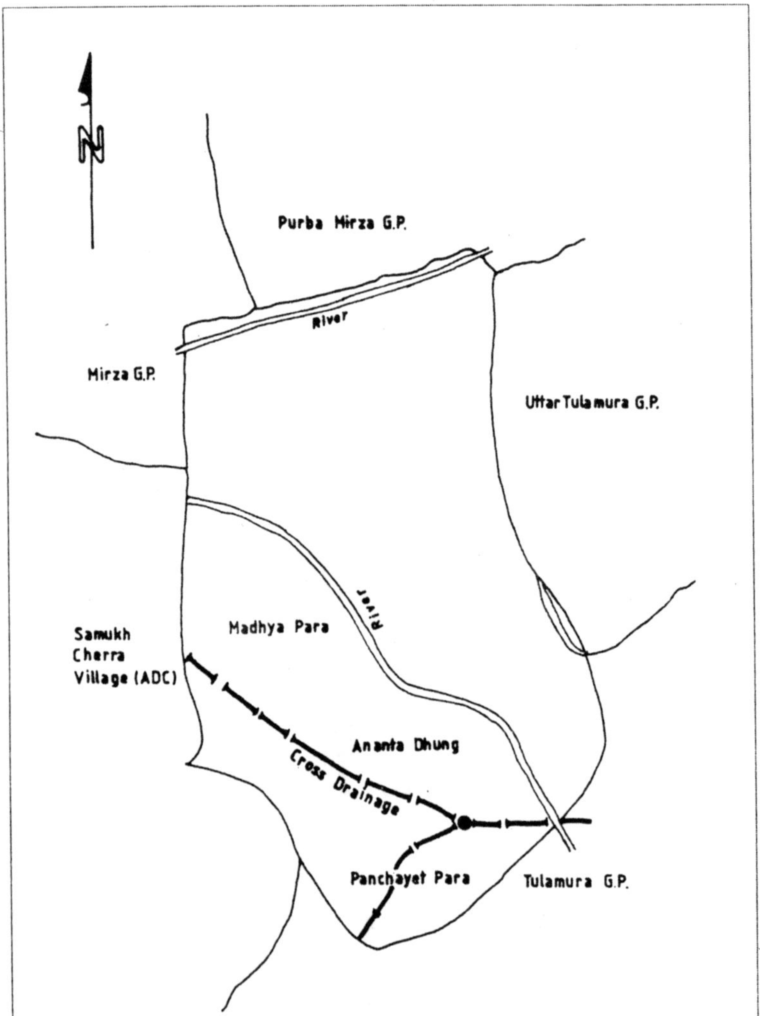

Map 6: Purba Mirza Gram Panchayat

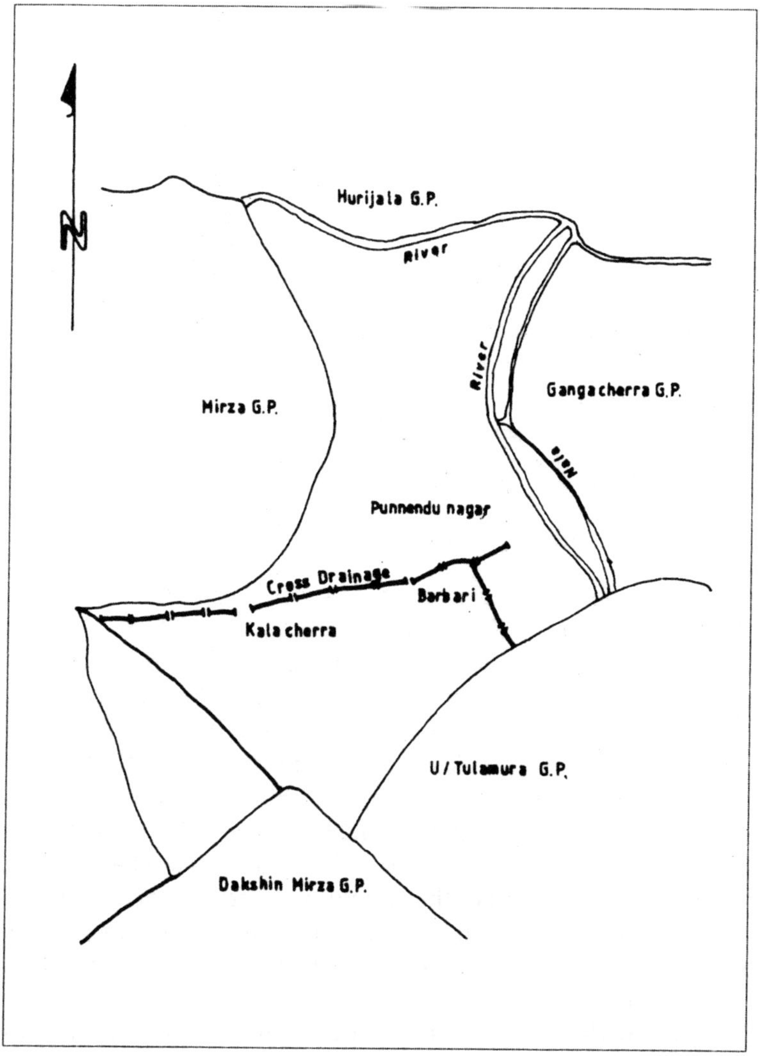

6

Socio-Economic Profile of Panchayat Members

Gram Panchayats are said to be the Local Self-government-cum-village level administrative unit in Tripura. These have been functioning since the establishment of Left Front government in Tripura. Following analysis relates to profiles of Gram Panchayat members their socio-economic and political background.

Gender and Age

The three Gram Panchayats of district West Tripura had 42 members of whom 57.14 per cent are male and 42.86 per cent female. Three Gram Panchayats of West Tripura had different proportion of male and female Gram Panchayat members. Dukli had 35.71 per cent members, Raj Lakshmipur have 28.57 per cent sample members and Paschim Pratappur had 35.71 per cent sample Gram-Panchayat members. Four categories of age distribution have been made, 64.29 per cent of the total Gram Panchayat members were from 36-50 age group in West Tripura district. 88.89 per cent of the females were from that age group. 62.07 per cent of the total members in that age group are female, so female are taking more active participation in the Panchayat (*Vide* Table & Fig. 1 & 2).

In South Tripura, 45.45 per cent female members belonged to 26-35 age-group. 18.18 per cent of them were in 36-50 age-group, 18.18 per cent in 51-60 age group and more than 60 age group. The distributions of male members are different.

Table 1: Distribution of Gram Panchayat Members by Gender

District	*Gram Panchayat*	*Sex*		*Total*
		Male	*Female*	
West Tripura	Dukli	10	5	15(35.71)
	Raj Lakshminagar	6	6	12(28.57)
	Paschim Pratappur	8	7	15(35.71)
	Total	24(57.14)	18(42.86)	42(100%)
South Tripura	Mirza	8	4	12
	Purba Mirza	5	4	9
	Dakshin Mirza	6	3	9
	Total	19(63.33)	11(36.67)	30(100%)
Grand Total		43(59.72)	29(40.28)	72(100%)

Source: Survey 2001-2002.

Table 2: Distribution of Gram Panchayat Members by Age group

District	*Gram Panch-ayat*	*Sex*	*Age Group*				*Sub-Total*	*Total*
			26-35	*36-50*	*51-60*	*More than 60*		
West Tripura	Dukli	Male	3	6	—	1	10	
		Female	1	4	—	—	5	15
	Raj Lakshmi-nagar	Male	3	2	1	—	6	
		Female	1	5	—	—	6	12
	Paschim Pratappur	Male	1	3	2	2	8	
		Female	—	7	—	—	7	15
	Total	Male	7	11	3	3	24	
		Female	2(11.11)	16(88.89)	—	—	18(100%)	
		Total	9(21.43)	27(64.29)	3(7.14)	3(7.14)	42(100%)	42
South Tripura	Mirza	Male	2	3	—	3	8	
		Female	2	—	1	1	4	12
	Purba Mirza	Male	1	3	—	1	5	
		Female	2	1	—	1	4	9
	Dakshin Mirza	Male	1	3	1	1	6	
		Female	1	1	1	—	3	9
	Total	Male	4(21.05)	9(47.36)	1(5.26)	5(26.31)	19(100)%	
		Female	5(45.46)	2(18.18)	2(18.18)	2(18.18)	11(100%)	
		Total	9(30.00)	11(36.67)	3(10.00)	7(23.33)	30(100%)	30
Grand Total		Male	11	20	4	8	43	
		Female	7(24.13)	18(62.07)	2(6.90)	2(2.90)	29(100%)	
		Total	18(25.00)	38(52.78)	6(8.33)	10(13.89)	72(100%)	72

Source: Survey 2001-2002.

Of the 19 members, 21.05 per cent belong to 26-35 age-group, 47.36 per cent belong to 36-50 age-group and 31.58 per cent belong to older age-group, i.e. more than 50 years of age.

It should be admitted here that there are inter-Panchayats variations in distribution of members but a common trend can be observed that younger persons belonging to 26-50 years of age have outnumbered the older ones.

Fig. 1. Distribution of Gram Panchayat Members by Gender

Fig. 1.1: Gram Panchayat Member by Gender (West Tripura and Total)

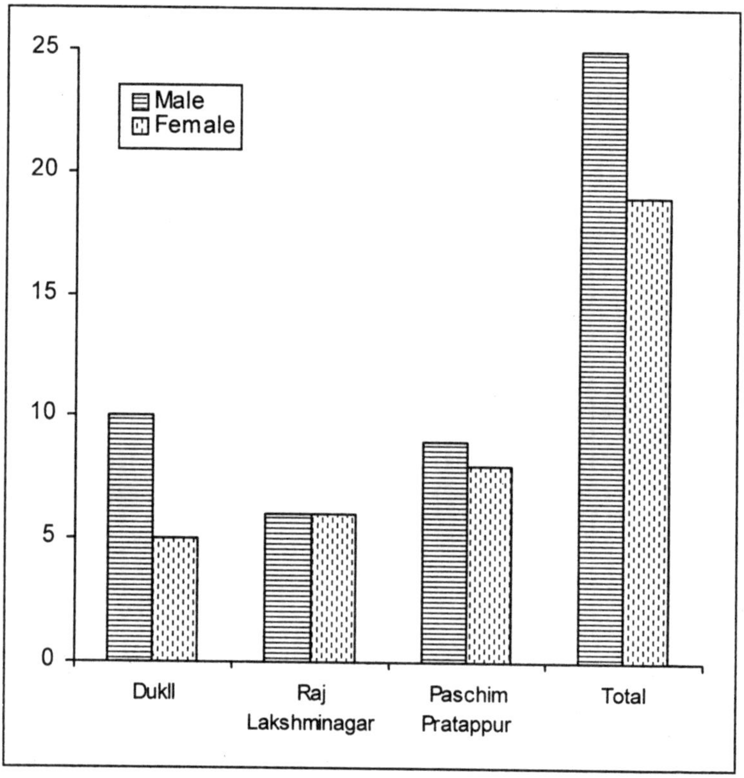

Fig. 1.2: Gram Panchayat Member by Gender
(South Tripura and Total)

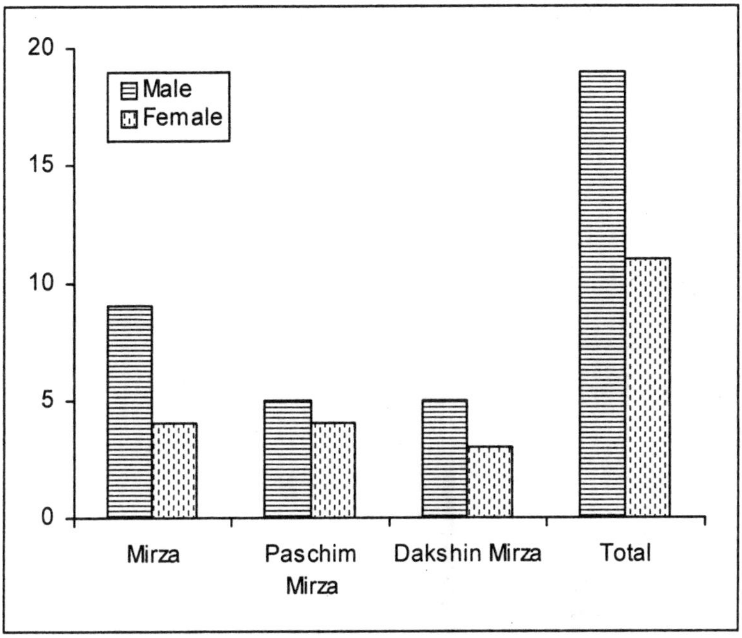

Fig. 1.3: Gram Panchayat Member by Gender
(Grand Total of West and South Tripura)

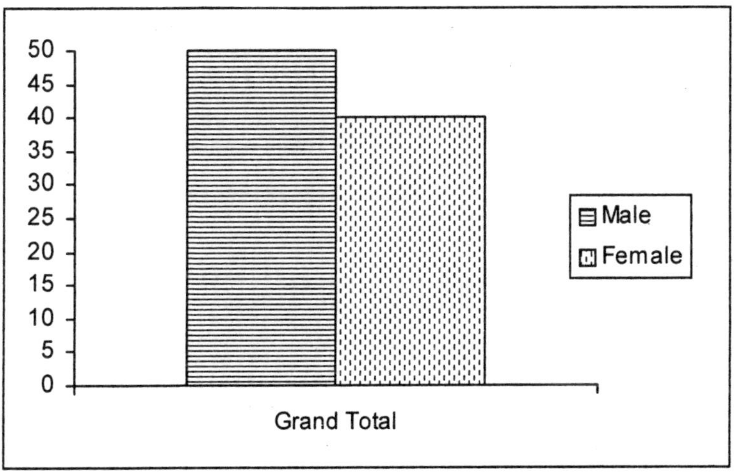

Fig. 2. Distribution of Gram Panchayat Members by Age-group

Fig. 2.1: Gram Panchayat Member by Age-group
(West Tripura andTotal)

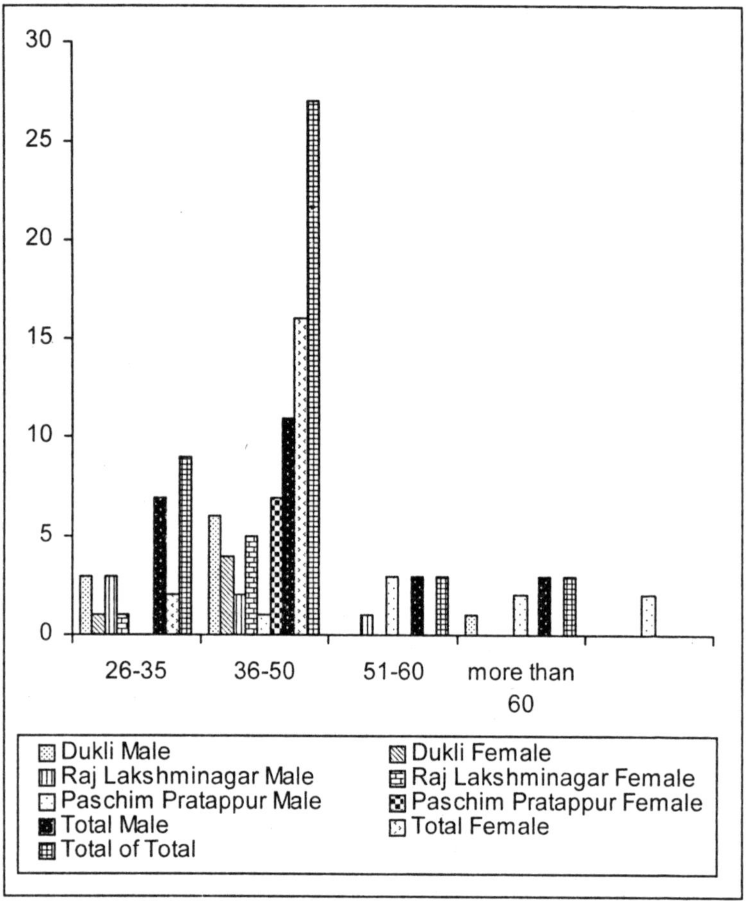

Fig. 2.2: Gram Panchayat Member by Age-group
(South Tripura and Total)

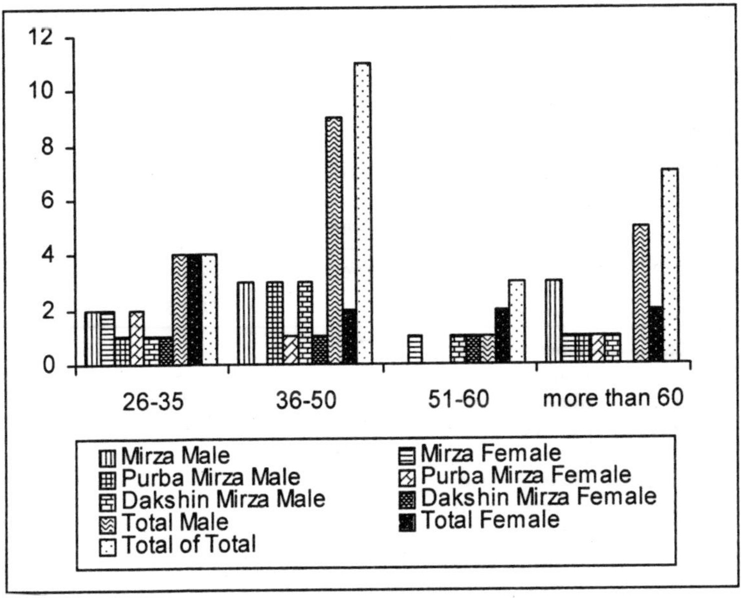

Fig. 2.3: Gram Panchayat Member by Age-group
(Grand Total of West and South Tripura)

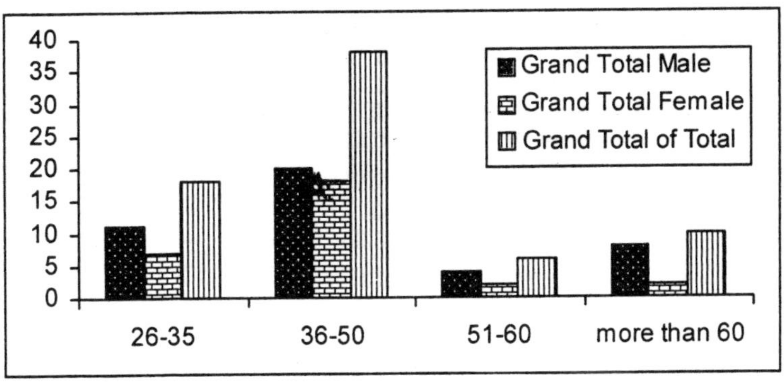

Marital Status

Marriage is a universal institution, which admits men and women into family life. It is stable relationship in which a man and a woman are socially permitted to have children implying the right to sexual relations. Gram Panchayat members of Tripura are no exception to this social rule.

In Table 3, we have figures in both absolute number and in terms of percentages the marital status of the men and women Gram Panchayat members. A martial profile often is given below:

Table 3: Distribution of Gram Panchayat Members by Marriage

District	*Gram Panchayat*	*Sex*	*Marital Status*				*Sub-Total*	*Total*
			Never Married	*Married*	*Widow*	*Divorced/ Separated*		
West Tripura	Dukli	Male	3	7	—	—	10	
		Female		5	—	—	5	15
	Raj Lakshmi-nagar	Male	3	2	—	1	6	
		Female	—	6	—	—	6	12
	Paschim Pratappur	Male	3	5	—	—	8	
		Female	1	5	1	—	7	15
	Total	Male	9(37.50)	14(58.33)	—	1	24	
		Female	1(5.56)	16(88.89)	1(5.55)	—	18(100%)	
		Total	*10(23.81)*	*30(71.43)*	*1(2.38)*	*1(2.38)*	*42(100%)*	*42*
South Tripura	Mirza	Male	—	8	—	—	8	
		Female	1	3	—	—	4	12
	Purba Mirza	Male	—	5	—	—	5	
		Female	—	4	—	—	4	9
	Dakshin Mirza	Male	—	6	—	—	6	
		Female	—	3	—	—	3	9
	Total	Male	—	19	—	—	19	
		Female	1(9.09)	10(90.91)	—	—	11(100%)	
		Total	*1(3.33)*	*29(96.67)*	—	—	*30(100%)*	*30*
Grand Total		Male	9	33	—	1	43	
		Female	2(6.90)	26(86.65)	1(3.45)	—	29(100%)	
		Total	*11(15.28)*	*59(81.94)*	*1(1.39)*	*1(1.39)*	*72(100%)*	*72*

Source: Survey 2001-2002.

In Gram Panchayats of West Tripura, 58.33 per cent of male members are married whereas 88.89 per cent female members are married. So a greater number of female are married. 37.5 per cent male members are not married. Why such a considerable number of male members in the Panchayat are unmarried? The possible reason may be attributed firstly the lack of adequate financial strength individually and that eventually earns less social prestige for an individual in a society. Secondly, a sense of social security and uncertainty prevails in Bengali society particularly among the younger people who does not want to take risk. Had this been a stable agricultural society, the amount of risk in taking decision of marriage would have been less. So a fragile marriage relation is prominent in the society, particularly among the Bengalis of today and the reflection of it has been on the Gram Panchayat members as well.

In South Tripura, 96.97 per cent Gram Panchayat male members are fortunately married. So, they are free from uncertainty of their social life comparatively to those who are not married. Among the female members, 91 per cent is married and 9 per cent is unmarried. 1 Widow and 1 divorced or separated male were also found.

Fig. 3. Distribution of Gram Panchayat Members by Marital Status

Fig. 3.1: Gram Panchayat Members by Marital Status (West Tripura and Total)

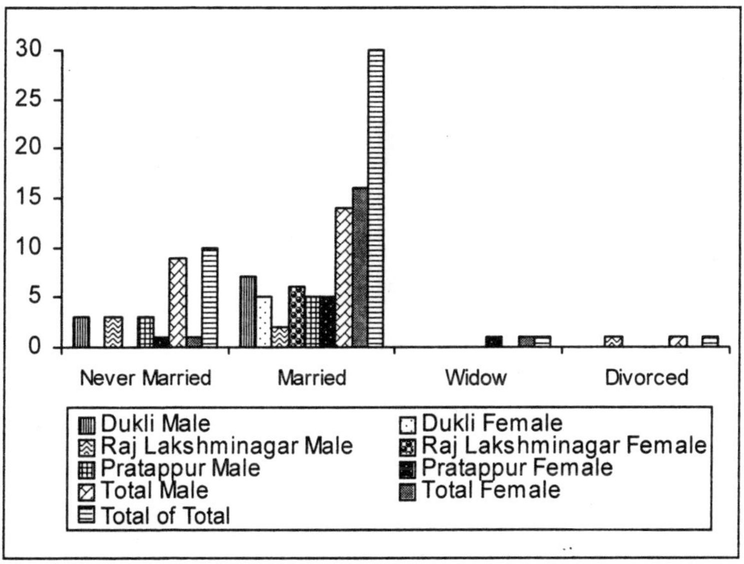

Fig. 3.2: Gram Panchayat Members by Marital Status (South Tripura and Total)

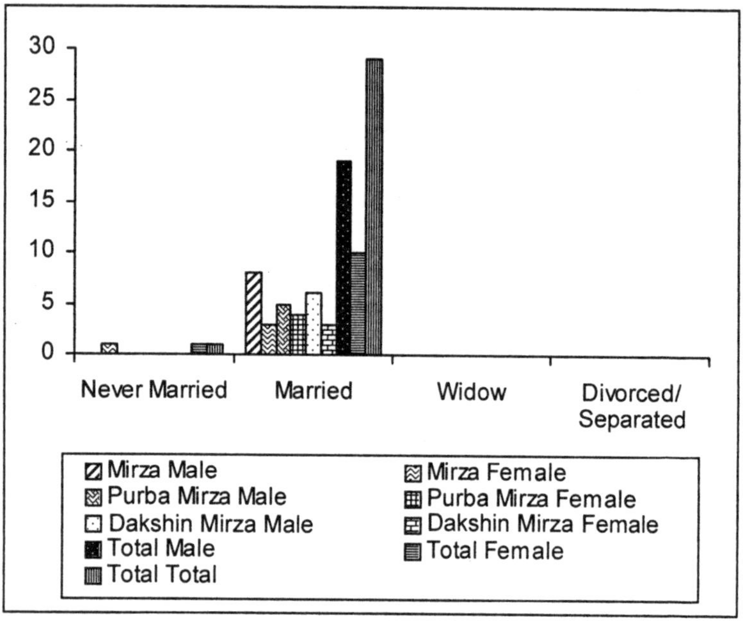

Fig. 3.3: Gram Panchayat Members by Marital Status (Grand Total of South & West Tripura)

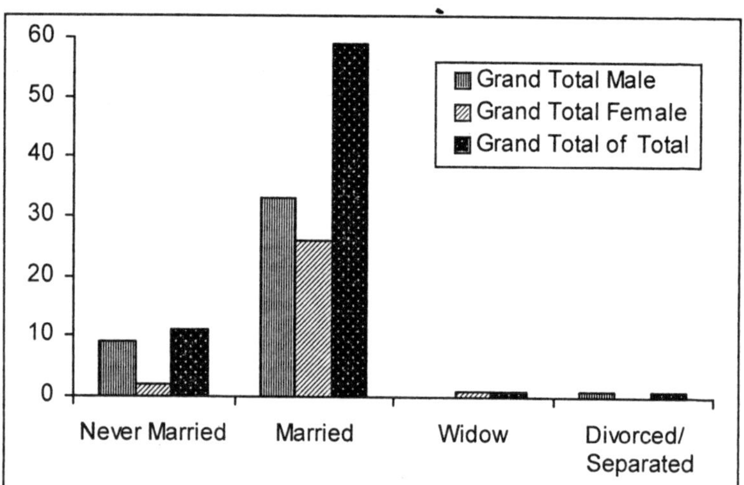

Type of Family

In Table 4 Gram Panchayat Members are classified by the type of family they belong. Two types of families are found in which members are distributed. These are joint and extended type. Interestingly, 54.16 per cent male members belong to nuclear families and 45.83 per cent belong to extended families. Among the females 66.67 per cent nuclear and 33.33 per cent have extended families.

Table 4: Distribution of Gram Panchayat Members by Type of Family

District	*Gram Panchayat*	*Sex*	*Type of family*		*Sub-Total*	*Total*
			Nuclear	*Extended*		
West Tripura	Dukli	Male	8	2	10	
		Female	4	1	5	15
	Raj	Male	1	5	6	
	Lakshminagar	Female	3	3	6	12
	Paschim	Male	4	4	8	
	Pratappur	Female	5	2	7	15
	Total	Male	13	11	24	
		Female	12(66.67)	6(33.33)	18(100%)	
		Total	*25(59.52)*	*17(40.48)*	*42(100%)*	*42*
South Tripura	Mirza	Male	2	6	8	
		Female	1	3	4	12
	Purba Mirza	Male	2	3	5	
		Female	1	3	4	9
	Dakshin	Male	2	4	6	
	Mirza	Female	–	3	3	9
	Total	Male	6(31.58)	13(68.42)	19(100%)	
		Female	2(18.18)	9(81.82)	11(100%)	
		Total	*8(26.67)*	*22(73.33)*	*30(100%)*	*30*
Grand Total		Male	19	24	43	
		Female	14(48.28)	15(51.72)	29(100%)	
		Total	*33(45.83)*	*39(54.17)*	*72(100%)*	*72*

Source : Survey 2001-2002.

But in South Tripura, predominance of extended families among both male and female members are found 81.82 per cent female members belong to extended families and 68.44 per cent among the male members belong to extended type. So remaining 18.18 per cent and 31.58 per cent among the female and male belong to nuclear type of families.

Variations can also be observed among according to family types of the Gram Panchayat members. In West Tripura, Dukli village is dominated by nuclear type of families.

But Raj Lakshmipur GP is characterized by extended type, on the other hand, Paschim Pratappur is nuclear.

South Tripura Gram Panchayats are dominated by extended type of families. Most of the members belong to extended type in Mirza, Purba Mirza and Dakshin Mirza Gram Panchayats.

Family Size

West Tripura Gram Panchayat members mostly have 3-4 and 5-7 member family sizes.

Fig. 4. Distribution of Gram Panchayat Member by Type of Family

Fig. 4.1: Gram Panchayat Members by Type of Family (West Tripura and Total)

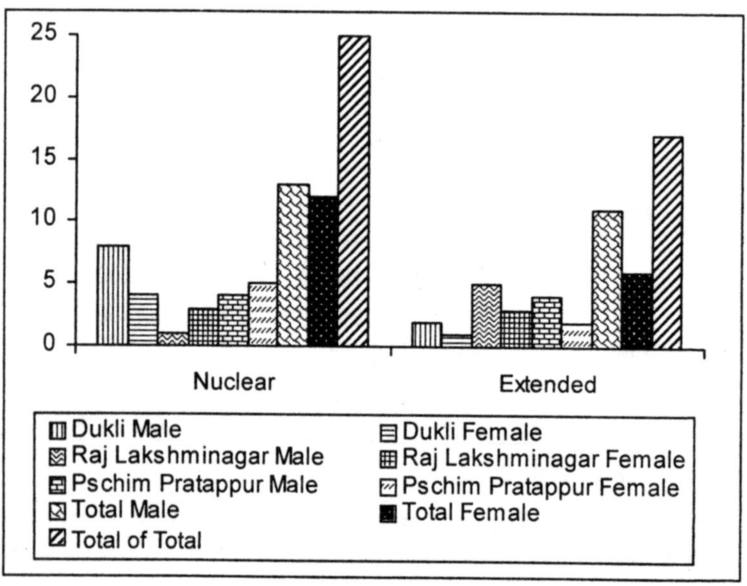

On the other hand, South Tripura Gram Panchayat members mainly have 5-7 members' family. A small number has 8-9 members and 10-11 members in their families. Percentage of such bigger household in West Tripura is 4.76 per cent (2 hhs.) with 8-9 members and 2.38 per cent (1 hh.) with 10-11 members.

In South Tripura 6.67 per cent households have 8-9 members and another 6.67 per cent households have 10-11 heads in their families.

Fig. 4.2: Gram Panchayat Member by Type of Family (South Tripura and Total)

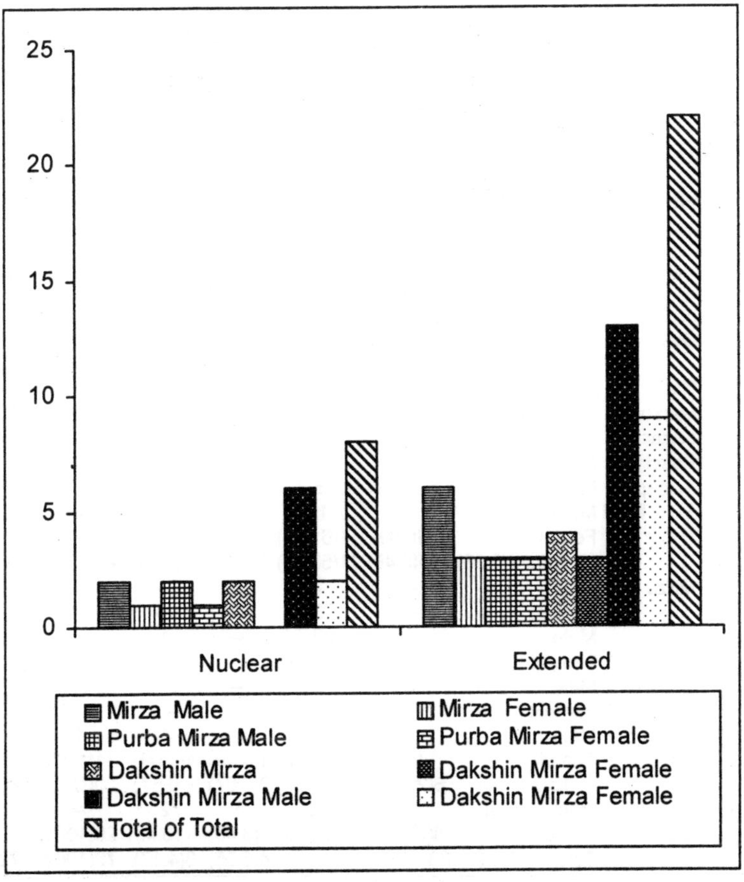

Fig. 4.3: Gram Panchayat Members by Type of Family (Grand Total West and South Tripura Total)

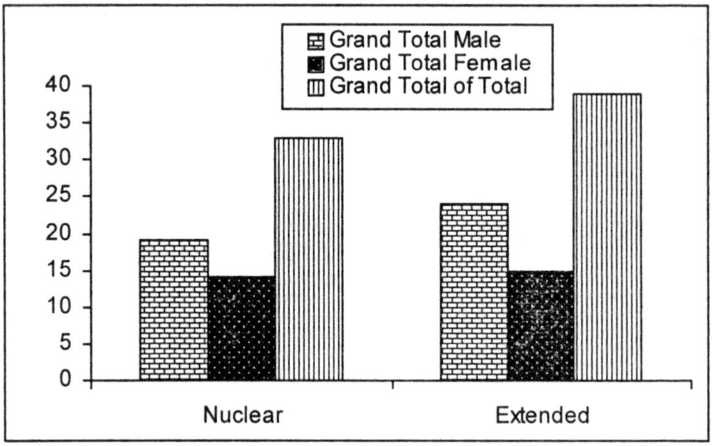

Table 5: Distribution of Gram Panchayat Members by Family Size

District	Gram Panchayat	Sex	Family Size 1-2	3-4	5-7	8-9	10-11	Sub-Total	Total
West Tripura	Dukli	Male	1	3	5	—	1	10	
		Female	—	4	1	—	—	5	15
	Raj	Male	—	4	1	1	—	6	
	Lakshmi-nagar	Female	—	1	5	—	—	6	12
	Paschim	Male	—	3	4	1	—	8	
	Pratappur	Female	—	2	5	—	—	7	15
	Total	Male	1	10	10	2	1	24	
		Female	—	7(38.89)	11(61.11)	—	—	18(100%)	
		Total	1(2.38)	17(40.48)	21(50.00)	2(4.76)	1(2.38)	42(100%)	42
South Tripura	Mirza	Male	—	—	7	1	—	8	
		Female	—	—	3	1	—	4	12
	Purba	Male	—	2	2	—	1	5	
	Mirza	Female	—	—	3	—	1	4	9
	Dakshin	Male	—	3	3	—	—	6	
	Mirza	Female	—	1	2	—	—	3	9
	Total	Male	—	5	12	1	1	19	
		Female	—	1(9.09)	8(72.73)	1(9.09)	1(9.09)	11(100%)	
		Total	—	6(20.00)	19(63.33)	2(6.67)	2(6.67)	30(100%)	30
Grand Total		Male	1	15	22	3	2	43	
		Female	—	8(27.58)	19(65.52)	1(3.45)	1(13.45)	29(100%)	
		Total	1(1.39)	23(31.94)	41	4(5.55)	3(4.17)	72(100%)	72

Source: Survey 2001-2002.

Castes/Tribes

Gram Panchayat members in West Tripura and South Tripura district belonged to Scheduled Castes, Scheduled Tribes, Other Backward Communities, General and Muslims.

In West Tripura, 42.86 per cent of the members are Scheduled Castes (18 out of 42). 19.05 per cent are Other Backward Communities and 33.33 per cent are General while 4.76 per cent are Muslims. Among the Females, 44.44 per cent are Scheduled Castes, 16.67 per cent belong to Other Backward Communities, 33.33 per cent of the female members are in General Categories and 4.76 per cent of them are Muslims.

In South Tripura, proportions of Scheduled Caste members are comparatively higher. It is 56.67 per cent out of members of 30 heads. 13.33 per cent belong to Scheduled Tribe and 13.33 per cent belong to Other Backward Communities as well as to General Castes and 3.34 per cent belong to Muslims.

Fig. 5. Distribution of Gram Panchayat Members by Family Size

Fig. 5.1: Gram Panchayat Members by Family Size (West Tripura and Total)

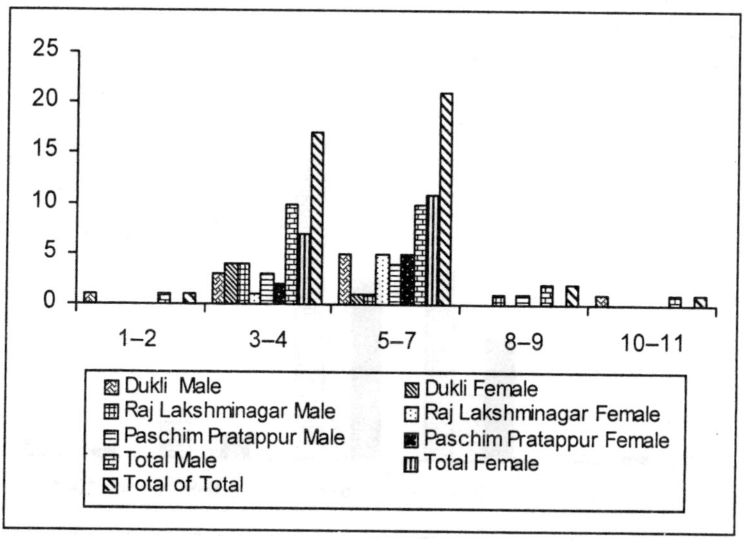

Fig. 5.2: Gram Panchayat Members by Family Size (South Tripura and Total)

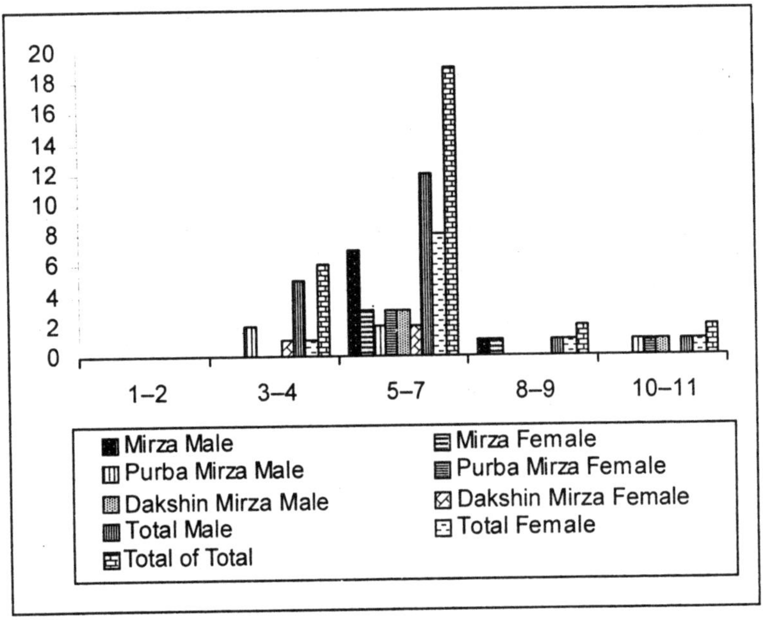

Fig. 5.3: Gram Panchayat Members by Family Size (Grand Total of West and South Tripura)

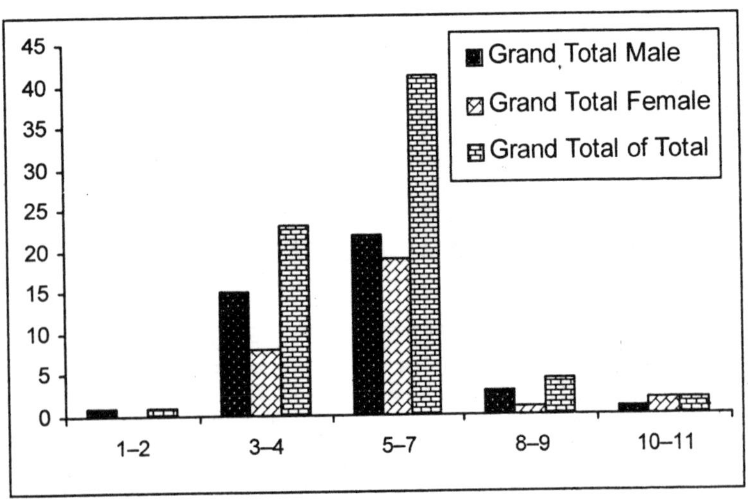

Table 6: Distribution of Gram Panchayat Members by Caste/Tribe/Religion

District	*Gram Panchayat*	*Sex*	*Caste/Tribe/Religion*					*Sub-Total*	*Total*
			SC	*ST*	*OBC*	*General*	*Muslim*		
West Tripura	Dukli	Male	5	—	4	1	—	10	
		Female	2	—	2	1	—	5	15
	Raj Lakshminagar	Male	2	—	1	3	—	6	
		Female	2	—	—	4	—	6	12
	Paschim Pratappur	Male	3	—	—	4	1	8	
		Female	4	—	1	1	1	7	15
	Total	Male	10	—	5	8	1	24	
		Female	8(44.44)	—	3(16.67)	6(33.33)	1(5.56)	18(100%)	
		Total	18(42.86)	—	8(19.05)	14(33.33)	2(4.76)	42(100%)	42
South Tripura	Mirza	Male	4	1	2	—	1	8	
		Female	2	—	1	1	—	4	12
	Purba Mirza	Male	1	1	—	3	—	5	
		Female	2	1	1	—	—	4	9
	Dakshin Mirza	Male	6	—	—	—	—	6	
		Female	2	1	—	—	—	3	9
	Total	Male	11	2	2	3	1	19	
		Female	6(54.55)	2(18.18)	2(18.18)	1(9.09)	—	11(100%)	
		Total	17(56.67)	4(13.33)	4(13.33)	4(13.33)	1(3.34)	30(100%)	30
Grand Total		Male	21	2	7	11	2	43	
		Female	14(48.27)	2(6.90)	5(17.24)	7(24.14)	1(3.45)	29(100%)	
		Total	35(48.61)	4(5.55)	12(16.67)	18(25.00)	3(4.17)	72(100%)	72

Source: Survey 2001-02.

Among the female members 50 per cent are Scheduled Castes, 20 per cent belong to Scheduled Tribes, 20 per cent belong to Other Backward Communities and 10 per cent belong to General members. Only minor percentages (3.34%) are Muslims.

Economic Class by Landholdings

Most Gram Panchayat members are characterized by landlessness and marginal landholding. Data show 92.44 per cent of the total members are landless in West Tripura and 7.14 per cent are marginal landholder. There is not even small landowner member in the Gram panchayats of West Tripura. 94.44 per cent female members are landless and 5.56 per cent female members have marginal holdings. The presence of marginal landowner among members can be observed in Dukli Gram Panchayat where 2 male and 1 female members belong to that category.

Fig. 6. Distribution of Gram Panchayat Members by Caste/Tribe/Religion

Fig. 6.1: Gram Panchayat Members by Caste/Tribe/Religion (West Tripura and Total)

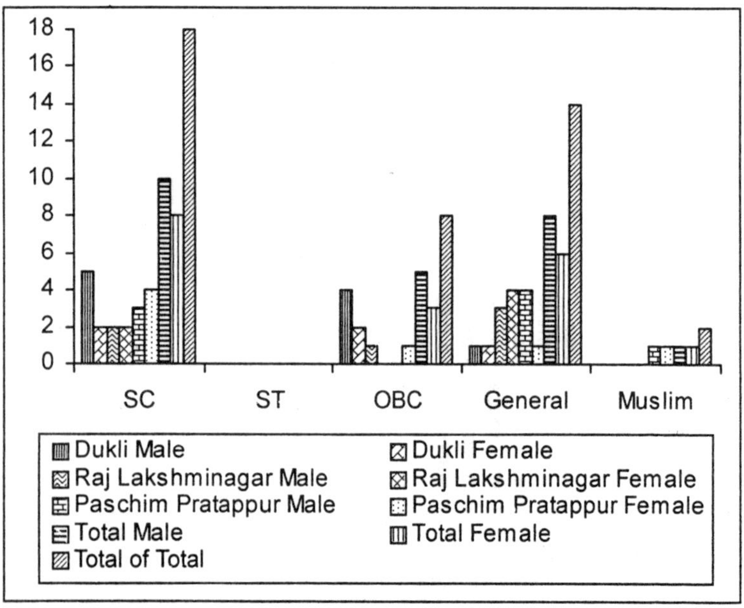

Fig. 6.2: Gram Panchayat Members by Caste/Tribe/Religion
(South Tripura and Total)

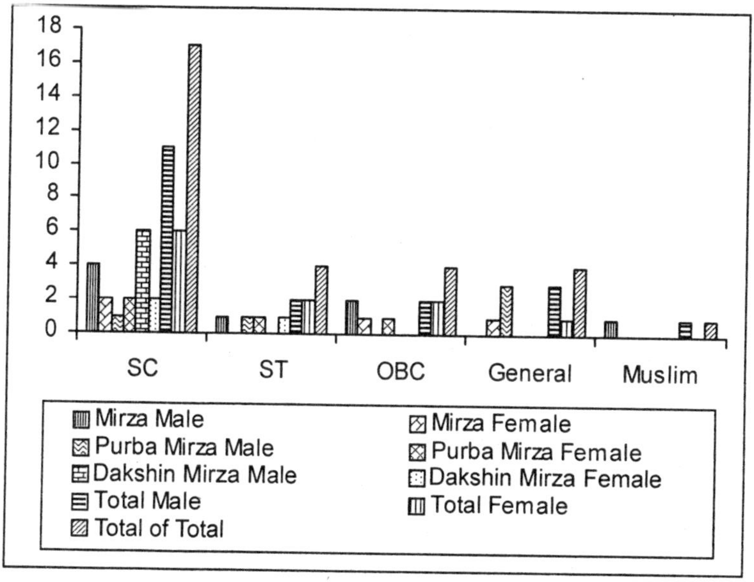

Fig. 6.3: Gram Panchayat Members by Caste/Tribe/Religion
(Grand Total of South and West Tripura)

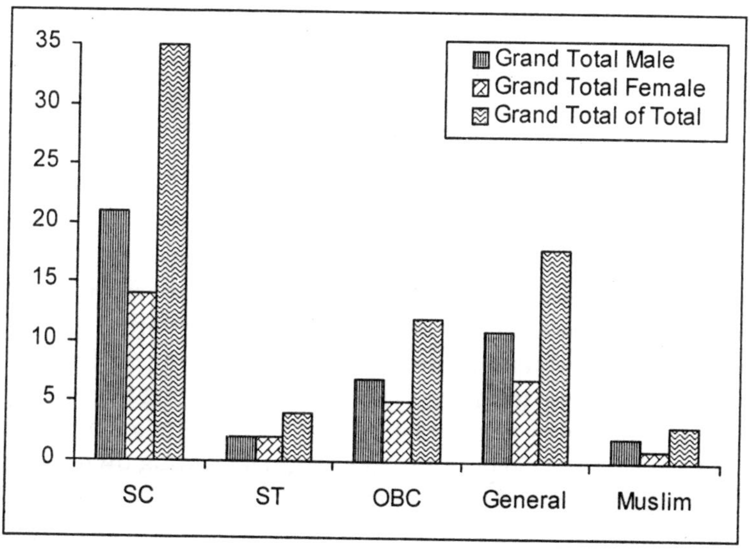

Table 7: Distribution of Gram Panchayat Members by their Economic Class

District	Gram Panchayat	Sex	Economic Class			Sub-Total	Total
			Landless	Marginal (<7.5)	Small (7.5-15)		
West Tripura	Dukli	Male	8	2	—	10	
		Female	4	1	—	5	15
	Raj Lakshminagar	Male	6	—	—	6	
		Female	6	—	—	6	12
	Paschim Pratappur	Male	8	—	—	8	
		Female	7	—	—	7	15
	Total	Male	22	2	—	24	
		Female	17(94.44)	1(5.56)	—	18(100%)	
		Total	39(92.86)	3(7.14)	—	42(100%)	42
South Tripura	Mirza	Male	4	4	—	8	
		Female	2	2	—	4	12
	Purba Mirza	Male	1	2	2	5	
		Female	2	2	—	4	9
	Dakshin Mirza	Male	3	3	—	6	
		Female	1	2	—	3	9
	Total	Male	8	9	2	19	
		Female	5(45.45)	6(54.55)	—	11(100%)	
		Total	13(43.33)	15(50.00)	2(6.67)	30(100%)	30
	Grand Total	Male	30	11	2	43	
		Female	22(75.86)	7(24.14)	—	29(100%)	
		Total	52(72.22)	18(25.00)	2(2.78)	72(100%)	72

Source: Survey 2001-2002.

Economic status according to the landless in South Tripura is different form that of West Tripura. Distributions of economic stratum are as follows. 43.33 per cent members of Gram Panchayats are landless, 50 per cent members are marginal farmers and 6.67 per cent are small farmers. Among the females, 50 per cent belong to landless and 50 per cent belong to marginal farming members. In contrast, among the male member, 40 per cent are landless, 50 per cent are marginal farming owner and 10 per cent are small farmer members.

Fig. 7. Distribution of Gram Panchayat Members by Economic Class

Fig. 7.1: Gram Panchayat Members by Economic Class (West Tripura and Total)

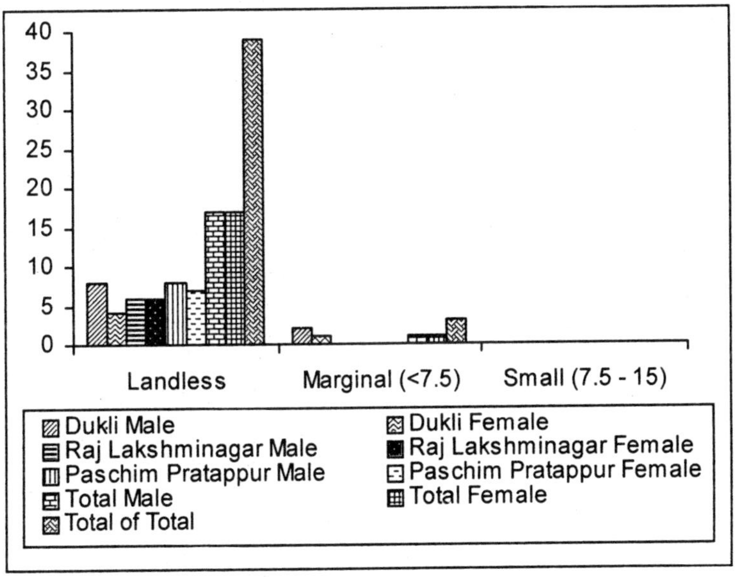

Fig. 7.2: Gram Panchayat Members by Economic Class (South Tripura and Total)

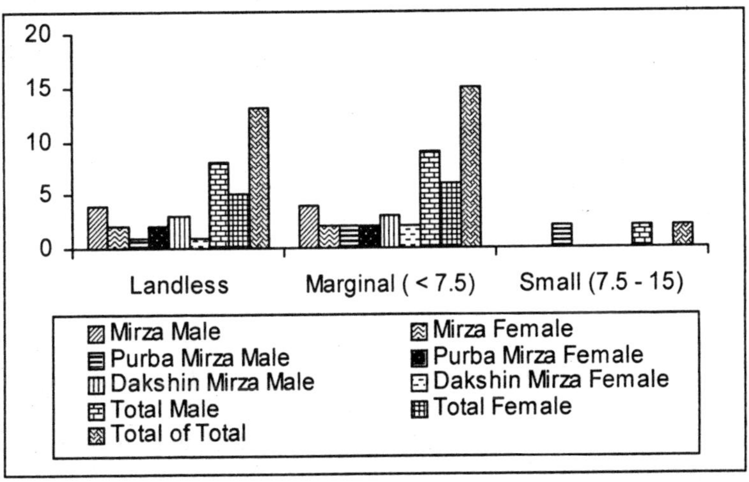

Fig. 7.3: Gram Panchayat Members by Economic Class (Grand Total of West and South Tripura)

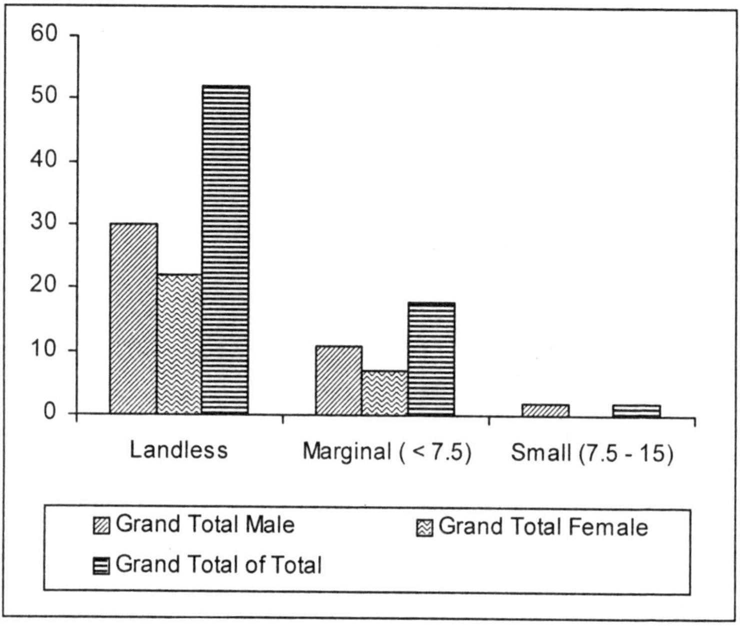

Two districts together, 72.22 per cent members are landless, 25 per cent are marginal farmers and 2.78 per cent are small owners. 78.57 per cent female members of the total are found to be landless and 21.43 per cent of them are marginal. 68.18 per cent male belong to landless and 27.27 per cent are marginal farmers and 4.54 per cent belong to small farmers.

Education

Apart from just literates (16.67%) members in West Tripura others were educated differently. Only 9.52 per cent Gram Panchayat members are reported to be Graduate and 2.38 per cent of the total members are educated above graduation level. So major numbers of people at Panchayat administration are literate between V to class XI-XII standard. The percentage of such members is 71.43 per cent.

Table 8: Distribution of Gram Panchayat Members by Education

District	Gram Panchayat	Sex	Education						Sub-Total	Total
			Upto V	VI-X	XI-XII	Graduate	Above Graduate	Just Literate		
West Tripura	Dukli	Male	1	5	1	—	1	2	10	
		Female	—	3	1	—	—	1	5	15
	Raj Lakshminagar	Male	—	4	—	2	—	—	6	
		Female	—	6	—	—	—	—	6	12
	Paschim Pratappur	Male	—	5	—	2	—	1	8	
		Female	1	3	—	—	—	3	7	15
	Total	Male	1	14	1	4	1	3	24	
		Female	1(5.55)	12(66.67)	1(5.56)	—	—	49(22.22)	18(100%)	
		Total	*2(4.76)*	*26(61.91)*	*2(4.76)*	*4(9.52)*	*1(2.38)*	*7(16.67)*	*42(100%)*	*42*
South Tripura	Mirza	Male	2	5	1	—	—	—	8	
		Female	—	2	1	1	—	—	4	12
	Purba Mirza	Male	—	4	—	—	1	—	5	
		Female	—	4	—	—	—	—	4	9
	Dakshin Mirza	Male	—	6	—	—	—	—	6	
		Female	—	2	—	1	—	—	3	9
	Total	Male	2	15	1	—	1	—	19	
		Female	—	8(72.73)	1(9.09)	2(18.18)	—	—	11(100%)	
		Total	*2(6.67)*	*23(76.66)*	*2(6.67)*	*2(6.67)*	*1(3.33)*	—	*30(100%)*	*30*
	Grand Total	Male	3	29	2	4	2	3	43	
		Female	1(3.45)	20(68.96)	2(6.90)	2(6.90)	—	4(13.79)	29(100%)	
		Total	*4(5.55)*	*49(68.06)*	*4(5.56)*	*6(8.33)*	*2(2.78)*	*7(9.72)*	*72(100%)*	*72*

Source: Survey 2001-02.

South Tripura also shows similar pattern of literacy. 76.66 per cent are educated up to VI-X. 6.67 per cent are literate up to XI-XII. Very small numbers of persons are literate up to class V standard.

Members of two districts taken together, 5.55 per cent are literate up to V standard, 68.55 per cent have read between VI to X class. 5.56 per cent are literate between XI to XII. 8.33 per cent members are Graduate 2.72 per cent amongst all Gram Panchayat members are literate above Graduation level.

It is important to note that 9.72 per cent of all GP member are just literate after a long exercise, i.e. it happened due to implementation of literacy programme at the village level.

Fig. 8. Distribution of Gram Panchayat Members by Education

Fig. 8.1: Gram Panchayat Members by Education (West Tripura and Total)

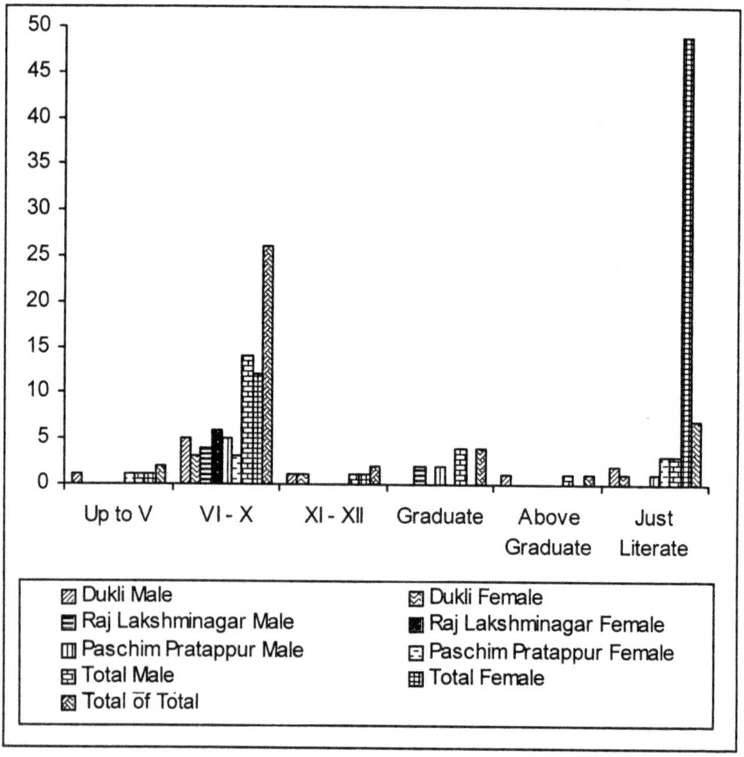

Fig. 8.2: Gram Panchayat Members by Education
(South Tripura and Total)

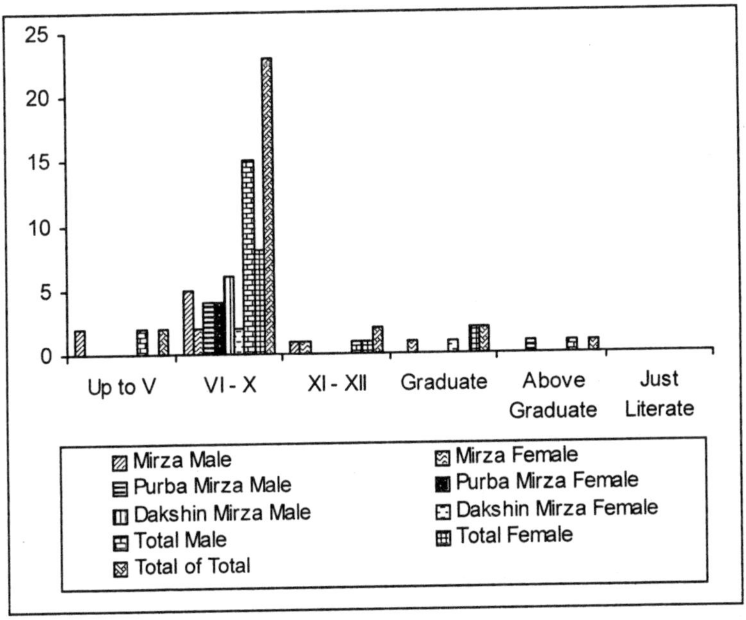

Fig. 8.3: Gram Panchayat Members by Education
(Grand Total of West and South Tripura)

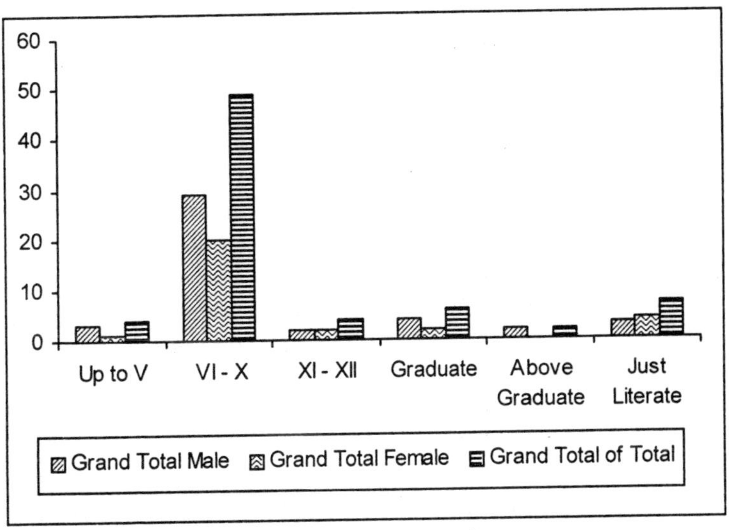

Annual Income

Table 9 deals with the annual income of the Gram Panchayat members in two districts of Tripura, viz. West and South Tripura. Members were found to have no income with a percentage of 42.86 per cent in West Tripura. 7.14 per cent has income below Rs. 600 per annum. 11.9 per cent members (both male and female) have income between Rs. 6001-15000 per annum. Another 11.9 per cent have income with Rs. 15001-25000 annually. 7.14 per cent with an income Rs. 25001-36000 annually. 11.90 per cent members have income ranging from Rs. 36001-55000 annually. 7.14 per cent members in Gram Panchayats of West Tripura have better income which is more than Rs. 55000 annually. More acute is the condition of the women of whom 77.78 per cent do not have income at all. Only 4 of them have income, 3 have low income and 1 is better off with income of 36001-55000 annually.

16.67 per cent has income below Rs. 6000 per annum. 3.33 per cent have income between Rs. 6001-15000 and 26.67 per cent members' income is between Rs. 15001-25000. Only 6 members have slightly better income with 16.67 per cent (5) between Rs. 36001-55000 and 3.33 per cent (1) having income more than Rs. 55000 annually.

Household Annual Income

Household income is different from that of the individual income. Table 10 deals with the annual income of Gram Panchayat members in Tripura. Household income is not so miserable as the individual member's income. When individual income is combined with household income then it looks workable for family maintenances.

40.47 per cent members' household have income which is more than Rs. 55000 per annum, 16.67 per cent households with an income falling between Rs. 36001-55000. Rs. 25001-36000 income bracket includes 16.67 per cent households. 21.43 per cent households having income between Rs. 15001-25000 per annum. 4.76 per cent households have income between Rs. 6001-15000 per annum. These figures relate to West Tripura district comprising 3 sample Gram Panchayats.

Table 9: Distribution of Gram Panchayat of Members by Annual Income

District	Gram Panchayat	Sex	*Annual Income of Leader*							Sub-Total	Total
			No Income	*Below 6000*	*6001-15000*	*15001-25000*	*25001-36000*	*36001-55000*	*More than 55000*		
West Tripura	Dukli	Male	1	—	2	3	2	1	1	10	
		Female	2	1	1	—	—	1	—	5	15
	Raj	Male	1	1	1	2	—	1	—	6	
	Lakshminagar	Female	5	—	1	—	—	—	—	6	12
	Paschim	Male	2	1	—	—	1	2	2	8	
	Pratappur	Female	7	—	—	—	—	—	—	7	12
	Total	Male	4	2	3	5	3	4	3	24	
		Female	14(77.78)	1(5.55)	2(11.11)	—	—	1(5.56)	—	18(100%)	
	Total		*18(42.86)*	*3(7.14)*	*5(11.91)*	*5(11.91)*	*3(7.14)*	*5(11.90)*	*3(7.14)*	*42(100%)*	42
South Tripura	Mirza	Male	1	2	1	2	—	2	—	8	
		Female	2	1	—	1	—	—	—	4	12
	Purba Mirza	Male	—	—	—	4	—	1	—	5	
		Female	4	—	—	—	—	—	—	4	9
	Dakshin	Male	1	1	—	1	—	2	1	6	
	Mirza	Female	2	1	—	—	—	—	—	3	9
	Total	Male	2	3	1	7	—	5	1	19	
		Female	8(72.73)	2(18.18)	—	1(9.09)	—	—	—	11(100%)	
	Total		*10(33.33)*	*5(16.67)*	*1(3.33)*	*8(26.67)*	—	*5(16.67)*	*1(3.33)*	*30(100%)*	*30*
	Grand Total	Male	6	5	4	12	3	9	4	43	
		Female	22(75.86)	3(10.34)	2(6.90)	1(3.45)	—	1(3.45)	—	29(100%)	
	Total		*28(38.89)*	*8(11.11)*	*6(8.33)*	*13(18.06)*	*3(4.17)*	*10(13.89)*	*4(5.55)*	*72(100%)*	72

Source: Survey 2001-02.

Fig. 9. Distribution of Gram Panchayat Members by Annual Income

Fig. 9.1: Gram Panchayat Members by Annual Income (West Tripura and Total)

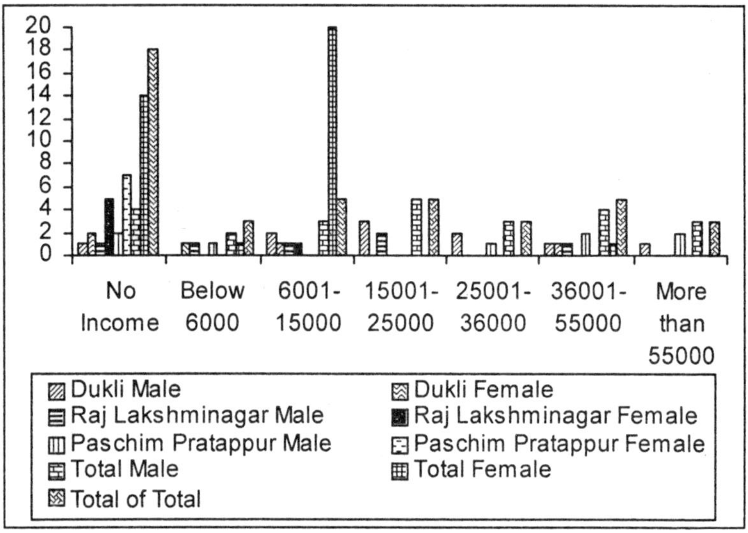

Fig. 9.2: Gram Panchayat Members by Annual Income (South Tripura and Total)

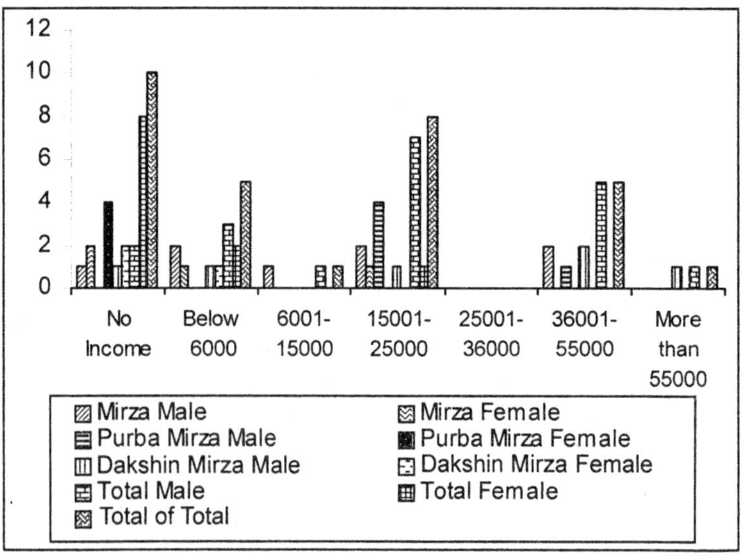

Fig. 9.3: Gram Panchayat Members by Annual Income
(Grand Total of West and South Tripura)

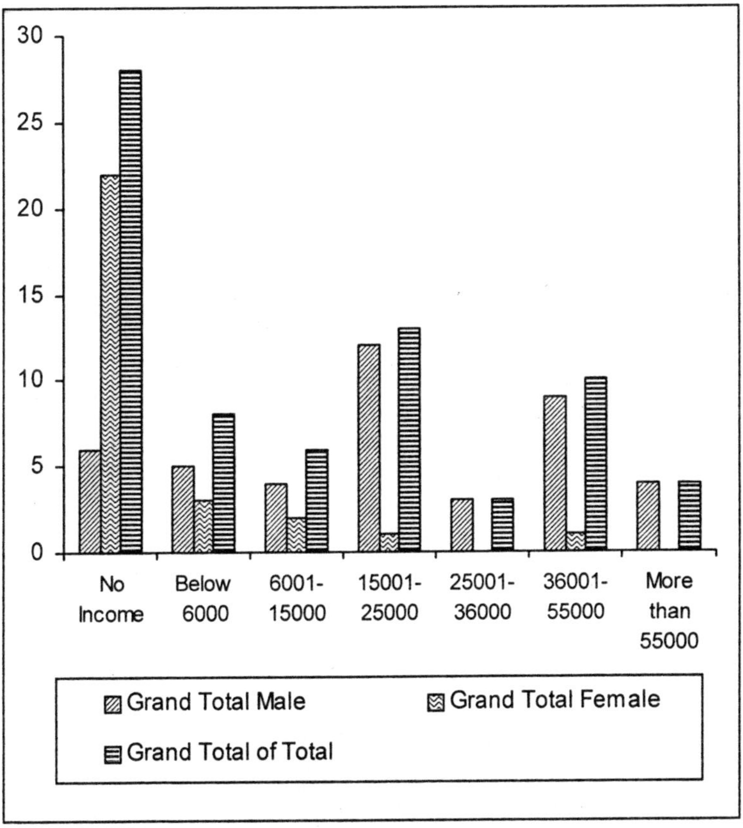

South Tripura comprises 3 Panchayats with a total no. members 30. Of them 10 per cent have Rs. 6001-15000, 23.33 per cent have 15001-25000 rupees per annum, 13.33 per cent have income between 25001-36000 rupees, 26.67 per cent households have Rs. 36001-55000 and another 26.67 per cent have income more than Rs. 55000 annually.

Its important that 30 per cent female are with more than Rs. 55000 and 10 per cent have income with Rs. 36001-55000 annually, 30 per cent with 25001-30000 rupees per annum. 20 per cent with Rs. 15001-25000 and 10 per cent members have Rs. 6001-15000 annually.

Table 10: Distribution of Gram Panchayat Members by Household Annual Income

District	Gram Panchayat		Sex	Household Annual Income					Sub-Total	Total
				6001-15000	15001-25000	25001-36000	36001-55000	More than 55000		
West Tripura	Dukli		Male	1	3	—	1	5	10	
			Female	—	2	1	—	2	5	15
	Raj Lakshminagar		Male	—	2	—	2	2	6	
			Female	—	—	2	1	3	6	12
	Paschim Pratappur		Male	1	1	1	2	3	8	
			Female	—	1	3	1	2	7	15
		Total	Male	2	6	1	5	10	24	
			Female	—	3(16.67)	6(33.33)	2(11.11)	7(38.89)	18(100%)	
		Total		*2(4.76)*	*9(21.43)*	*7(16.67)*	*7(16.67)*	*17(40.47)*	*42(100%)*	*42*
South Tripura	Mirza		Male	2	1	—	3	2	8	
			Female	1	1	1	—	1	4	12
	Purba Mirza		Male	—	3	1	1	—	5	
			Female	—	1	1	1	1	4	9
	Dakshin Mirza		Male	—	1	—	3	2	6	
			Female	—	—	—	—	2	3	9
		Total	Male	2	5	1	7	4	19	
			Female	1(9.09)	2(18.18)	3(27.27)	1(9.09)	4(36.37)	11(100%)	
		Total		*3(10.00)*	*7(23.33)*	*4(13.33)*	*8(26.67)*	*8(26.67)*	*30(100%)*	*30*
	Grand	Total	Male	4	11	2	12	14	43	
			Female	1(3.45)	5(17.24)	9(31.04)	3(10.34)	11(37.93)	29(100%)	
		Total		*5(6.95)*	*16(22.22)*	*11(15.28)*	*15(20.83)*	*25(34.72)*	*72(100%)*	*72*

Source: Survey 2001-02.

Household Annual Expenditure

Household expenditure was grouped in six Categories. 5.56 per cent female members' annual expenditure of household is below 6000. 26.19 per cent is between 15001-25000. 21.43 per cent between 25001-36000 and 14.29 per cent between 36001-55000 and finally 33.33 per cent families expenditure exceeds more than Rs. 55000 annually. These date relate to Gram Panchayats of West Tripura.

Fig. 10. Distribution of Gram Panchayat Members by Household Annual Income

Fig. 10.1: Gram Panchayat Member by Household Annual Income (West Tripura and Total)

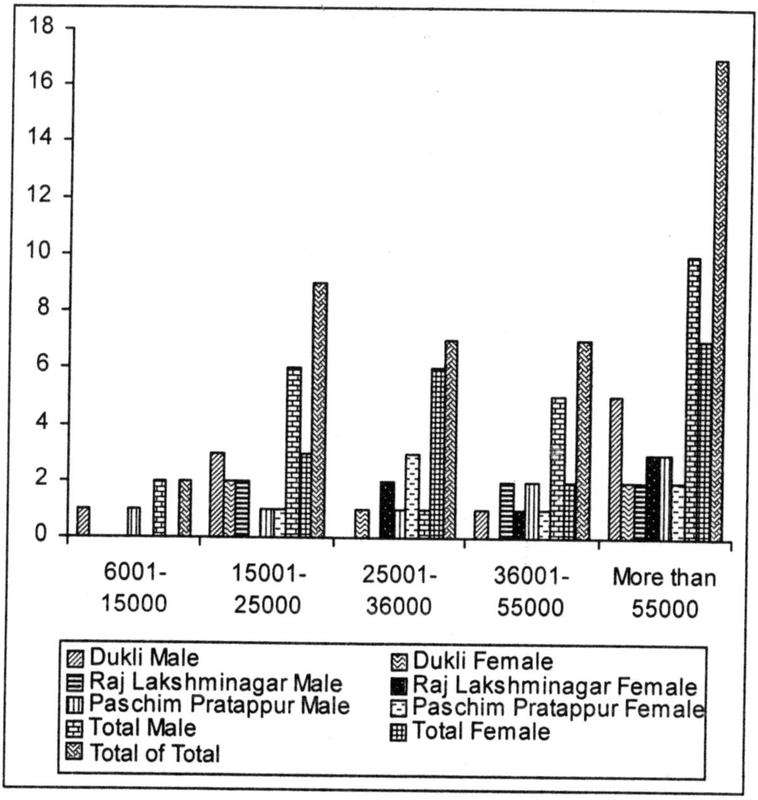

Fig. 10.2: Gram Panchayat Member by Household Annual Income (South Tripura and Total)

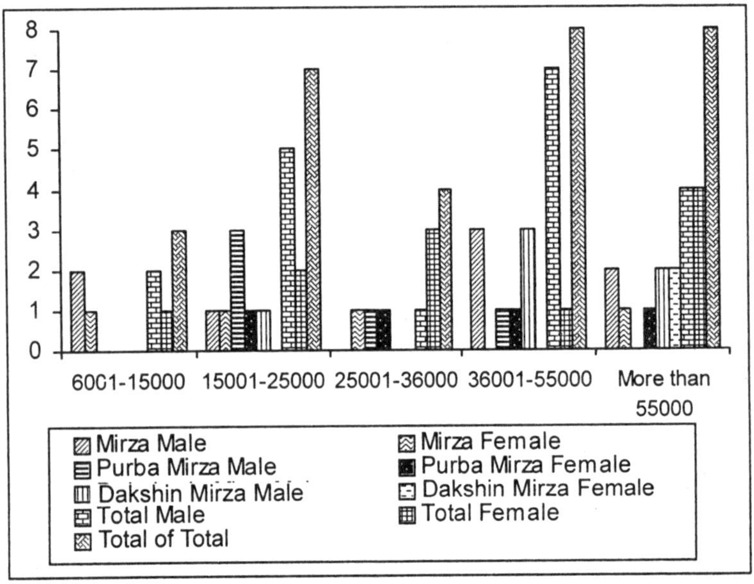

Fig. 10.3: Gram Panchayat Member by Household Annual Income (Grand Total of West and South Tripura)

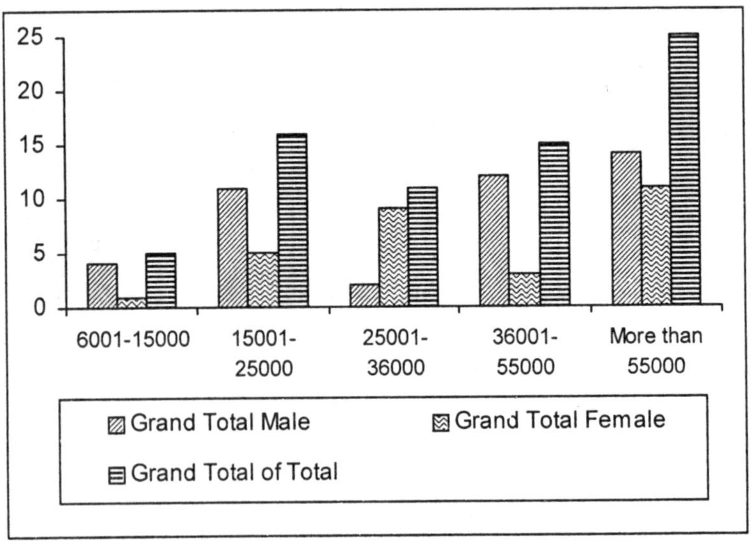

Table 11: Distribution of Gram Panchayat Member by Household Annual Expenditure

District	Gram Panchayat	Sex	Household Annual Expenditure						Sub-Total	Total
			Below 6000	6001-15000	15001-25000	25001-36000	36001-55000	More than 55000		
West Tripura	Dukli	Male	1	—	4	2	1	2	10	
		Female	1	—	2	—	—	2	5	15
	Raj	Male	—	—	2	—	1	3	6	
	Lakshminagar	Female	—	—	—	2	1	3	6	12
	Paschim	Male	—	—	2	1	2	3	8	
	Pratappur	Female	—	—	1	4	1	1	7	15
	Total	Male	1	—	8	3	4	8	24	
		Female	1(5.56)	—	3(16.67)	6(33.33)	2(11.11)	6(33.33)	18(100%)	
		Total	*2(4.76)*	—	*11(26.19)*	*9(21.43)*	*6(14.29)*	*14(33.33)*	*42(100%)*	*42*
South Tripura	Mirza	Male	—	2	1	2	1	2	8	
		Female	—	1	1	1	—	1	4	12
	Purba Mirza	Male	—	1	3	1	—	—	5	
		Female	—	—	2	—	1	1	4	9
	Dakshin	Male	—	1	—	1	2	2	6	
	Mirza	Female	—	—	1	—	—	2	3	9
	Total	Male	—	4	4	4	3	4	19	
		Female	—	1(9.09)	4(36.37)	1(9.09)	1(9.09)	4(36.36)	11(100%)	
		Total	—	*5(16.67)*	*8(26.66)*	*5(16.67)*	*4(13.33)*	*8(26.67)*	*30(100%)*	*30*
	Grand Total	Male	1	4	12	7	7	12	43	
		Female	1(3.45)	1(3.45)	7(24.14)	7(24.13)	3(10.35)	10(34.48)	29(100%)	
		Total	*2(2.78)*	*5(6.94)*	*19(26.39)*	*14(19.44)*	*10(13.89)*	*22(30.56)*	*72(100%)*	*72*

Source: Survey 2001-02.

In South Tripura, 16.67 per cent members' household expenditure is within Rs. 6001-15000 and 26.66 per cent members' household expenditure is between Rs. 15001-25000 and 16.67 per cent members household expenditure is between Rs. 25001-36000. 13.33 per cent household members expended between 36001-55000 and 26.67 per cent households have made expenditure exceeding Rs. 55000 or more.

Of the total 72 members in both the districts of Tripura only 2.78 per cent have expenditure below Rs. 6000 per annum and 6.94 per cent belong to annually 6001-15000 annual expenditure. 26.39 per cent members have annual expenditure with Rs. 15001 to 26000. 19.44 per cent members' household expenditure has been Rs. 25001-36000 annually. 13.89 per cent members' expenditure remains within 36001-55000 and 30.56 per cent members household expenditure exceeded beyond Rs. 55000 per annum.

Fig. 11. Distribution of Gram Panchayat Members by Household Annual Expenditure

Fig. 11.1: Gram Panchayat Members by Household Annual Expenditure (West Tripura and Total)

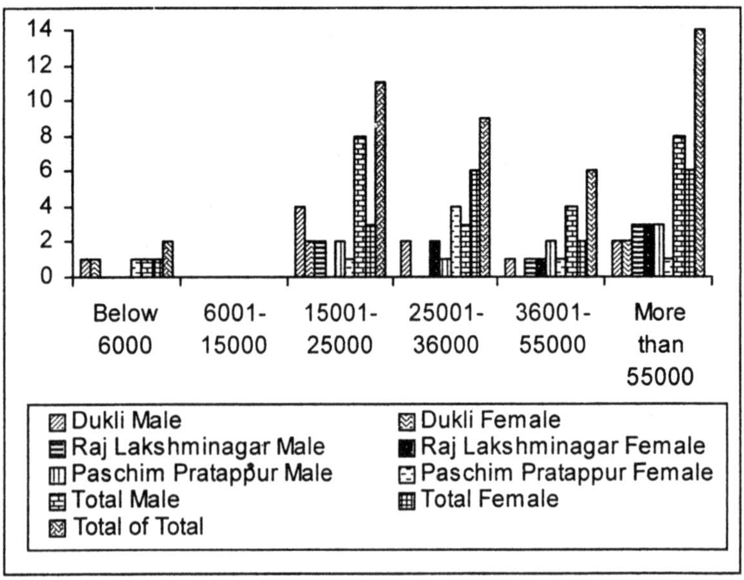

Fig. 11.2: Gram Panchayat Members by Household Annual Expenditure (South Tripura and Total)

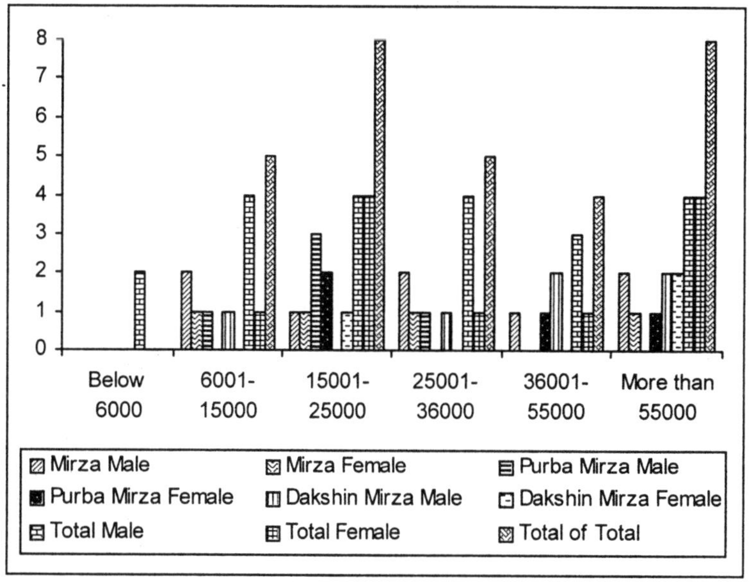

Fig. 11.3: Gram Panchayat Members by Household Annual Expenditure (Grand Total of West and South Tripura)

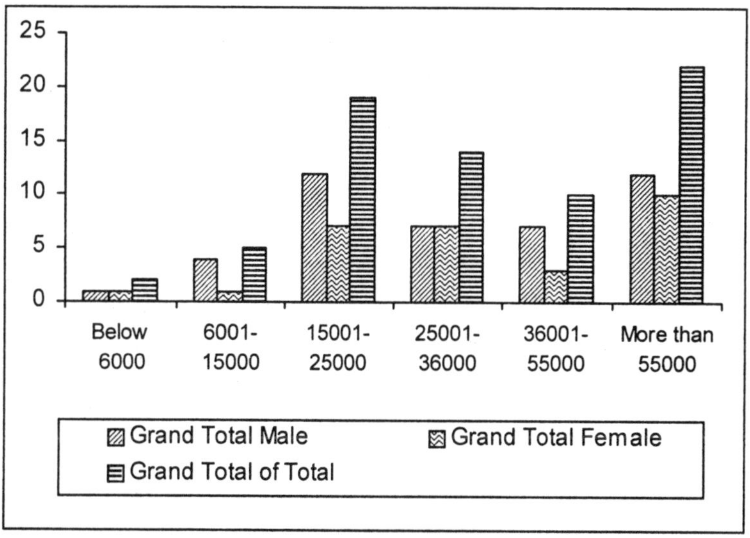

Affiliation to Mass Front

Gram Panchayat is the smallest administrative body at the Grassroots; its members belong to political parties. That is why they are found to have inclination and affiliation to different mass front of political parties. There are varieties of mass fronts where the members work.

Panchayat members work in some mass fronts, which are, affiliated mainly to Communist Party of India (Marxist). We find that Krishak Sabha, Democratic Youth Federation of India, and Women's Organization such as AIDWA, SC/ST/OBC Organization, CITU, Labour Union, Social Welfare etc.

It may be observed that 2.38 per cent members do not have any affiliation to any particular mass front. 14.29 per cent have affiliation to Krishak Sabha, the peasants' organization. 23.8 per cent members in West Tripura Gram Panchayats belong to DYFI. 40.48 per cent are affiliated to Women's Organizations, namely AIDWA. 4.76 per cent members owe its allegiance to SC/ST/OBC Organization. 2.38 per cent work with Social Welfare Organization. 9.52 per cent members belong to CITU. 2.38 per cent affiliates to Labour Union whose identity is unknown.

In South Tripura, 6.67 per cent do not have affiliation to any political party. 40 per cent members are affiliated to Krishak Sabha, 3.33 per cent are affiliated to DYFI. Interestingly 33.34 per cent members are active in Women's Front. 3.33 per cent members affiliate to SC/ST/OBC front. 3.3 per cent is affiliated to Social Welfare Organization 10 per cent members are affiliated to Labour Union.

Party Affiliation

In Tripura, three major national political parties, such as CPI(M), Congress and Forward Block have their members elected to the Panchayat administration. In West Tripura, 95.24 per cent members are elected from CPI(M) and 4.76 per cent are elected from Forward Block.

96.67 per cent members of the Gram Panchayats are elected from CPI(M) and 1, i.e. 3.33 per cent members is elected from National Congress in South Tripura district.

Table 12: Distribution of Gram Panchayat Members by Affiliation to Mass Front

District	Gram Panchayat	Sex	Affiliation to Mass Front								Sub-Total
			No Affiliation	Krishak Sabha	DYFI	Women Front	SC/ST/OBC Front	Social Welfare	CITU	Labour Union	
West Tripura	Dukli	Male	1	3	3	—	2	—	1	—	10
		Female	—	—	—	5	—	—	—	—	5
	Raj Lakshminagar	Male	—	—	5	—	—	—	—	1	6
		Female	—	—	1	5	—	—	—	—	6
	Paschim Pratappur	Male	—	3	1	—	—	1	3	—	8
		Female	—	—	—	7	—	—	—	—	7
	Total	Male	1	6	9	—	2	1	4	1	24
		Female	—	—	1(5.56)	17(94.44)	—	—	—	—	18(100%)
	Total		*1(2.38)*	*6(14.29)*	*10(23.81)*	*17(40.48)*	*2(4.76)*	*1(2.38)*	*4(9.52)*	*1(2.38)*	*42(100%)*
South Tripura	Mirza	Male	1	3	—	—	1	—	—	3	8
		Female	—	1	1	2	—	—	—	—	4
	Purba Mirza	Male	—	4	—	—	—	1		—	5
		Female	—	—	—	4	—	—	—	—	4
	Dakshin Mirza	Male	1	4	—	1	—	—		—	6
		Female	—	—	—	3	—	—	—	—	3
	Total	Male	2	11	—	1	1	1		3	19
		Female	—	1(9.09)	1(9.09)	9(81.82)	—	—	—	—	11(100%)
	Total		*2(6.67)*	*12(40.00)*	*1(3.33)*	*10(33.34)*	*1(3.33)*	*1(3.33)*		*3(10.00)*	*30(100%)*
	Grand Total	Male	3	17	9	1	3	2	4	4	43
		Female	—	1(3.45)	2(6.90)	26(89.65)	—	—	—	—	29(100%)
	Total		*3(4.17)*	*18(25.00)*	*11(15.28)*	*27(37.50)*	*3(4.17)*	*2(2.78)*	*4(5.55)*	*4(5.55)*	*72(100%)*

Source: Survey 2001-02.

Fig. 12. Distribution of Gram Panchayat Members by Affiliation to Mass Front

Fig. 12.1: Gram Panchayat Members by Affiliation to Mass Front (West Tripura and Total)

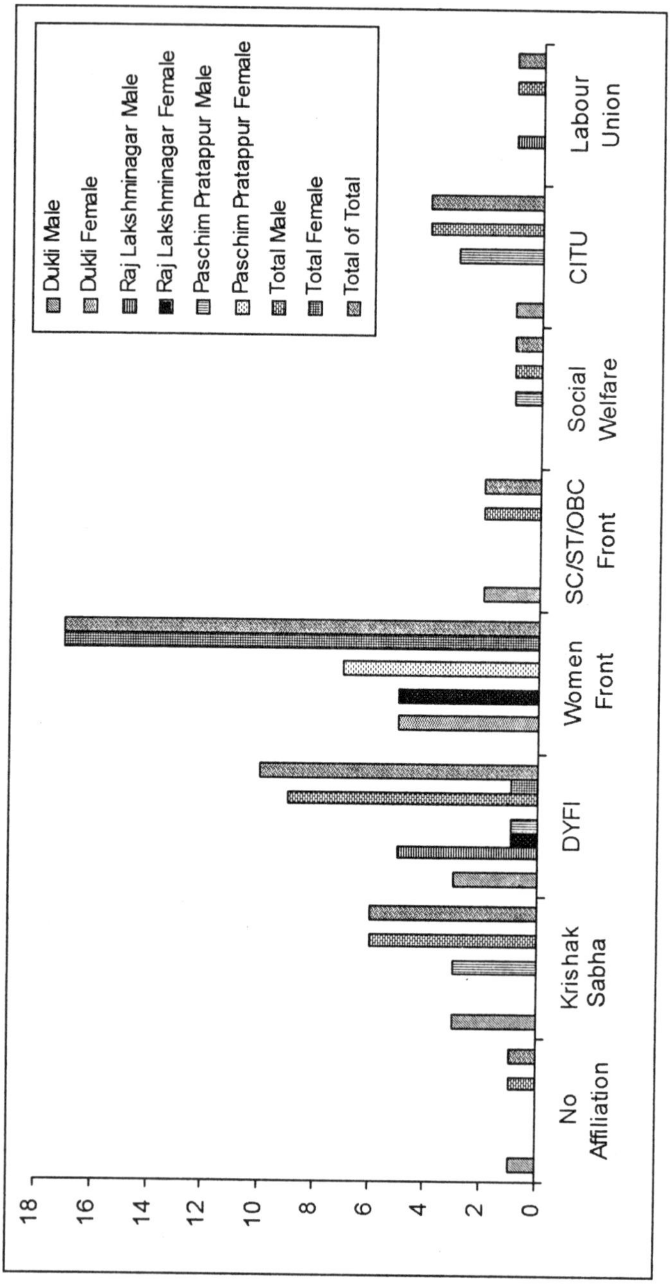

Fig. 12.2: Gram Panchayat Members by Affiliation to Mass Front (South Tripura and Total)

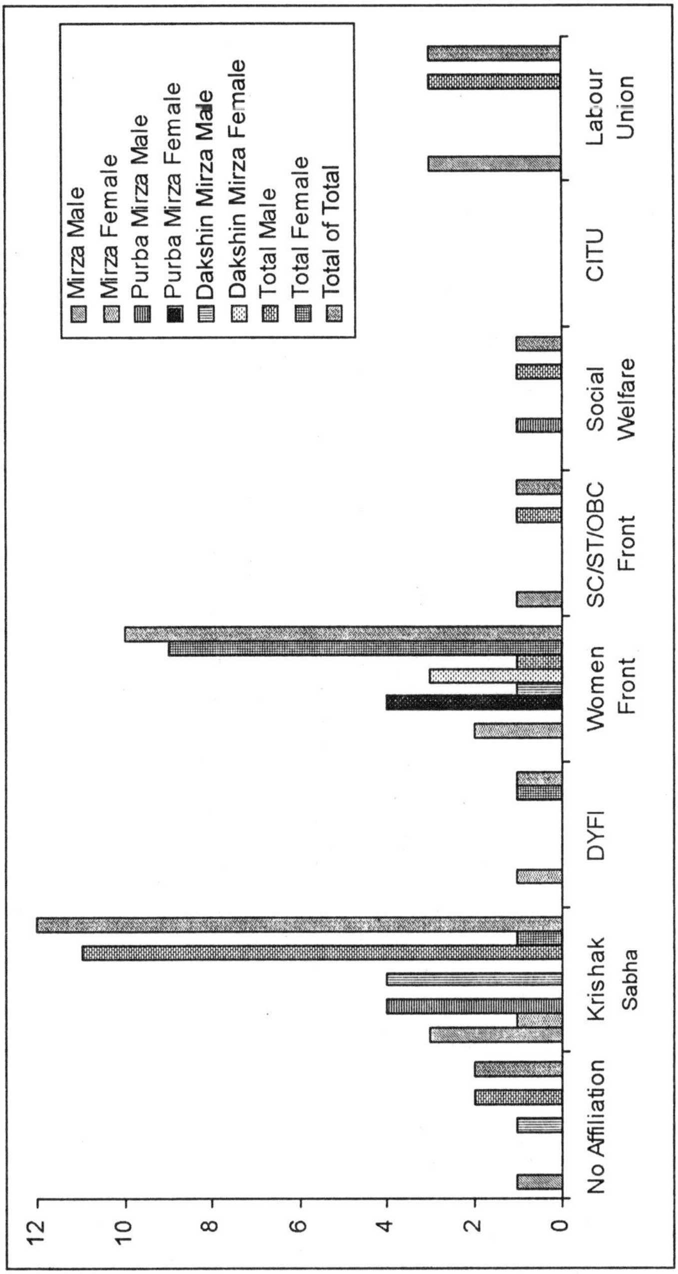

Fig. 12.3: Gram Panchayat Members by Affiliation to Mass Front (Grand Total of West and South Tripura)

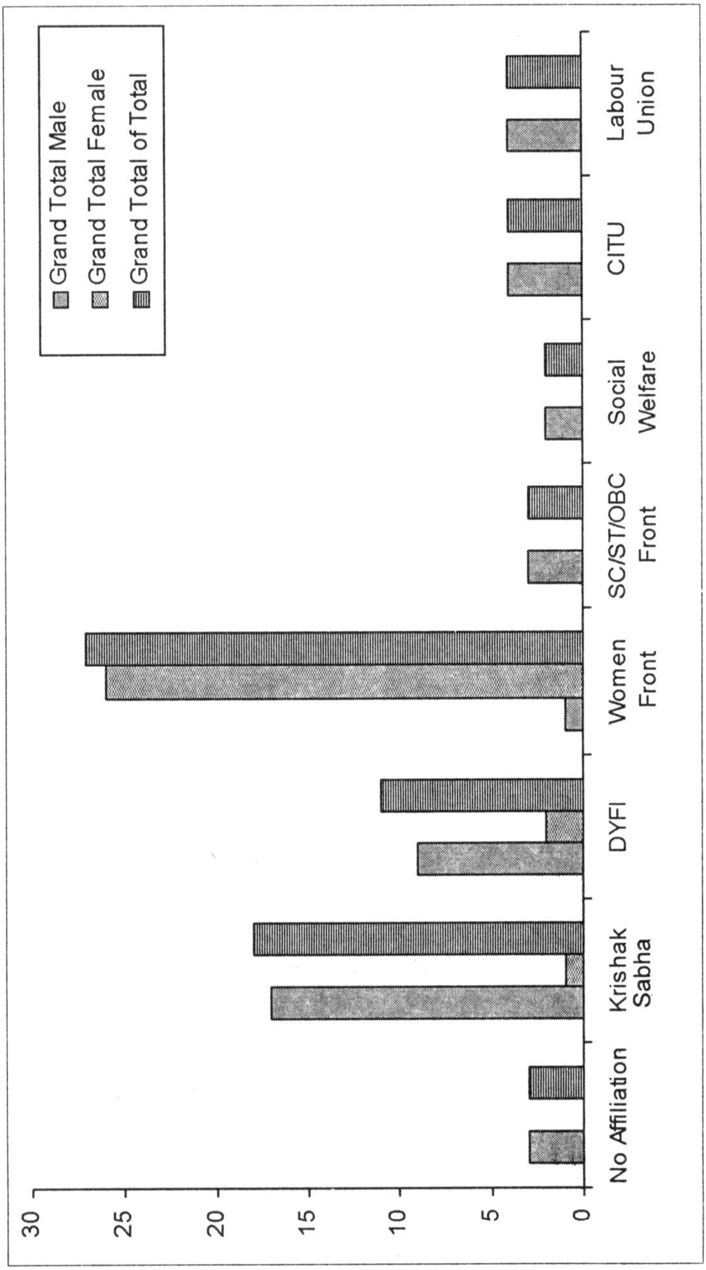

In West Tripura, parity cannot be observed in the proportion of both male and female candidates. Except in Raj Lakshminagar Gram Panchayats, nowhere female representation was equal to that of the male. This is applicable for CPI(M). In South Tripura, among the CPI(M) members, equal representation of female to the Gram Panchayats did not happen. In all cases, females were less represented among the CPI(M) elected members. Why it is so, may be the point of further enquiry. But 33 per cent reservation of seats for women in Gram Panchayats was observed.

Table 13: Distribution of Gram Panchayat Members by their Party Affiliation

District	*Gram Panchayat*	*Sex*	*Party Affiliation*			*Sub-Total*	*Total*
			C.P.I.(M)	*Congress*	*F.B.*		
West Tripura	Dukli	Male	10	—	—	10	
		Female	5	—	—	5	15
	Raj Lakshminagar	Male	6	—	—	6	
		Female	6	—	—	6	12
	Paschim Pratappur	Male	7	—	1	8	
		Female	6	—	1	7	15
	Total	Male	23	—	1	24	
		Female	17(94.44)	—	1(5.56)	18(100%)	
	Total		*40(95.24)*	—	*2(4.76)*	*42(100%)*	*42*
South Tripura	Mirza	Male	7	1	—	8	
		Female	4	—	—	4	12
	Purba Mirza	Male	5	—	—	5	
		Female	4	—	—	4	9
	Dakshin Mirza	Male	6	—	—	6	
		Female	3	—	—	3	9
	Total	Male	18	1	—	19	
		Female	11(100.00)	—	—	11(100%)	
	Total		*29(96.67)*	*1(3.33)*	—	*30(100%)*	*30*
	Grand Total	Male	41	1	1	43	
		Female	28(96.55)	—	1(3.45)	29(100%)	
	Total		*69(95.83)*	*1(1.39)*	*2(2.78)*	*72(100%)*	*72*

Source: Survey 2001-02.

Fig. 13. Distribution of Gram Panchayat Members by their Party Affiliation

Fig. 13.1: Gram Panchayat Members by their Party Affiliation (West Tripura and Total)

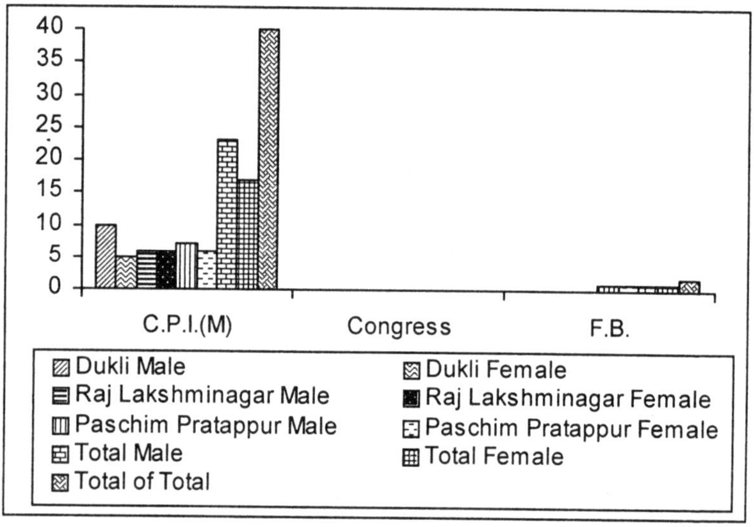

Fig. 13.2: Gram Panchayat Members by their Party Affiliation (South Tripura and Total)

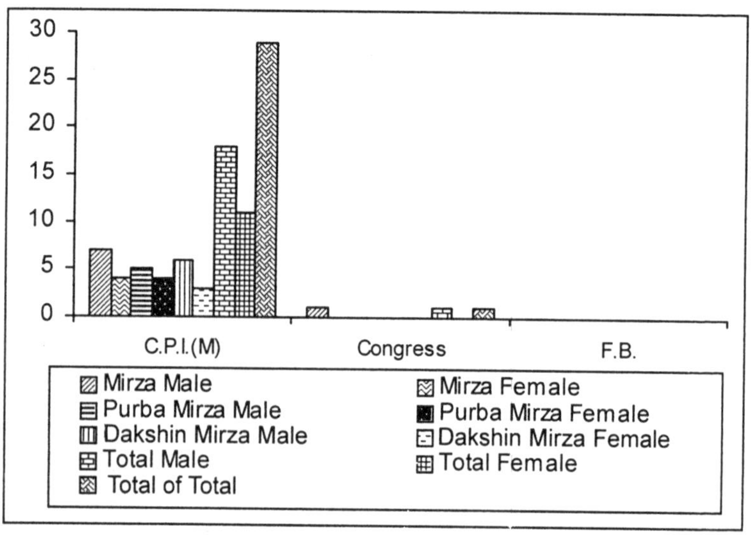

Fig. 13.3: Gram Panchayat Members by their Party Affiliation (Grand Total of West and South Tripura Total)

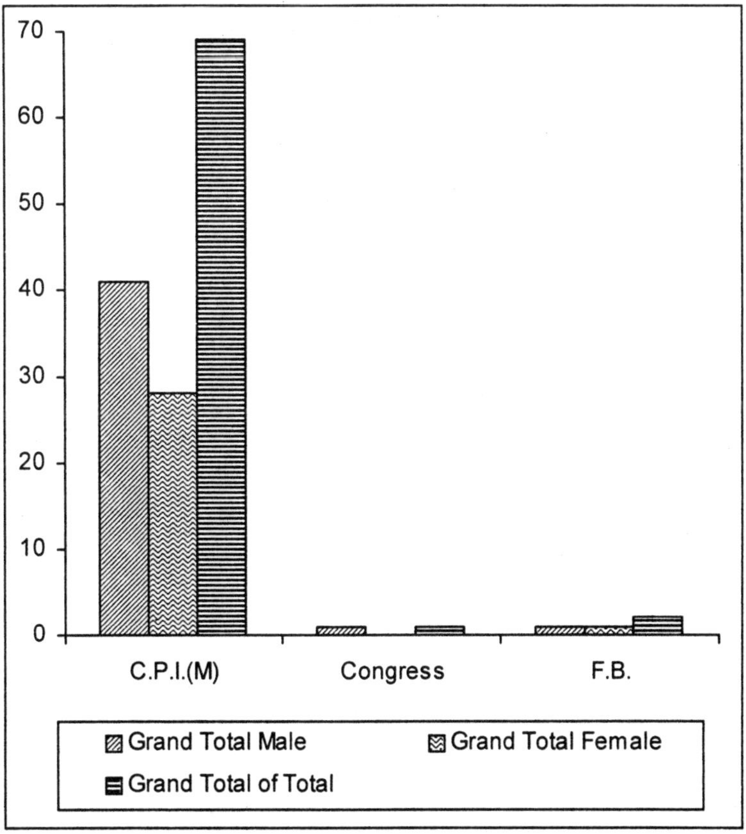

Number of Adult Male in their Family

Size of the family is one of the main criteria to judge the awareness about family planning among the members. Number of dependants per earner is one of the major issues in development and economic management. Traditional concept—who has given the life, he will provide food—is not working now-a-days and the society has been more rational today. In view of this, we have tried to assess the dependency among the Panchayat members.

Table 14: Distribution of Gram Panchayat Member by the Number of Adult Male in their Family

District	Gram Panchayat	Sex	Adult Male				Sub-Total	Total
			1	2	3	More than 3		
West Tripura	Dukli	Male	3	4	2	1	10	
		Female	1	4	—	—	5	15
	Raj Lakshminagar	Male	1	3	1	1	6	
		Female	2	—	1	3	6	12
	Paschim Pratappur	Male	1	3	3	1	8	
		Female	1	—	5	1	7	15
	Total	Male	5	10	6	3	24	
		Female	4(22.22)	4(22.22)	6(33.33)	4(22.22)	18(100%)	
		Total	*9(21.43)*	*14(33.33)*	*12(28.57)*	*7(16.67)*	*42(100%)*	*42*
South Tripura	Mirza	Male	—	1	4	3	8	
		Female	—	1	2	1	4	12
	Purba Mirza	Male	2	1	—	2	5	
		Female	1	1	—	2	4	9
	Dakshin Mirza	Male	3	2	1	—	6	
		Female	—	2	1	—	3	9
	Total	Male	5	4	5	5	19	
		Female	1(9.09)	4(36.37)	3(27.27)	3(27.27)	11(100%)	
		Total	*6(20.00)*	*8(26.67)*	*8(26.66)*	*8(26.67)*	*30(100%)*	*30*
	Grand Total	Male	10	14	11	8	43	
		Female	5(17.24)	8(27.59)	9(31.03)	7(24.14)	29(100%)	
		Total	*15(20.83)*	*22(30.56)*	*20(27.28)*	*15(20.83)*	*72(100%)*	*72*

Source: Survey 2001-02.

Fig. 14. Distribution of Gram Panchayat Members by the number of Adult Male in their Family

Fig. 14.1: Gram Panchayat Members by the number of Adult Male in their family (West Tripura and Total)

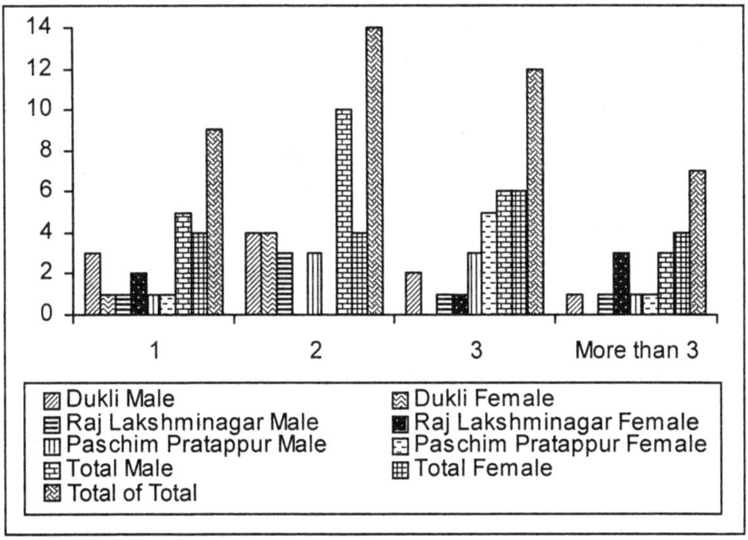

Fig. 14.2: Gram Panchayat Members by the number of Adult Male in their family (South Tripura and Total)

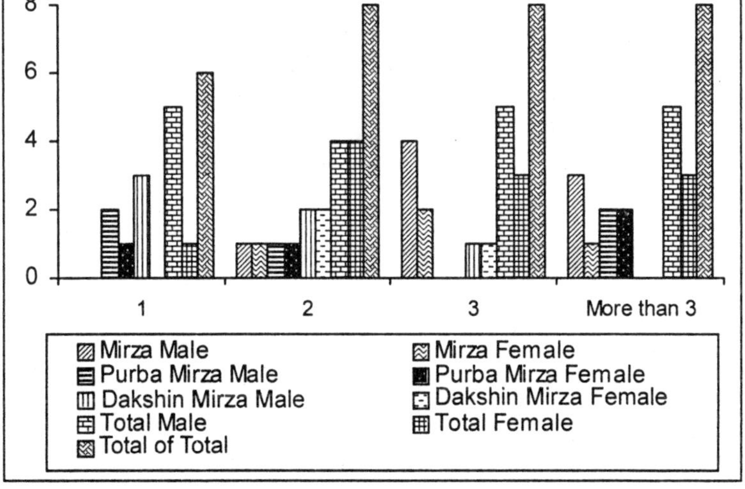

Fig. 14.3: Gram Panchayat Members by the number of Adult Male in their family (Grand Total West and South Tripura)

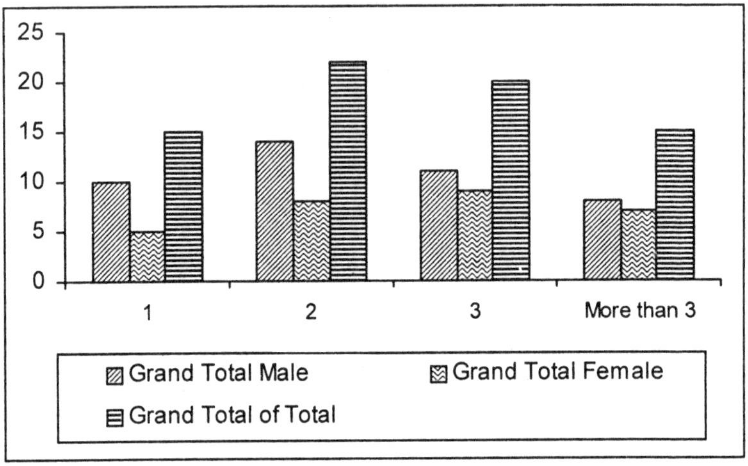

Let us see, the number of working hands who are adult males and who may be absorbed.

In West Tripura, 21.43 per cent members have 1 adult male in their family. 33.33 per cent members have 2 adult males in their families. 28.57 per cent members in the Panchayat have 3 adult males in their families. 16.67 per cent member have more than 3 adult males in the families.

In South Tripura, 20 per cent of the members have 1 adult male in the family, 26.67 per cent members have 2 adult males in their families and 26.66 per cent members have 3 adult males in the families. 26.67 per cent members have more than 3 adult males in the families. 26.67 per cent member have more adult males in their families.

Number of Adult Female in their Family

Adult male is considered to be socially providing working hands. Females are supposed to perform domestic chore. Only female hands also may produce, a number of commodities of productive as Commercial and use value Panchayat system is basically related to agrarian production process or household

Table 15: Distribution of Gram Panchayat Members by the Number of Adult Female in their Family

District	Gram Panchayat	Sex	Adult Female					Sub-Total	Total
			0	1	2	3	More than 3		
West Tripura	Dukli	Male	1	5	3	—	1	10	
		Female	—	2	3	—	—	5	15
	Raj Lakshminagar	Male	—	2	3	—	1	6	
		Female	—	4	—	2	—	6	12
	Paschim Pratappur	Male	—	3	3	—	2	8	
		Female	—	4	1	2	—	7	15
	Total	Male	1	10	9	—	4	24	
		Female	—	10(55.56)	4(22.22)	4(22.22)	—	18(100%)	
		Total	*1(2.38)*	*20(47.62)*	*13(30.96)*	*4(9.52)*	*4(9.52)*	*42(100%)*	*42*
South Tripura	Mirza	Male	—	2	6	—	—	8	
		Female	—	2	1	1	—	4	12
	Purba Mirza	Male	—	3	1	1	—	5	
		Female	—	2	1	1	—	4	9
	Dakshin Mirza	Male	—	2	4	—	—	6	
		Female	—	1	1	1	—	3	9
	Total	Male	—	7	11	1	—	19	
		Female	—	5(45.46)	3(27.27)	3(27.27)	—	11(100%)	
		Total	—	*12(40.00)*	*14(46.67)*	*4(13.33)*	—	*30(100%)*	*30*
	Grand Total	Male	1	17	20	1	4	43	
		Female	—	15(51.72)	7(24.14)	7(24.14)	—	29(100%)	
		Total	*1(1.39)*	*32(44.44)*	*27(37.50)*	*8(11.11)*	*4(5.56)*	*72(100%)*	*72*

Source: Survey 2001-02.

industry based production organization. Female hands can be fruitfully utilized in such household industry.

Though, where these household industries are absent, adult females are tied with domestic work mainly. But their labour with domestic work is considered to be productive, as it does not bring economic value or surplus value. But none can deny the necessity of their labour in the domestic front. There have been numerous debates in this issue very recently. Male take over the work of women and process of emancipation accelerates thereby. So that increasing leisure time can be utilized by women rationally and fruitfully. But our society has not given emphasis with full effort to this area. As a result discussion and debate has not attracted the women.

Some figures on dependency of adult female in the families of the Gram Panchayat members has been presented. 1 member in West Tripura district did not have any adult female in the household. 47.62 per cent members have 1 adult female in femily. 30.96 per cent have 2 adult females in family. 9.52 per cent members have 3 females in household. 9.52 per cent members have more than 3 females in their families. So, 1-2 adult female/s per member's family is the common pattern. Very few families, about 19 per cent members have 3 or above number of adult females.

In South Tripura, 40 per cent members have 1 adult female per family. 46.67 per cent members have 3 females per family. 13.33 per cent members have 3 adult females per family. But there are no member who have more than 3 adult females in their families.

We find that out of total 72 in two districts, 44.44 per cent and 37.50 per cent members have 1 and 2 adult females per family. 11.11 per cent and 5.56 per cent have 2 and 3 adult females per family. Only 1 member has no adult female in the family.

Fig. 15. Distribution of Gram Panchayat Members by the number of Adult Female in their Family

Fig. 15.1: Gram Panchayat Members by the number of Adult Female in their Family (West Tripura and Total)

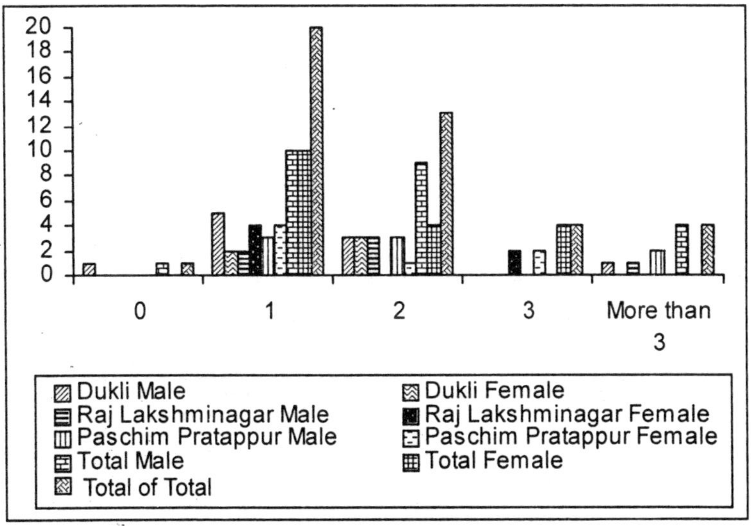

Fig. 15.2: Gram Panchayat Members by the number of Adult Female in their Family (West Tripura and Total)

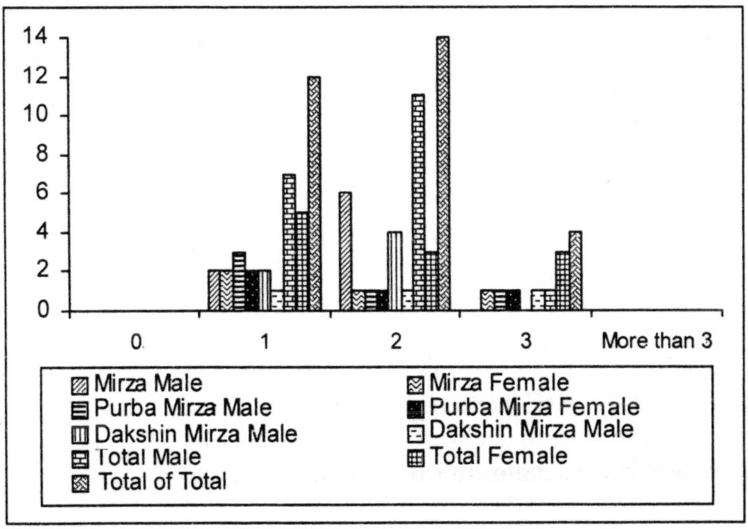

Fig. 15.3: Gram Panchayat Member by the number of Adult Females in their Family (Grand Total of West and South Tripura)

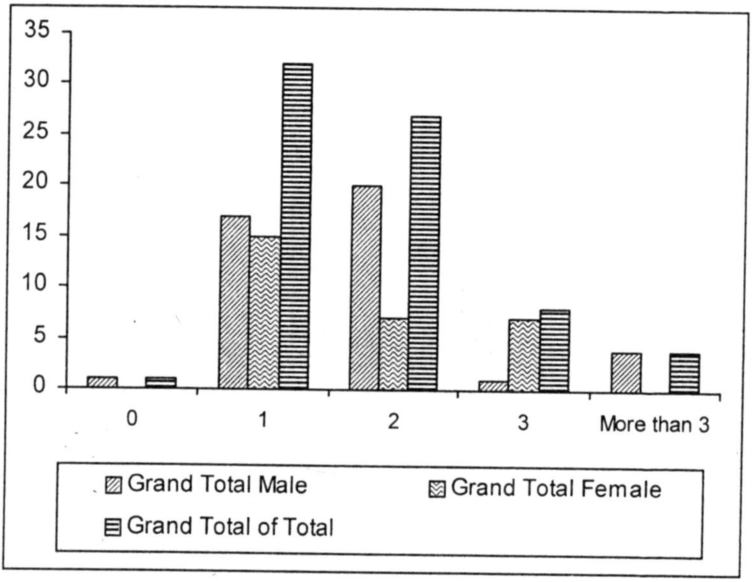

Number of Male Children in their Family

Male female Child differentiation still exists in our society. Preference to male children among the mothers can be observed. That is why, male children's and female children's number in family is taken into consideration. 61.91 per cent members do not have more male children in their families in West Tripura Gram Panchayats. 33.33 per cent members have 1 male child in their families. 4.76 per cent members do have 2 male children in their families. 72.22 per cent female members do not have children. 22.22 per cent female members have 1 male child each in their families. 5.56 per cent of the female members have 2 children in the family.

In South Tripura, 46.67 per cent members have no male child in the family. 36.67 per cent of them have 1 male child. 10 per cent of them have 2 children in their home. 6.66 per cent members have 3 male children in their families.

Table 14: Distribution of Gram Panchayat Member by the Number of Adult Male in their Family

District	Gram Panchayat	Sex	Adult Male				Sub-Total	Total
			1	2	3	More than 3		
West Tripura	Dukli	Male	3	4	2	1	10	
		Female	1	4	—	—	5	15
	Raj Lakshminagar	Male	1	3	1	1	6	
		Female	2	—	1	3	6	12
	Paschim Pratappur	Male	1	3	3	1	8	
		Female	1	—	5	1	7	15
	Total	Male	5	10	6	3	24	
		Female	4(22.22)	4(22.22)	6(33.33)	4(22.22)	18(100%)	
		Total	*9(21.43)*	*14(33.33)*	*12(28.57)*	*7(16.67)*	*42(100%)*	*42*
South Tripura	Mirza	Male	—	1	4	3	8	
		Female	—	1	2	1	4	12
	Purba Mirza	Male	2	1	—	2	5	
		Female	1	1	—	2	4	9
	Dakshin Mirza	Male	3	2	1	—	6	
		Female	—	2	1	—	3	9
	Total	Male	5	4	5	5	19	
		Female	1(9.09)	4(36.37)	3(27.27)	3(27.27)	11(100%)	
		Total	*6(20.00)*	*8(26.67)*	*8(26.66)*	*8(26.67)*	*30(100%)*	*30*
	Grand Total	Male	10	14	11	8	43	
		Female	5(17.24)	8(27.59)	9(31.03)	7(24.14)	29(100%)	
		Total	*15(20.83)*	*22(30.56)*	*20(27.28)*	*15(20.83)*	*72(100%)*	*72*

Source: Survey 2001-02.

Among the female member, 40 per cent do not have male children, 30 per cent of them have 1 child in each family. 20 per cent female members have 2 male children in each family. 10 per cent of them have 3 children (male) in each family.

Number of Female Child/Children in their Family

In West Tripura, 76.19 per cent members have no female child in their family. 16.67 per cent members of the Gram Panchayat have got 1 female child each, 2.38 per cent have 2 children (female) per household. 4.76 per cent have 3 children (female) in their household. 88.89 per cent female members have two female children. 11.11 per cent female members in West Tripura have 2 female children in their homes.

Fig. 16. Distribution of Gram Panchayat Members by the Number of Male Child/Children in their Family

Fig. 16.1: Gram Panchayat Members by the Number of Male Children in their Family (West Tripura and Total)

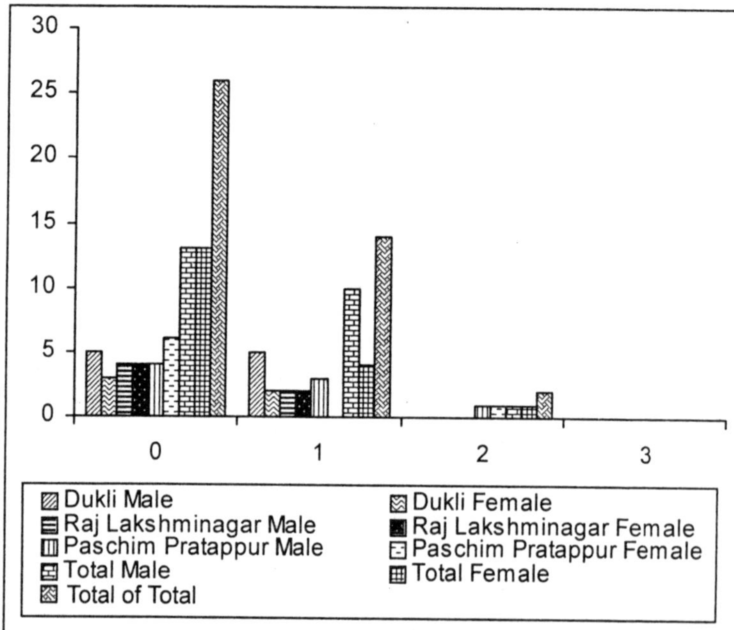

Fig. 16.2: Gram Panchayat Members by the Number of Male Child/ Children in their Family (South Tripura and Total)

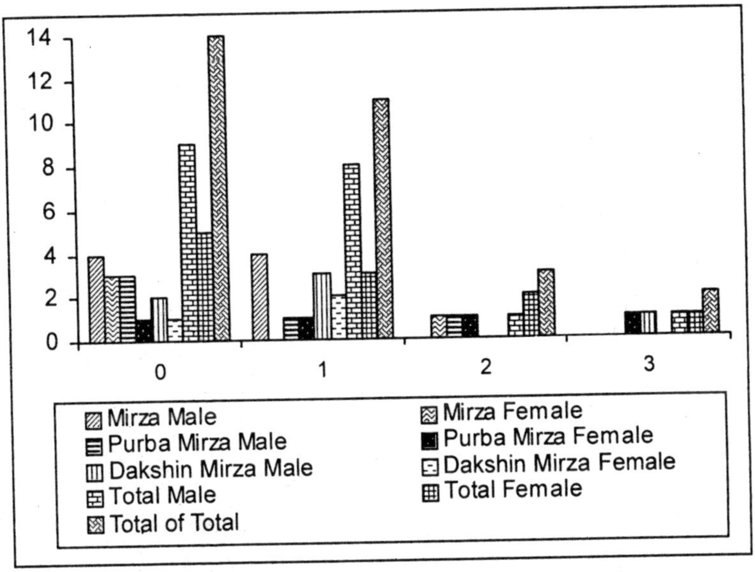

Fig. 16.3: Gram Panchayat Members by the Number of Male Child/ Children in their Family (Grand Total of West and South Tripura)

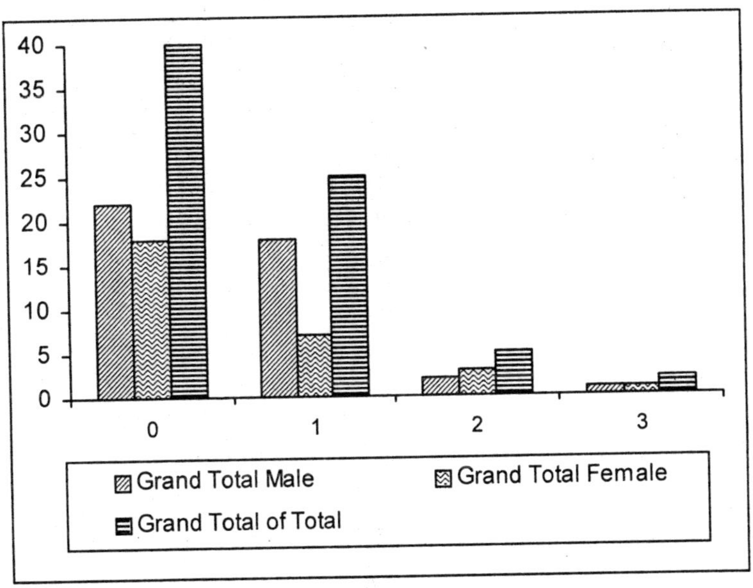

Table 17: Distribution of Gram Panchayat Members by the Number of Female Child/children in their Family

District	*Gram Panchayat*	*Sex*		*Female Child*				*Sub-Total*	*Total*
				0	*1*	*2*	*3*		
West Tripura	Dukli	Male		4	4	—	2	10	
		Female		5	—	—	—	5	15
	Raj Lakshmi-nagar	Male		6	—	—	—	6	
		Female		6	—	—	—	6	12
	Paschim Pratappur	Male		6	1	1	—	8	
		Female		5	2	—	—	7	15
	Total	Male		16	5	1	2	24	
		Female		16(88.89)	2(11.11)	—	—	18(100%)	
			Total	*32(76.19)*	*7(16.67)*	*1(2.38)*	*2(4.76)*	*42(100%)*	*42*
South Tripura	Mirza	Male		3	3	2	—	8	
		Female		2	—	2	—	4	12
	Purba Mirza	Male		1	4	—	—	5	
		Female		2	2	—	—	4	9
	Dakshin Mirza	Male		4	2	—	—	6	
		Female		2	1	—	—	3	9
	Total	Male		8	9	2	—	19	
		Female		6(54.55)	3(27.27)	2(18.18)	—	11(100%)	
			Total	*14(46.67)*	*12(40.00)*	*4(13.33)*	—	*30(100%)*	*30*
	Grand Total	Male		24	14	3	2	43	
		Female		22(75.86)	5(17.24)	2(6.90)	—	29(100%)	
			Total	*46(63.89)*	*19(26.39)*	*5(6.94)*	*2(2.78)*	*72(100%)*	*72*

Source: Survey 2001-02.

In South Tripura 46.67 per cent members have no female child, 40 per cent members have 1 female child in each household. 13.33 per cent have 2 female children in each household. In case of female members: 60 per cent of them have no female child and 30 per cent of the members have 1 female child in each household and 10 per cent only of them have 2 female children.

63.89 per cent of total 72 members have no female children and 26.39 per cent of the members have 1 female child in each household. 6.94 per cent with 2 female children in each household and 2.78 per cent of them have 3 female children.

Fig. 17. Distribution of Gram Panchayat Members by the number of Female Child/Children in their Family

Fig. 17.1: Gram Panchayat Members by the number of Female Child/ Children in their Family (West Tripura and Total)

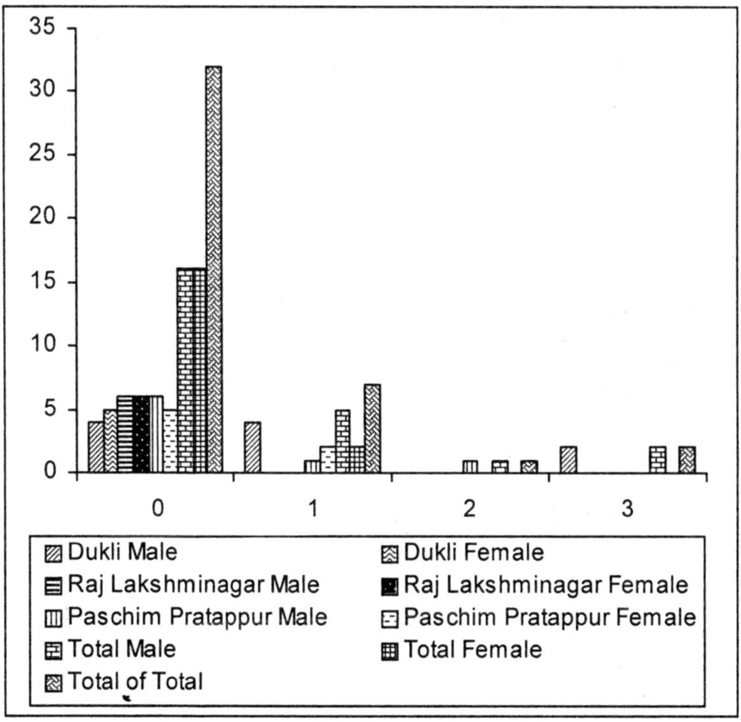

Fig. 17.2: Gram Panchayat Members by the number of Female Child/ Children in their Family (South Tripura and Total)

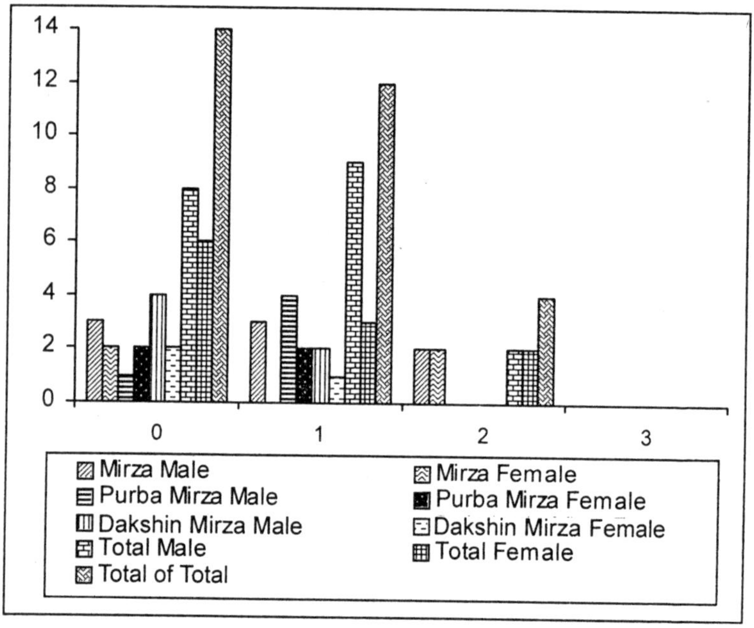

Fig. 17.3: Gram Panchayat Members by the number of Female Child/ Children in their Family (Grand Total of West and South Tripura)

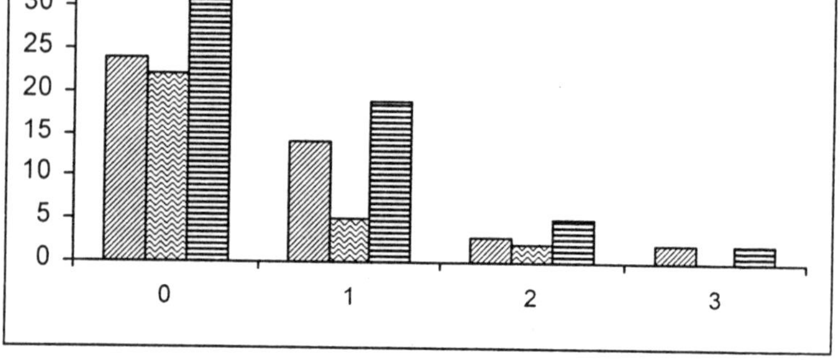

Earning Status

Earning is a usual habit of human being. In Table 18, Panchayat members have been classificd as main earners.

Table 18: Distribution of Gram Panchayat Members by their Earning-Status

Dist-rict	Gram Panchayat	Sex	Main Earner		Sub-Total	Total
			Yes	No		
West Tripura	Dukli	Male	8	2	10	
		Female	—	5	5	15
	Raj Lakshmi-nagar	Male	5	1	6	
		Female	—	6	6	12
	Paschim Pratappur	Male	4	4	8	
		Female	—	7	7	15
	Total	Male	17	7	24	
		Female	—	18(100.00)	18(100%)	
		Total	*17(40.48)*	*25(59.52)*	*42(100%)*	*42*
South Tripura	Mirza	Male	6	2	8	
		Female	1	3	4	12
	Purba Mirza	Male	5	—	5	
		Female	—	4	4	9
	Dakshin Mirza	Male	5	1	6	
		Female	1	2	3	9
	Total	Male	16	3	19	
		Female	2(18.18)	9(81.82)	11(100%)	
		Total	*18(60.00)*	*12(40.00)*	*30(100%)*	*30*
	Grand Total	Male	33	10	43	
		Female	2(6.90)	27(93.10)	29(100%)	
		Total	*35(48.61)*	*37(51.39)*	*72(100%)*	*72*

Source: Survey 2001-02.

It is worth mentioning that 40.48 per cent of the members are main earners and all of them are male. No female members in West Tripura have been main earners. Total percentage of main earner is 59.52 per cent among the total 42 members.

In South Tripura Gram Panchayats, 60 per cent of the members are main earner and 2 female members have been found to be main earners. 40 per cent of them are not main earner. Among the female members, 20 per cent are main earner and 80 per cent females are not main earners.

Fig. 18. Distribution of Gram Panchayat Members by their Earning Status

Fig. 18.1: Gram Panchayat Members by their Earning Status (West Tripura and Total)

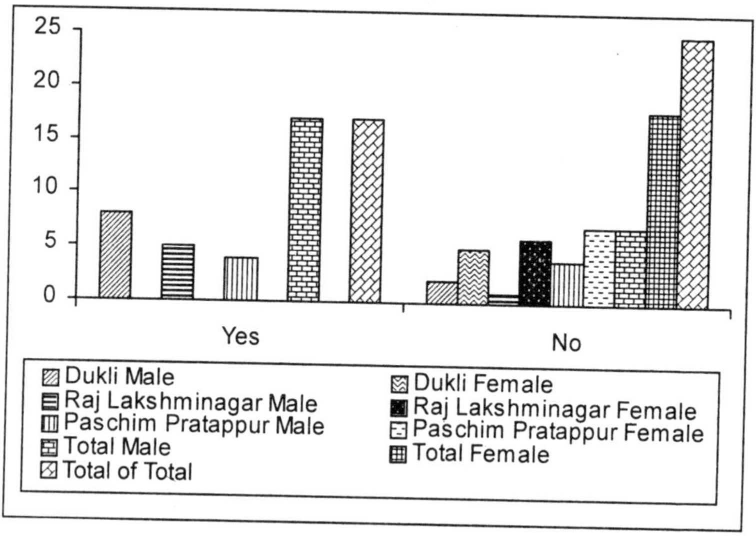

Fig. 18.2: Gram Panchayat Members by their Earning Status (South Tripura and Total)

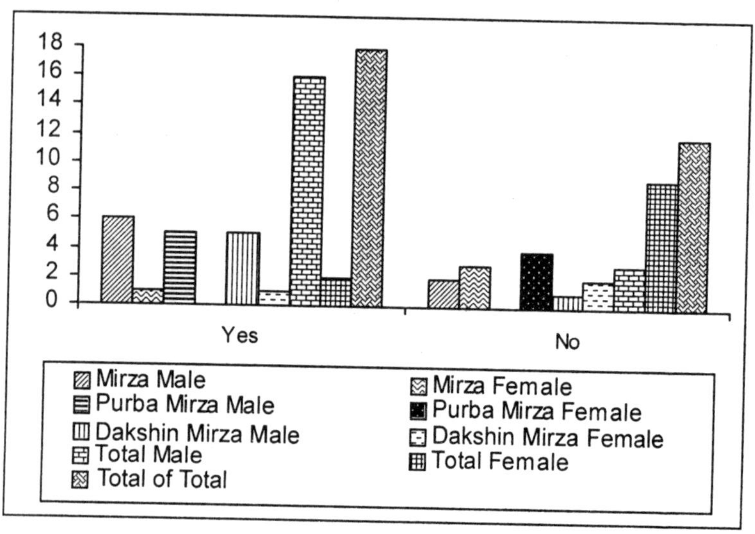

Fig. 18.3: Gram Panchayat Members by their Earning Status (Grand Total of West and South Tripura)

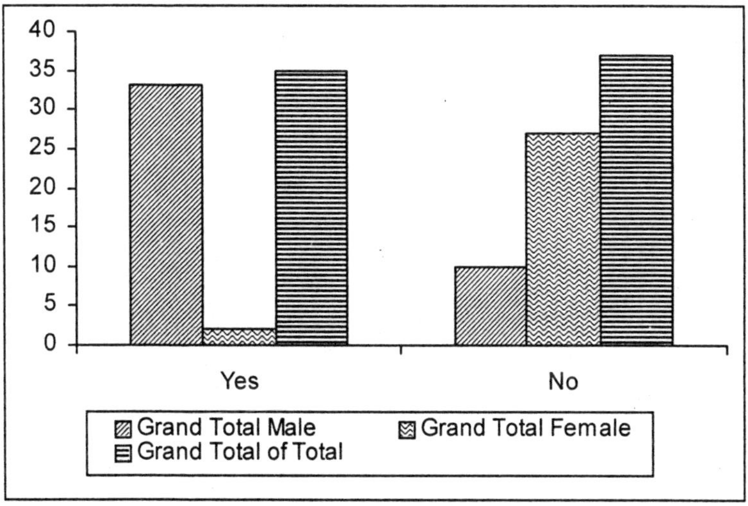

Main Occupation

Ten types of main occupation were found among Tripura Gram Panchayat members. 50 per cent of the members have no occupation. 4.76 per cent members' main occupation is Industrial labour followed by 9.53 per cent daily labour, 9.53 per cent members have service, either government or private. 7.14 per cent of the members have business as main occupation. 4.76 per cent are housewives. 4.76 per cent are mason. 2.38 per cent have tailoring shop as main occupation. Another 2.38 per cent have cultivation as their main occupation. Also similar portions of members are professionally Political Workers. 2.38 per cent of the members are retired person. Among the females, 6.67 per cent have no occupation and 5.56 per cent are industrial workers. These all figures pertain to West Tripura.

Gram Panchayats of South Tripura have 43.33 per cent members with no occupation, among the females 90 per cent members are with no occupation. 13.33 per cent are daily labour. 6.67 per cent have got business establishments. 36.67 per cent are cultivators. 10 per cent of the female members are daily labourers.

Table 19: Distribution of Gram Panchayat Members by their Main Occupation

District	*Gram Panch-ayat*	*Sex*	*Main Occupation 0*	*1*	*2*	*3*	*4*	*5*	*6*	*7*	*8*	*9*	*10*	*Sub-Total*	*Total*
West Tripura	Dukli	Male	1	1	—	2	3	—	1	—	1	1	—	10	
		Female	1	1	1	2	—	—	—	—	—	—	—	5	15
	Raj Lakshmi-nagar	Male	3	—	2	—	—	—	—	—	—	—	1	6	
		Female	4	—	—	—	—	2	—	—	—	—	—	6	12
	Paschim Pratappur	Male	5	—	1	—	—	—	1	1	—	—	—	8	
		Female	7	—	—	—	—	—	—	—	—	—	—	7	15
	Total	Male	9	1	3	2	3	—	2	1	1	1	1	24	
		Female	12(66.67)	1(5.56)	1(5.55)	2(11.11)	—	2(11.11)	—	—	—	—	—	18(100%)	
		Total	*21(50.00)*	*2(4.76)*	*4(9.53)*	*4(9.53)*	*3(7.14)*	*2(4.76)*	*2(4.76)*	*1(2.38)*	*1(2.38)*	*1(2.38)*	*1(2.38)*	*42(100%)*	*42*
South Tripura	Mirza	Male	2	—	3	—	2		—	—	1	—	—	8	
		Female	3	—	1	—	—	—	—	—	—	—	—	4	12
	Purba Mirza	Male	—	—	—	—	—	—	—	—	5	—	—	5	
		Female	4	—	—	—	—	—	—	—	—	—	—	4	9
	Dakshin Mirza	Male	1	—	—	—	—	—	—	—	5	—	—	6	
		Female	3	—	—	—	—	—	—	—	—	—	—	3	9
	Total	Male	3	—	3	—	2	—	—	—	11	—	—	19	
		Female	10(90.91)	—	1(9.09)	—	—	—	—	—	—	—	—	11(100%)	
		Total	*13(43.33)*	—	*4(13.33)*	—	*2(6.67)*	—	—	—	*11(36.67)*	—	—	*30(100%)*	*30*
	Grand Total	Male	12	1	6	2	2	—	2	1	12	1	1	43	
		Female	22(75.86)	1(3.44)	2(6.90)	2(6.90)	2(6.90)	—	—	—	—	—	—	29(100%)	
		Total	*34(47.22)*	*2(2.78)*	*8(11.11)*	*4(5.55)*	*5(6.94)*	*2(2.78)*	*2(2.78)*	*1(1.39)*	*12(16.67)*	*1(1.39)*	*1(1.39)*	*72(100%)*	*72*

Source: Survey 2001-02.

Note: 0. No occupation, 1. Industrial labour, 2. Daily labour, 3. Service, 4. Business, 5. House-wife, 6. Rajmistri, 7. Tailor, 8. Cultivator, 9. Professional Political Worker, 10. Retired person

Fig. 19. Gram Panchayat Members by their Main Occupation

Fig. 19.1: Members by their Main Occupation (West Tripura)

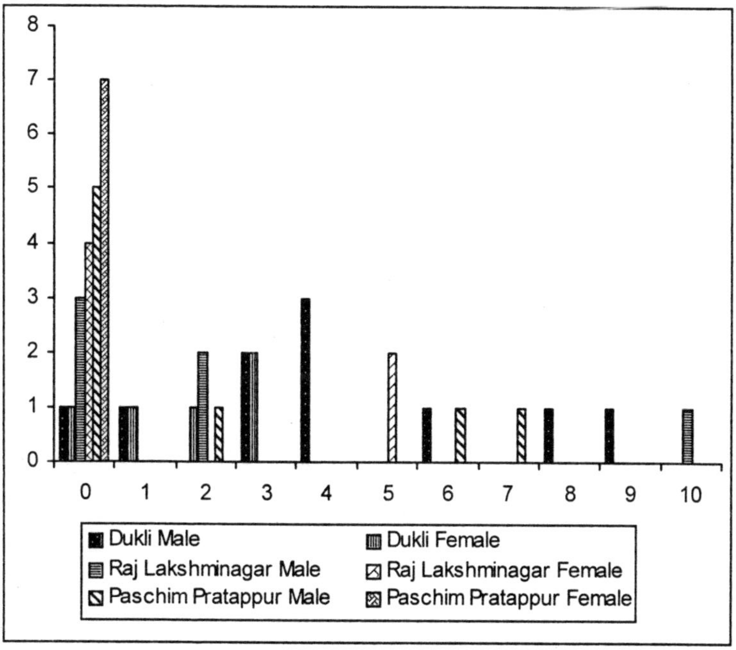

Fig. 19.2: Members by their Main Occupation (West Tripura Total)

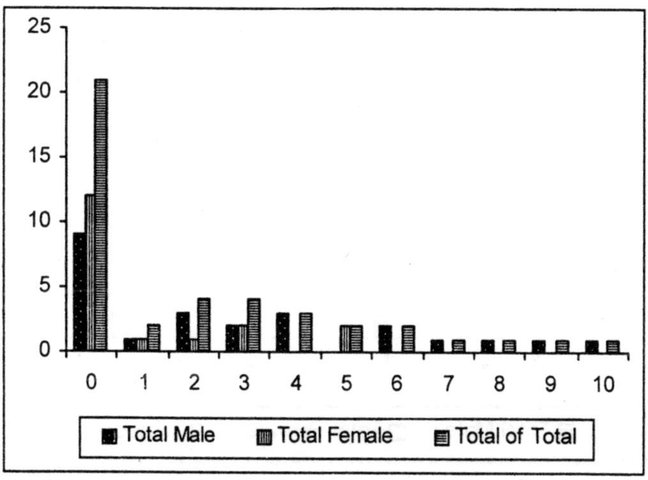

Fig. 19.3: Members by their Main Occupation (South Tripura)

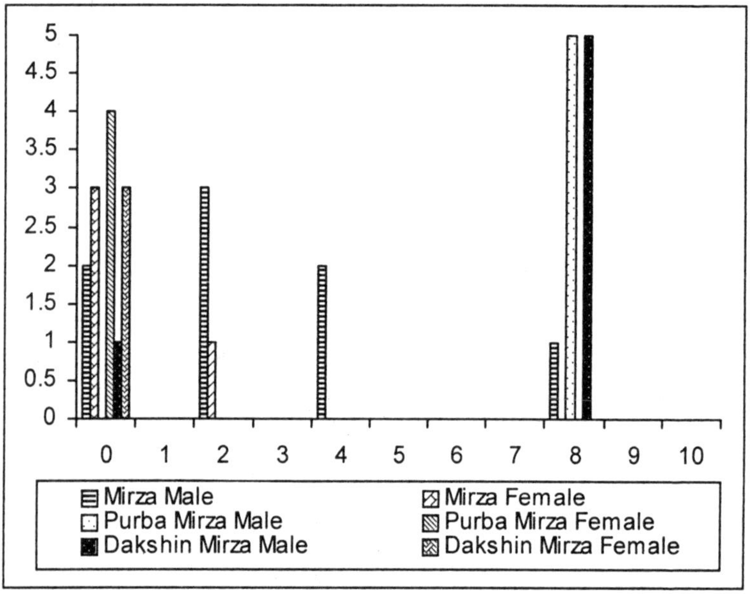

Fig. 19.4: Members by their Main Occupation (South Tripura Total)

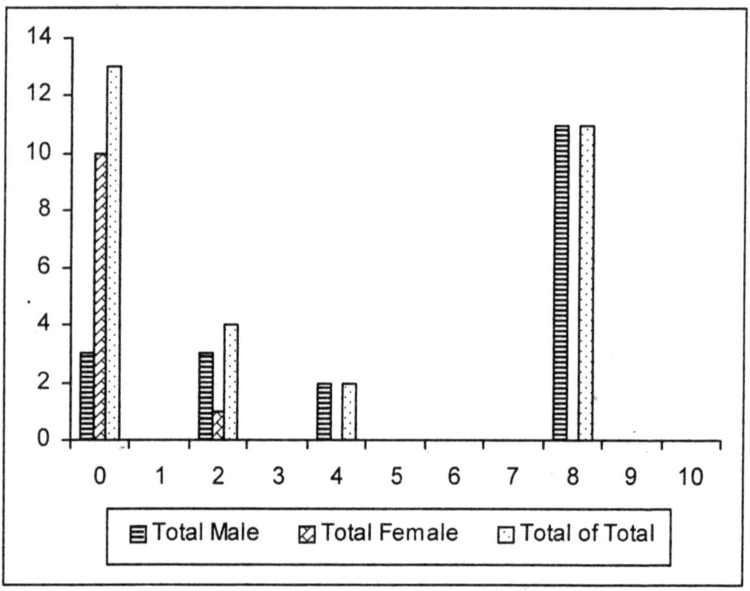

Fig. 19.5: Members by their Main Occupation
(Grand Total of West and South Tripura)

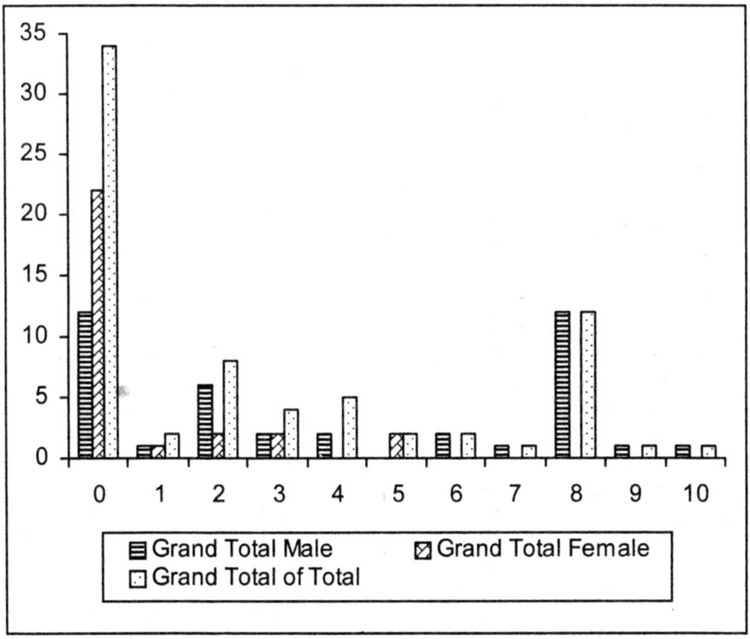

Subsidiary Occupation

Subsidiary occupation includes daily labour; Service; Business; Raj Mistri; Goatherd, Pigboy, Cowboy etc. Service; Business and Cultivator, Fisherman; Professional political workers. Retired person has no occupation but they have been categorized separately.

In West Tripura, 71.43 per cent members have no occupation. 2.38 per cent are daily labourer and 2.38 per cent have service as subsidiary occupation 7.14 per cent having business as subsidiary occupation. 4.76 per cent having cowboy etc. Members also have cultivation as subsidiary occupation and 4.77 per cent are engaged in it. 2.38 per cent members are fishermen. However, retired persons are also available in the Panchayat as member.

Table 19: Distribution of Gram Panchayat Members by their Main Occupation

District	Gram Panchayat	Sex	Main Occupation 0	1	2	3	4	5	6	7	8	9	10	Sub-Total	Total
West Tripura	Dukli	Male	1	1	—	2	3	—	1	—	1	1	—	10	
		Female	1	1	1	2	—	—	—	—	—	—	—	5	15
	Raj	Male	3	—	2	—	—	—	—	—	—	—	1	6	
	Lakshmi-nagar	Female	4	—	—	—	—	2	—	—	—	—	—	6	12
	Paschim	Male	5	—	1	—	—	—	1	1	—	—	—	8	
	Pratappur	Female	7	—	—	—	—	—	—	—	—	—	—	7	15
	Total	Male	9	1	3	2	3	—	2	1	1	1	1	24	
		Female	12(66.67)	1(5.56)	1(5.55)	2(11.11)	—	2(11.11)	—	—	—	—	—	18(100%)	
		Total	*21(50.00)*	*2(4.76)*	*4(9.53)*	*4(9.53)*	*3(7.14)*	*2(4.76)*	*2(4.76)*	*1(2.38)*	*1(2.38)*	*1(2.38)*	*1(2.38)*	*42(100%)*	*42*
South Tripura	Mirza	Male	2	—	3	—	2		—	—	1	—	—	8	
		Female	3	—	1	—	—	—	—	—	—	—	—	4	12
	Purba Mirza	Male	—	—	—	—	—	—	—	—	5	—	—	5	
		Female	4	—	—	—	—	—	—	—	—	—	—	4	9
	Dakshin Mirza	Male	1	—	—	—	—	—	—	—	5	—	—	6	
		Female	3	—	—	—	—	—	—	—	—	—	—	3	9
	Total	Male	3	—	3	—	2	—	—	—	11	—	—	19	
		Female	10(90.91)	—	1(9.09)	—	—	—	—	—	—	—	—	11(100%)	
		Total	*13(43.33)*	—	*4(13.33)*	—	*2(6.67)*	—	—	—	*11(36.67)*	—	—	*30(100%)*	*30*
	Grand Total	Male	12	1	6	2	2	—	2	1	12	1	1	43	
		Female	22(75.86)	1(3.44)	2(6.90)	2(6.90)	2(6.90)	—	—	—	—	—	—	29(100%)	
		Total	*34(47.22)*	*2(2.78)*	*8(11.11)*	*4(5.55)*	*5(6.94)*	*2(2.78)*	*2(2.78)*	*1(1.39)*	*12(16.67)*	*1(1.39)*	*1(1.39)*	*72(100%)*	*72*

Source: Survey 2001-02.

Note: 0. No occupation, 1. Industrial labour, 2. Daily labour, 3. Service, 4. Business, 5. House-wife, 6. Rajmistri, 7. Tailor, 8. Cultivator, 9. Professional Political Worker, 10. Retired person

Fig. 20. Distribution of Gram Panchayat Members by their Subsidiary

Fig. 20.1: Distribution of Gram Panchayat Members by their Subsidiary Occupations (West Tripura and Total)

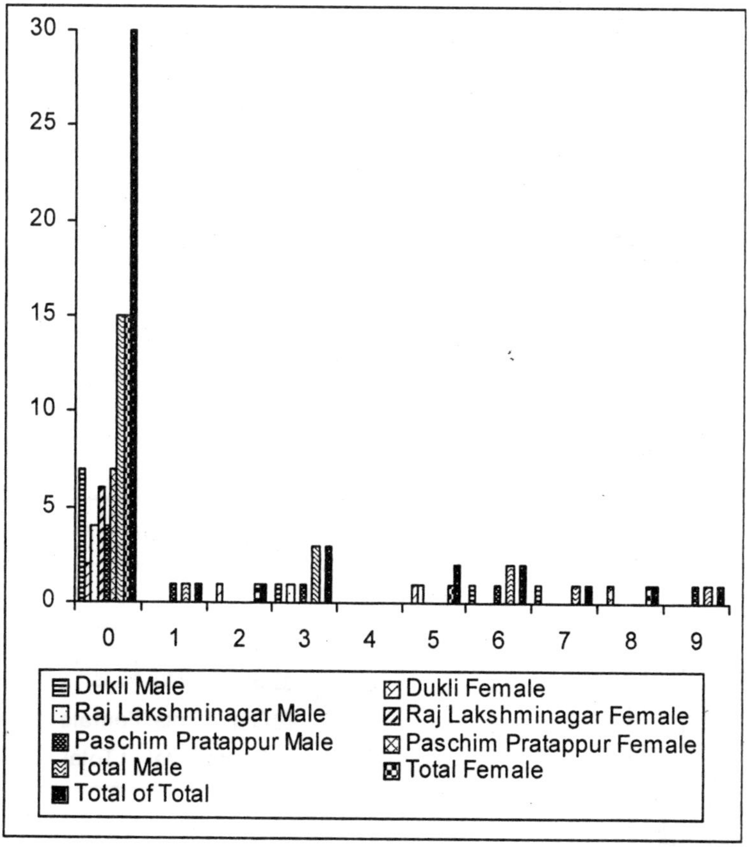

Fig. 20.2: Distribution of Gram Panchayat Members by their Subsidiary Occupations (South Tripura and Total)

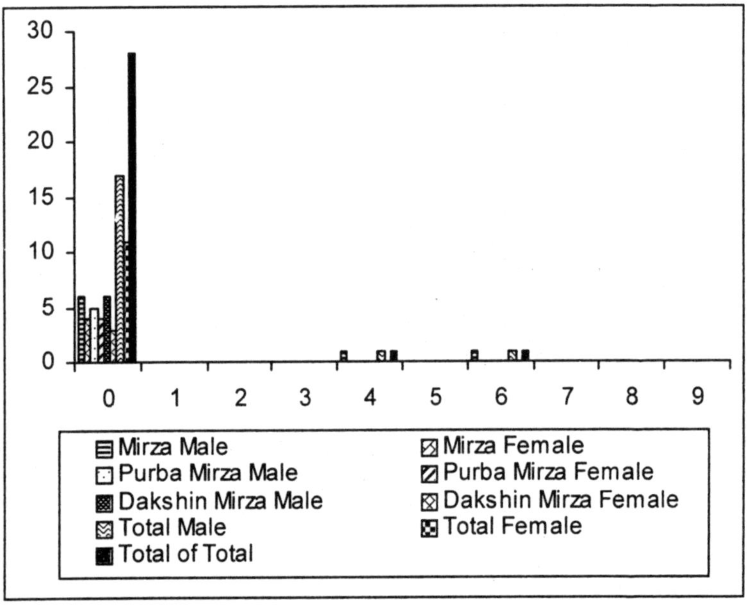

Fig. 20.3: Distribution of Gram Panchayat Members by their Subsidiary Occupations (Grand Total of West and South Tripura)

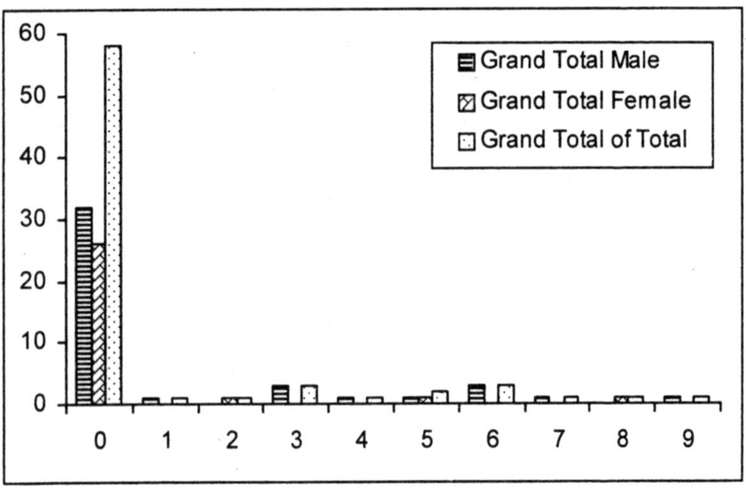

7

Participation, Activities and Achievements of Gram Panchayat Members Especially of Women

Panchayati Raj Institution

Before Tripura merged with the Indian Union in 1949, it was a princely state. There were traditional village level institutions based on tribal customs, which took important decisions on matters pertaining to tribal communities and to disputes among their members. But these institutions could hardly be described as democratic, depending as they did on the social legitimacy conferred on them by the existing power structure and social order. Women were denied the right to participate in these village councils.

The real breakthrough in democratic local self-government came with the accession to office of the Left Front Government in Tripura. For the first time, elections to panchayats were held through secret ballot and with open participation of political parties. Tripura had a single-tier system of village panchayats till 1978, when the left front Government brought forward legislation to constitute a two-tier panchayat system. The Tripura Panchayati Raj Act of 1983 reduced the voting age from 21 to 18 years, and made special provisions for the representation of Scheduled Castes (SCs) and Scheduled Tribes (STs). Democratic decentralization in Tripura suffered a setback when the Congress (I)-TUJS coalition came to power in the state in 1988. The Government superseded all 698 gaon Panchayats and appointed block development officers to supervise the functions of the panchayats. Following the 73rd Constitution Amendment Act of 1992, Tripura enacted the Tripura Panchayat

Act, 1993, and introduced a three-tier structure. Elections to all three tiers of Panchayats have been held on schedule in 1994, 1999 and 2004. There are at present four Zilla Parishads, 23 Panchayat Samitis and 513 Gram Panchayats under the Tripura Panchayat Act, 1993.

Political Participation of Women

The remarkable feature of women's political participation in Tripura is that the participation is very high and visible.

There has been no woman Member of Parliament from Tripura and there is only one woman in the Legislative Assembly.

The representation of women in panchayat institutions is closely tied to the enactment of the Tripura Panchayat Act, 1993 following the Constitution (73rd Amendment) Act, 1992. Here we have tried to mention the participation activities and achievements of gram panchayat women members.

Involvement (Number of Years) in Socio-Political Activities

The length of involvement of members has been 3-5 years, 6-10 years, 11-15 years and more than 15 years or so. 11.11 per cent of females served the Panchayats from 3-5 years and 6-10 years respectively. 77.78 per cent, i.e. 14 members out of 18 served consecutively for more than 15 years. To serve at a stretch for more than 15 years, is quite a satisfactory performance being women-members.

4.16 per cent male members have served between 3-5 years and 20.83 per cent male members have served 11-15 years duration. 75 per cent male members served in their respective Gram Panchayats for more than 15 years in Panchayats of West Tripura district.

In South Tripura, 18.18 per cent female members in Panchayats have rendered their service actively for 1-15 years. 81.82 per cent, i.e. 9 female members have given services to Panchayat for more than 15 years as well. On the contrary, 10.52 per cent have served within 6-10 years in different Panchayats of South Tripura. 10.52 per cent male members served between 11-15 years. 15 members, i.e. 78.95 per cent male members have served and still serving for more than 15 years.

Table 21: Distribution of Gram Panchayat Members by their Involvement (number of Years) in Socio-Political Activities

District	Gram Panchayat	Sex		Socio-Political Activities				Sub-Total	Total
				3—5	6—10	11—15	More than 15		
West Tripura	Dukli	Male		1	—	2	7	10	
		Female		1	—	—	4	5	15
	Raj Lakshminagar	Male		—	—	1	5	6	
		Female		1	—	—	5	6	12
	Paschim Pratappur	Male		—	—	2	6	8	
		Female		—	2	—	5	7	15
	Total	Male		1	—	5	18	24	
		Female		2(11.11)	2(11.11)	—	14(77.78)	18(100%)	—
			Total	*3(7.14)*	*2(4.76)*	*5(11.91)*	*32(76.19)*	*42(100%)*	*42*
South Tripura	Mirza	Male		—	1	—	7	8	
		Female		—	—	—	4	4	12
	Purba Mirza	Male		—	—	1	4	5	
		Female		—	—	2	2	4	9
	Dakshin Mirza	Male		—	1	1	4	6	
		Female		—	—	—	3	3	9
	Total	Male		—	2	2	15	19	
		Female		—	—	2(18.18)	9(81.82)	11(100%)	
			Total	—	*2(6.67)*	*4(13.33)*	*24(80.00)*	*30(100%)*	*30*
	Grand Total	Male		1	2	7	33	43	
		Female		2(6.90)	2(6.90)	2(6.90)	23(79.30)	29(100%)	
			Total	*3(4.17)*	*4(5.55)*	*9(12.50)*	*56(77.78)*	*72(100%)*	*72*

Source: Survey 2001-02.

Quite a small number of member, both male and female, served 6-15 years in their village Panchayats. But most of them in two districts have served for more than 15 years (*vide* Table and Figure 21).

Fig. 21. Distribution of Gram Panchayat Members by their Involvement (number of Years) in Socio-Political Activities

Fig. 21.1: Distribution of Gram Panchayat Members by their Involvement in Socio-Political Activities (West Tripura)

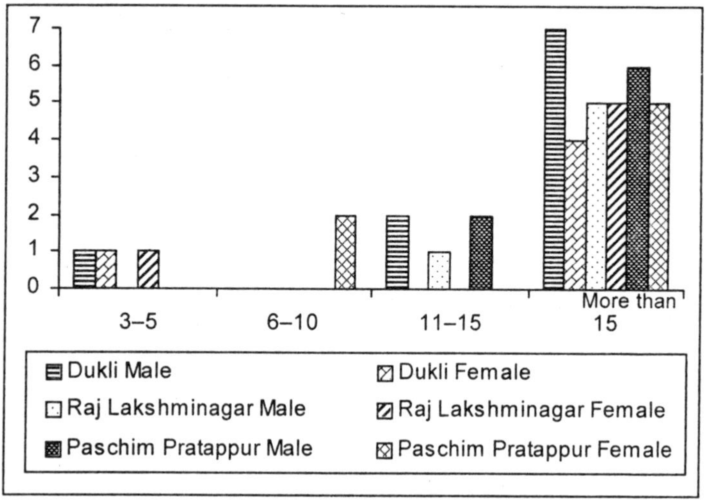

Fig. 21.2: Distribution of Gram Panchayat Members by their Involvement in Socio-Political Activities (West Tripura Total)

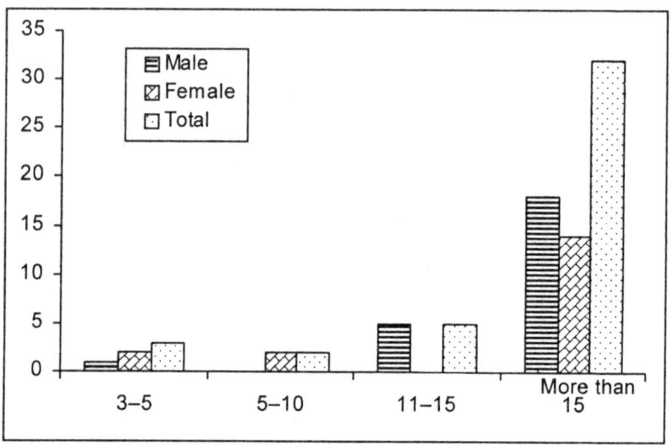

Fig. 21.3: Distribution of Gram Panchayat Members by their Involvement in Socio-Political Activities (South Tripura)

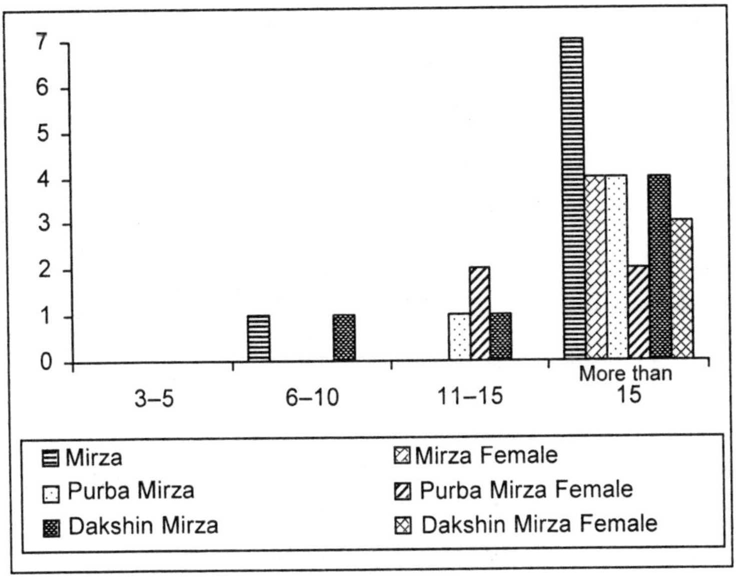

Fig. 21.4: Distribution of Panchayat Members by their Involvement in Socio-Political Activities (South Tripura Total)

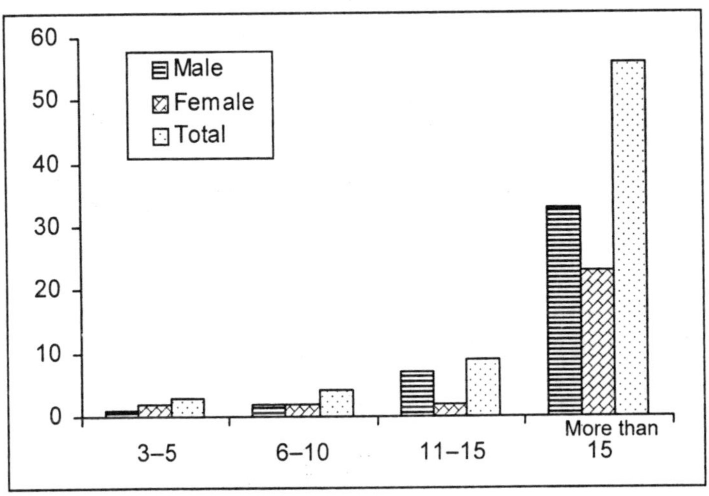

Fig. 21.5: Distribution of Panchayat Members by their Involvement in Socio-Political Activities
(Grand Total of West and South Tripura)

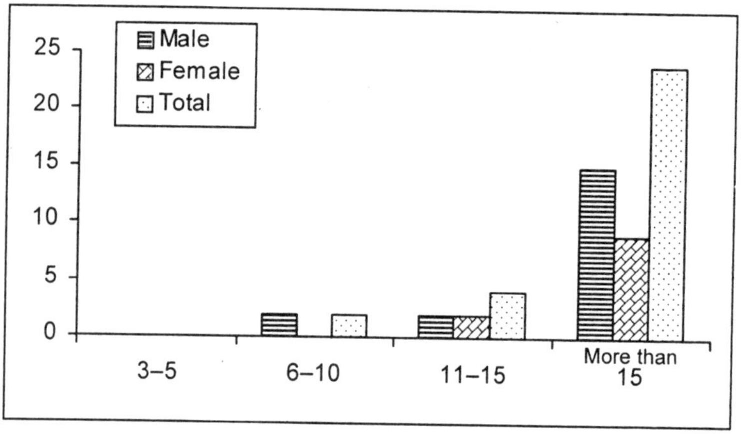

First Appearance in Contest in Gram Panchayat

Gram Panchayats in Tripura had regular elections during left-front rule. Contesting in the Gram Panchayats for being elected, is prestigious to the members as well as to their political party.

In West Tripura we studied Dukli, Raj Lakshminagar and Paschim Pratappur Gram Panchayats. In Table 22, we see that female panchayat members started contesting in West Tripura since the year 1994 and a large number of women contested in the year 1999 for the first time. As we see, 16.67 per cent Gram Panchayat members who were females contested in 1994. 83.33 per cent female members have contested in 1999. That is why, inspiration and interest to participate in the election held by the females are increasing though some other views may be obtained as to whether this participation is at all effective or it neatly counter the patriarchal structure of the society.

On the other hand, male members are strong in their participation in their Gram panchayat election. In 1984, 4 members had participated first in the election, 1 male member in 1989-contested first in 1989 and 2 males contested in 1994. Finally, 17 male members contested first in 1999 in West Tripura.

Table 22: Distribution of Gram Panchayat Members by their First Year of Contest (debutantes) in Gram Panchayat

District	*Gram Panchayat*	*Sex*	*First year of contest in Gram Panchayat*				*Sub-Total*	*Total*
			1984	*1989*	*1994*	*1999*		
West Tripura	Dukli	Male	2	1	1	6	10	15
		Female	—	—	1	4	5	
	Raj Lakshminagar	Male	—	—	1	5	6	12
		Female	—	—	2	4	6	
	Paschim Pratappur	Male	2	—	—	6	8	15
		Female	—	—	—	7	7	
	Total	Male	4	1	2	17	24	
		Female	—	—	3(16.67)	15(83.33)	18(100%)	
		Total	4(9.53)	1(2.38)	5(11.90)	32(76.19)	42(100%)	42
South Tripura	Mirza	Male	2	—	2	4	8	12
		Female	—	—	2	2	4	
	Purba Mirza	Male	2	—	—	3	5	9
		Female	—	—	1	3	4	
	Dakshin Mirza	Male	—	1	—	5	6	9
		Female	—	—	2	1	3	
	Total	Male	4	1	2	12	19	
		Female	—	—	5(45.45)	6(54.55)	11(100%)	
		Total	4(13.34)	1(3.33)	7(23.33)	18(60.00)	30(100%)	30
	Grand Total	Male	8	2	4	29	43	
		Female	—	—	8(27.59)	21(72.41)	29(100%)	
		Total	8(11.11)	2(2.78)	12(16.67)	50(69.44)	72(100%)	72

Source: Survey 2001-02.

In South Tripura, female members contested first election in 1994. The result we see, 45.45 per cent, i.e. 5 female members had contested first in that year. 6 female members in South Tripura, constituting 54.55 per cent are the first contestants in the year 1999 election in the Gram Panchayats.

In two districts together, 27.59 per cent female members contested first in 1994 and 72.41 per cent female members contested first 1999 respectively.

First Contest (Debutantes) in Social and Political Organization

Members of the Panchayat are not only contestants in Gram Panchayat but they are also seen to contest election at the school, co-operative, club and other organizations which include Barowari Puja Committee, Bazar Committee (Byabasahi Sanghatan) and Village Elder's Council, Water Users' Beneficiary Committee at the village, Rice Growers' Association or Crop Protection Committee etc.

Fig. 22. Distribution of Gram Panchayat Members by their First Year of Contest

Fig. 22.1: Distribution of Gram Panchayat Members by their First Year of Contest (West Tripura)

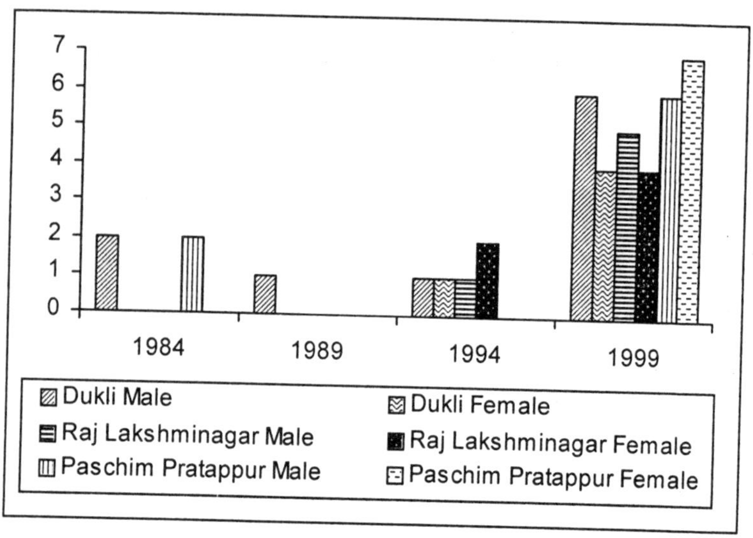

Fig. 22.2: Distribution of Gram Panchayat Members by their First Year of Contest (West Tripura Total)

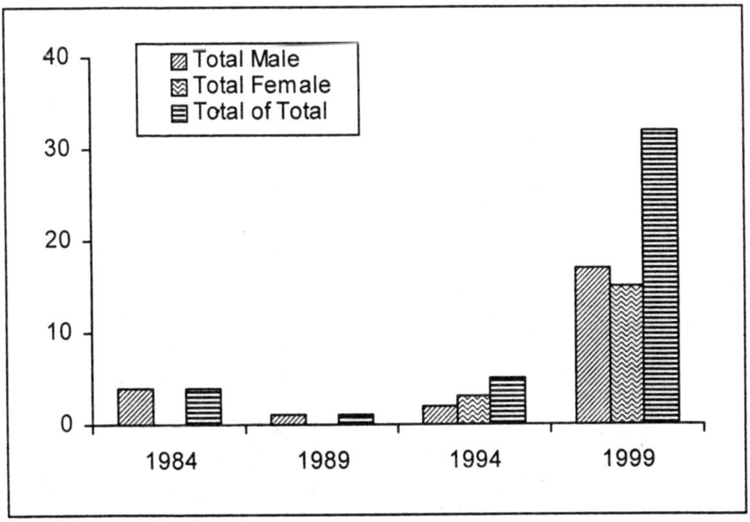

Fig. 22.3: Distribution of Gram Panchayat Members by their First Year of Contest (South Tripura)

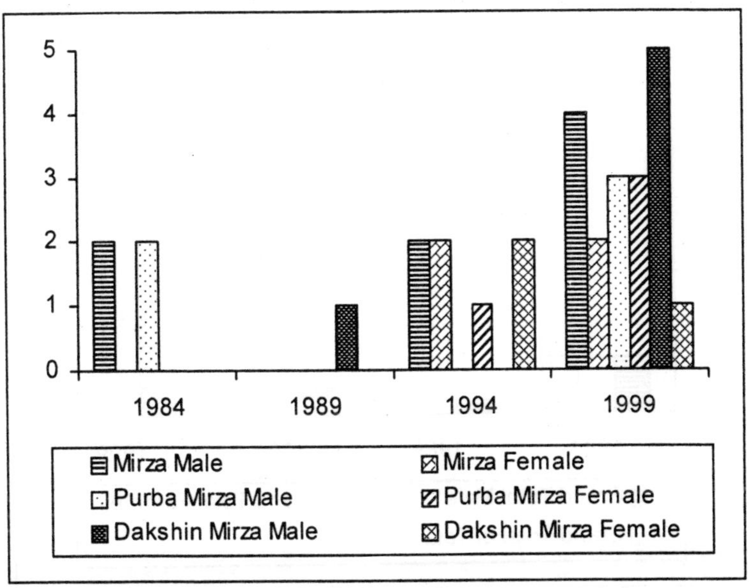

Fig. 22.4: Distribution of Gram Panchayat Members by their First Year of Contest (South Tripura Total)

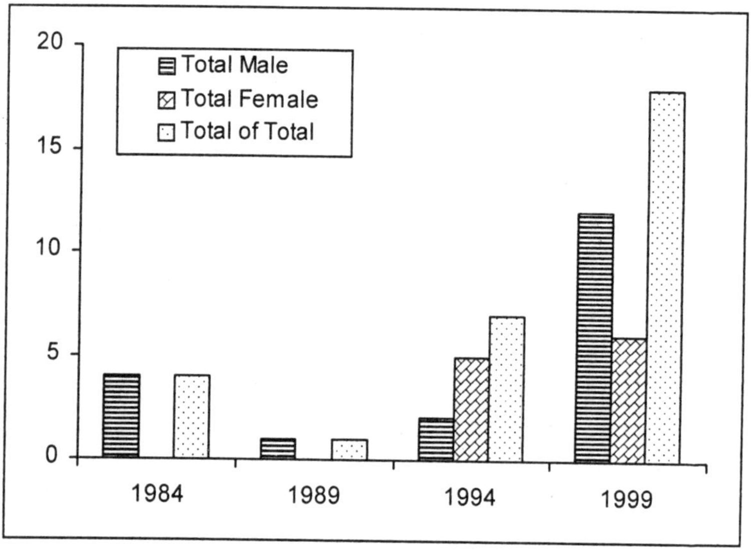

Fig. 22.5: Distribution of Gram Panchayat Members by their First Year of Contest (Grand Total West and South Tripura)

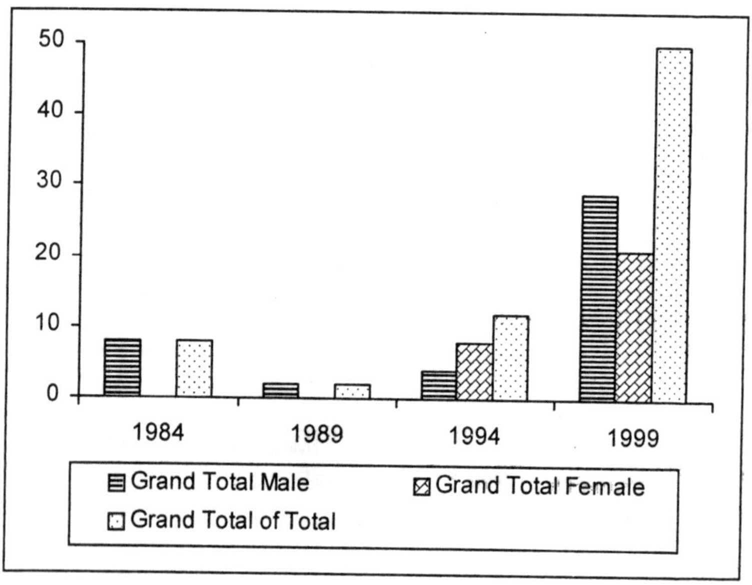

However, in West Tripura, female members are found to contest in Panchayat only whereas male members are found to contest in a club, Panchayat and other organizations.

South Tripura Panchayat women are seen to participate in the election to Gram Panchayats only. In Table 23, 100 per cent women members only contested in Panchayat. Male members are seen to contest in variety of organizations apart from the Panchayat.

Table 23: Distribution of Gram Panchayat Members by their First Contest (debutante) in Social and Political Organization

District	*Gram Panch-ayat*	*Sex*	*First year of contest in*					*Sub-Total*	*Total*
			School	*Co-op.*	*Club*	*Panchayat*	*Others*		
West Tripura	Dukli	Male	—	—	2	8	—	10	
		Female	—	—	—	5	—	5	15
	Raj Lakshmi-nagar	Male	—	—	—	6	—	6	
		Female	—	—	—	6	—	6	12
	Paschim Pratappur	Male	—	—	1	6	1	8	
		Female	—	—	—	7	—	7	15
	Total	Male	—	—	3	20	1	24	
		Female	—	—	—	18(100.00)	—	18(100%)	
		Total	—	—	*3(7.14)*	*38(90.48)*	*1(2.38)*	*42(100%)*	*42*
South Tripura	Mirza	Male	1	—	1	6	—	8	
		Female	—	—	—	4	—	4	12
	Purba Mirza	Male	1	—	—	4	—	5	
		Female	—	—	—	4	—	4	9
	Dakshin Mirza	Male	—	1	—	5	—	6	
		Female	—	—	—	3	—	3	9
	Total	Male	2	1	1	15	—	19	
		Female	—	—	—	11(100.00)	—	11(100%)	
		Total	*2(6.67)*	*1(3.33)*	*1(3.33)*	*26(86.67)*	—	*30(100%)*	*30*
Grand Total		Male	2	1	4	35	1	43	
		Female	—	—	—	29(100.00)		29(100%)	
		Total	*2(2.78)*	*1(1.39)*	*4(5.55)*	*64(88.89)*	*1(1.39)*	*72(100%)*	*72*

Source: Survey 2001-02.

Two male members contested in the school election; 1 member contested in Co-operative and 1 member contested in Club and remaining 15 members contested first time in Panchayats. 1 male member in Mirza and 1 male in Purba Mirza contested for the

School Committee. 1 male in Dakshmin Mirza contested in Co-operative, 1 male member contested in Club election.

Fig. 23. Distribution of Gram Panchayat Members by their First Contest in Social and Political Organization

Fig. 23.1: Gram Panchayat Members by their First Contest in Social and Political Organization (West Tripura)

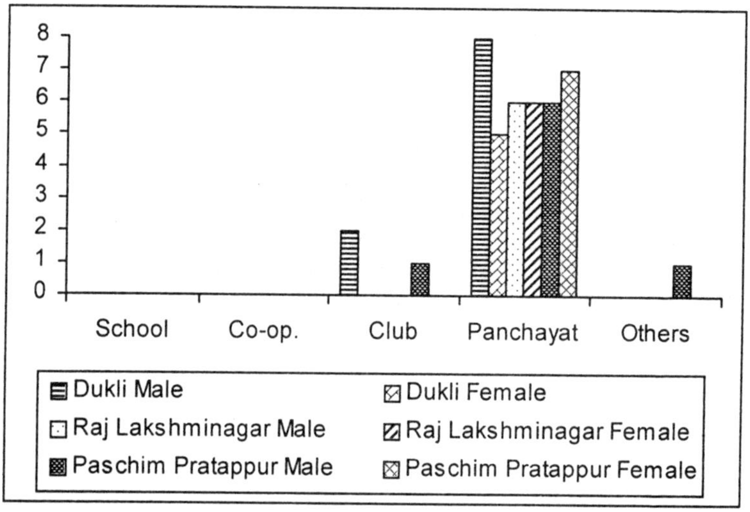

Fig. 23.2: Gram Panchayat Members by their First Contest in Social and Political Organization (West Tripura Total)

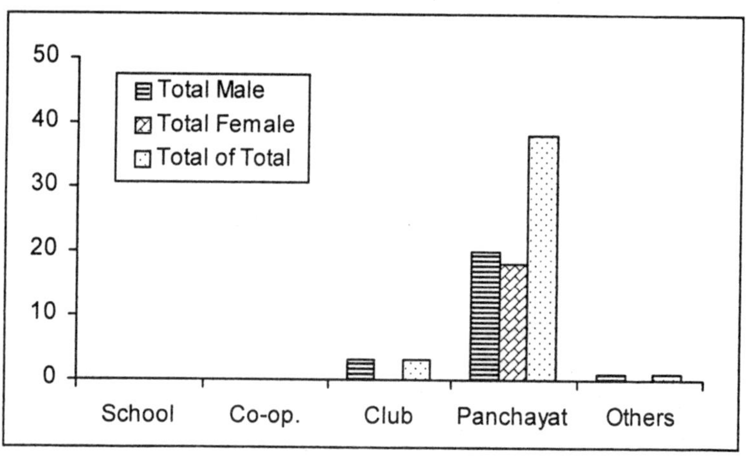

Fig. 23.3: Gram Panchayat Members by their First Contest in Social and Political Organization (South Tripura)

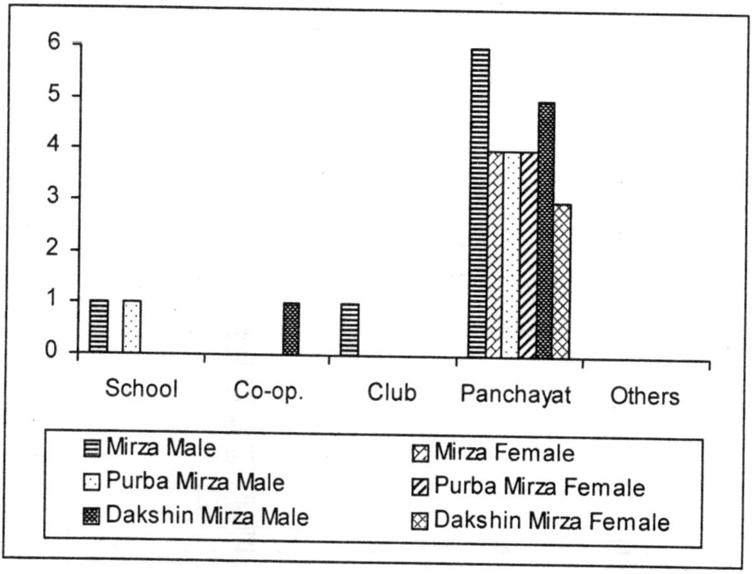

Fig. 23.4: Gram Panchayat Members by their First Contest in Social and Political Organization (South Tripura Total)

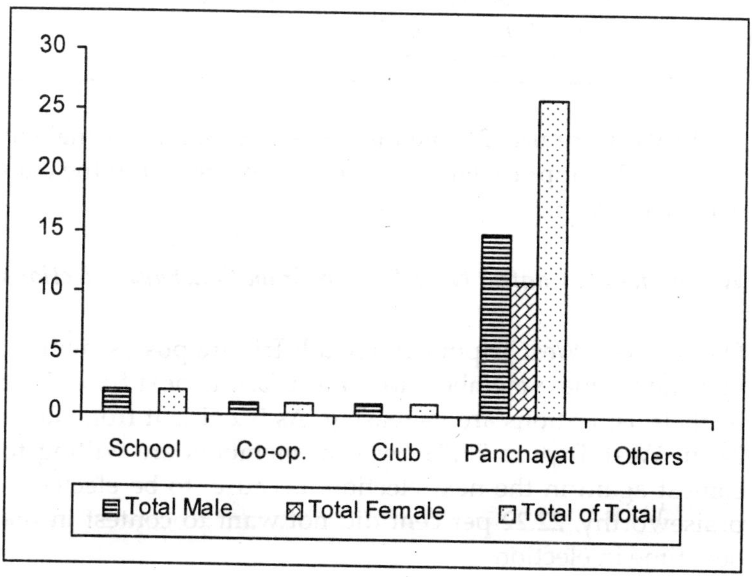

Fig. 23.5: Gram Panchayat Members by their First Contest in Social and Political Organization (Grand Total of West and South Tripura)

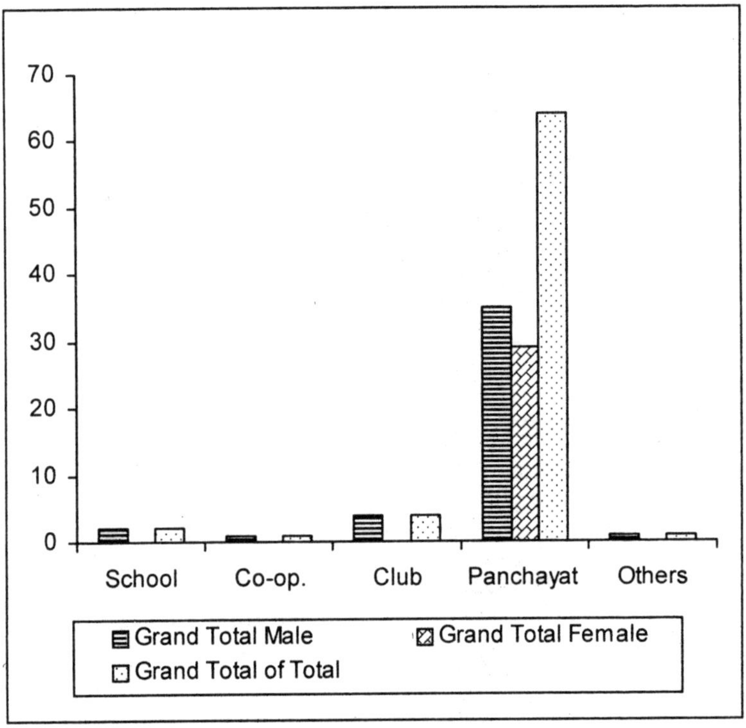

In West Tripura, 2 male members in Dukli and 1 male in Paschim Pratappur were found to have contested in the club general election.

Willingness to Contest Next Time in Gram Panchayat Elections

District-wise West Tripura and South Tripura possess willing male and female members to contest for the next time. That is, their aspirations are increasing. As is evident from Table 24, in West Tripura 77.78 per cent members are willing to contest again in the next election. Because, to be elected is praiseworthy, 22.22 per cent did not want to contest in the next time in election.

Table 24: Distribution of Gram Panchayat Members by their Willingness to Contest next Time in Gram Panchayat elections

District	Gram Panchayat	Sex	Willingness to contest next time		Sub-Total	Total
			Yes	No		
West Tripura	Dukli	Male	7	3	10	
		Female	4	1	5	15
	Raj Lakshminagar	Male	5	1	6	
		Female	4	2	6	12
	Paschim Pratappur	Male	5	3	8	
		Female	6	1	7	15
	Total	Male	17	7	24	
		Female	14(77.78)	4(22.22)	18(100%)	
		Total	31(73.81)	11(26.19)	42(100%)	42
South Tripura	Mirza	Male	7	1	8	
		Female	4		4	12
	Purba Mirza	Male	4	1	5	
		Female	4		4	9
	Dakshin Mirza	Male	6		6	
		Female	2	1	3	9
	Total	Male	17	2	19	
		Female	10(90.91)	1(9.09)	11(100%)	
		Total	27(90.00)	3(10.00)	30(100%)	30
Grand Total		Male	34	9	43	
		Female	24(82.76)	5(17.24)	29(100%)	
		Total	58(80.56)	14(19.44)	72(100%)	72

Source: Survey 2001-02.

Fig. 24. Distribution of Gram Panchayat Members by their Willingness to Contest next Consequent time in Gram Panchayat Elections.

Fig. 24.1. Gram Panchayat Members by their Willingness to Contest in next Panchayat Election (West Tripura)

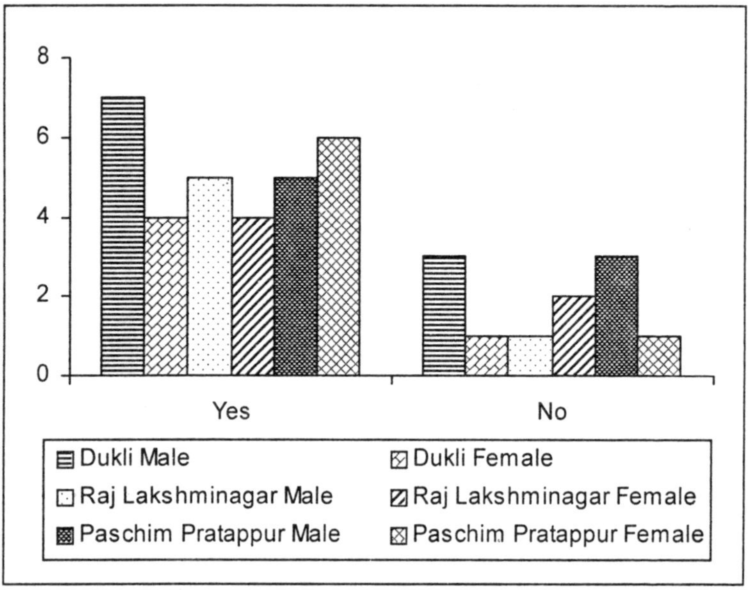

Fig. 24.2: Gram Panchayat Members by their Willingness to Contest in next Panchayat Election (West Tripura Total)

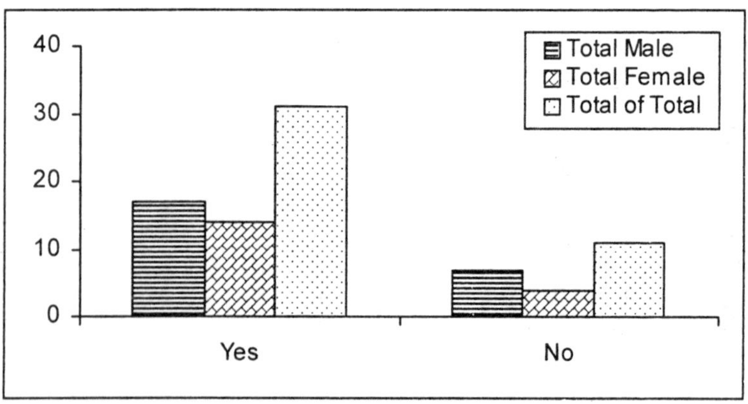

Fig. 24.3: Gram Panchayat Members by their Willingness to Contest in next Panchayat Election (South Tripura)

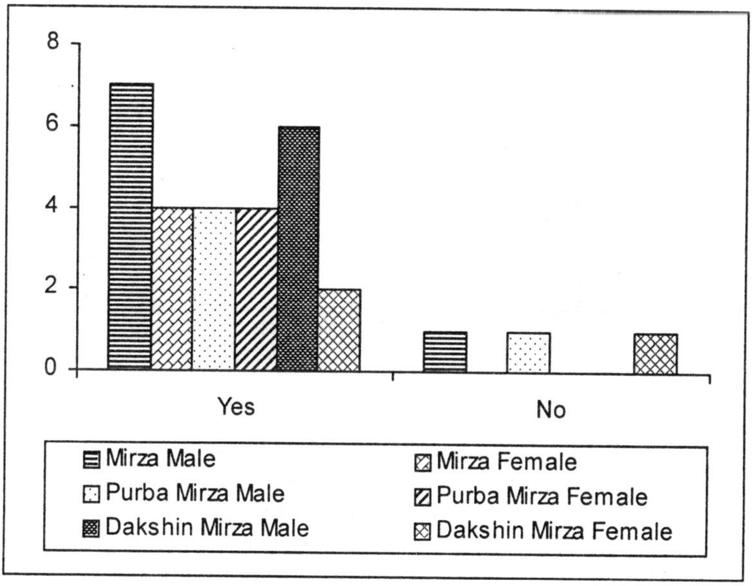

Fig. 24.4: Gram Panchayat Members by their Willingness to Contest in next Panchayat Election (South Tripura Total)

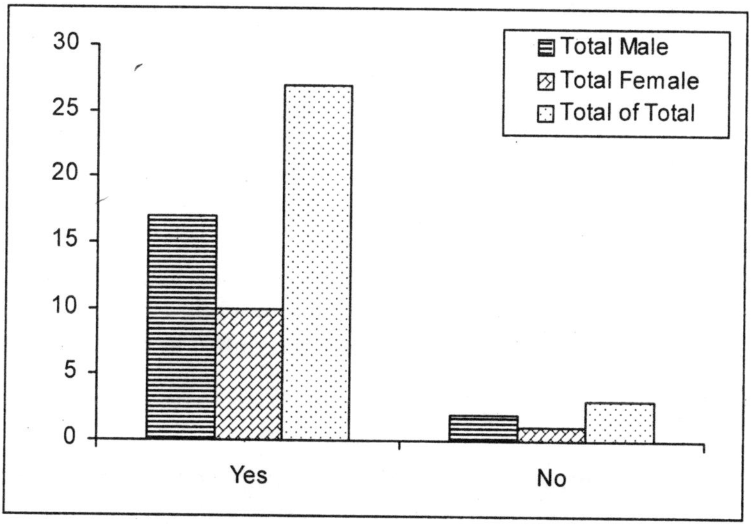

Fig. 24.5: Gram Panchayat Members by their Willingness to Contest in next Panchayat Election (Grand Total West and South Tripura Total)

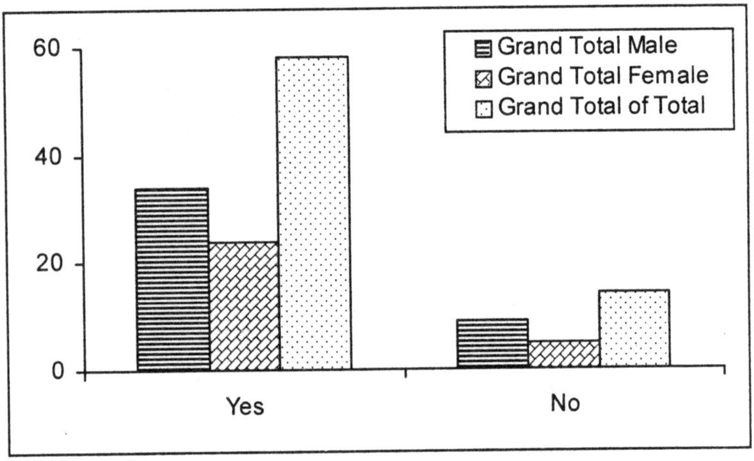

In South Tripura, 90.92 per cent members comprising females consented to contest next time by expressing their willingness. Only 9.09 per cent of them did not show willingness to contest in the next election. 89.47 per cent male did not agree to contest again in the next election. So 10.53 per cent wanted not to contest again in the next election as candidate. But, if we look in table we see that most of the members comprising both male and female in Mirza G.P., Purba Mirza G.P. and Dakshin Mirza G.P. favoured to contest again in next election.

A detail break up shows that among the females in Mirza and Purba Mirza, no one to contest again in the election. In Dakshin Mirza, 100 per cent male members wanted to contest again in the election.

Two districts taken together, we can see 82.76 per cent female members wanted to contest again while 17.24 per cent female members were not interested to contest in the election.

The Source of Initiative or Inspiration

Sources of initiative or inspiration to become Panchayat members are of great sociological interest. Because, in a bourgeois political party, membership to Panchayat is dependent upon many factors. Bourgeois political party structure is very much linked with aristocracy, political maturity and thoughts of subordination. Wise ruler and the ruled must have distance. Otherwise ruling cannot be done. Rulers are born to govern and leaders are chosen from those elite sections who were traditional elites.

The party structure influences the individual's motivation to become active in the politics. The CPI(M) wants to distribute the wealth equally among its constituent peoples of the society. great thinkers of the society in Europe always thought to remove the evils of the mal-distribution of wealth and disparity in slave society to feudal lords and the initiative was extended to remove the evils of capitalist society in order to make it an egalitarian society. Attempts were made towards such path but poverty and hunger remains as it was ever with the capitalist world. The appendages of influence of colonialism and imperialism are many. Trusts based on religion, charitable trusts, financial trusts to siphon off money from below to above in a hierarchical society, which is characteristic to inequity and exploitation in a capitalist society. Syndicate is one of them. Syndicalism was used to bring in money from members under umbrella. Trusts' role in Capitalism is not conducive to worker-employee relation but the main role of the trust is to promote pacifism and reformism.

Different sources of inspirations were found and those include party, to which members belong to, immediate friends circle, own initiative, party, friends own decision. In most cases, party directives are followed very keenly in this regard. But in out of West Tripura and South Tripura Gram Panchayats, 55.55 per cent in West Tripura were influenced by party, friends and own decision in order to being candidate in election and 33.33 per cent were motivated by party and friends both. Only 1 person was elected from initiative and insistence of party, friends' initiative was pivotal for another person although final affiliation remains to be approved by friends. This picture was available in West Tripura.

Table 25: Distribution of Gram Panchayat Members as per the Source of Initiative or Inspiration

District	Gram Panchayat	Sex	Contested on Whose Insistence						Sub-Total	Total
			Party	Friends	Own	Party, friends and own	Party & Friends	Friends & Own		
West Tripura	Dukli	Male	—	—	—	10	—	—	10	
		Female	—	1	—	3	1	—	5	15
	Raj	Male	—	—	—	5	1	—	6	
	Lakshminagar	Female	1	—	—	1	4	—	6	12
	Paschim	Male	1	—	1	5	—	1	8	
	Pratappur	Female	—	—	—	6	1	—	7	15
	Total	Male	1	—	1	20	1	1	24	
		Female	1(5.56)	1(5.56)	—	10(55.55)	6(33.33)	—	18(100%)	
		Total	2(4.76)	1(2.38)	1(2.38)	30(71.43)	7(16.67)	1 (2.38)	42(100%)	42
South Tripura	Mirza	Male	1	—	—	7	—	—	8	
		Female	—	—	—	4	—	—	4	12
	Purba Mirza	Male	—	—	—	5	—	—	5	
		Female	—	1	—	3	—	—	4	9
	Dakshin Mirza	Male	—	—	2	4	—	—	6	
		Female	—	—	—	3	—	—	3	9
	Total	Male	1	—	2	16	—	—	19	
		Female	—	1(9.09)	—	10(90.91)	—	—	11(100%)	
		Total	1(3.33)	1(3.33)	2(6.67)	26(86.67)	—	—	30(100%)	30
	Grand Total	Male	2	—	3	36	1	1	43	
		Female	1(3.45)	2(6.90)	—	20(68.96)	6(20.69)	—	29(100%)	
		Total	3(4.17)	2(2.78)	3(4.16)	56(77.78)	7(9.72)	1(1.39)	72(100%)	72

Source: Survey 2001-02.

In South Tripura, 90.91 per cent female candidates had mixed source of inspiration from party, friends and own decision. Normal trend that we locate is a mixed insistence combining party, friends and own will and wish. Only in case of 1 female member, friends were main inspiration in making her active in the party and Panchayats.

Willingness to Serve the Party Directly

Gender variation in response to the willingness to serve party directly or not was taken into consideration in Table 26. Total 94.44 per cent women in West Tripura expressed willingness to serve political party directly and 5.56 per cent did not want to serve directly.

100 per cent male members wanted to serve their political party directly.

In South Tripura, 100 per cent female and 100 per cent male members wanted to serve their political party directly.

Fig. 25. Gram Panchayat Members as per the Source of Initiative or Inspirations

Fig. 25.1: Gram Panchayat Members as per the Source of Initiative (West Tripura)

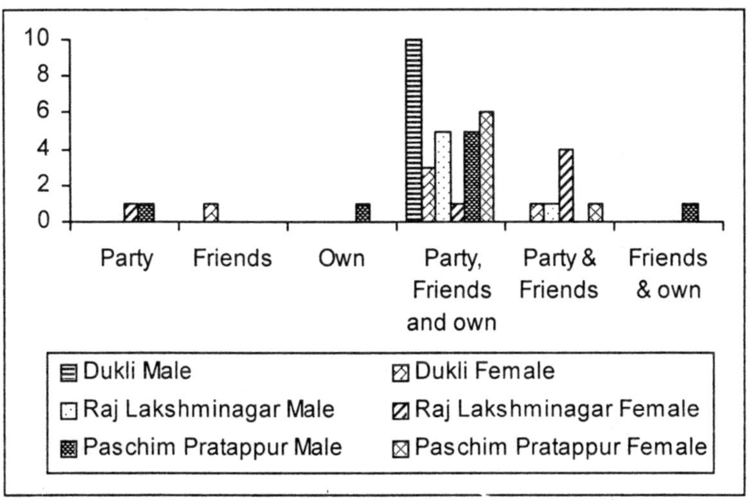

Fig. 25.2: Gram Panchayat Members as per the Source of Initiative (West Tripura Total)

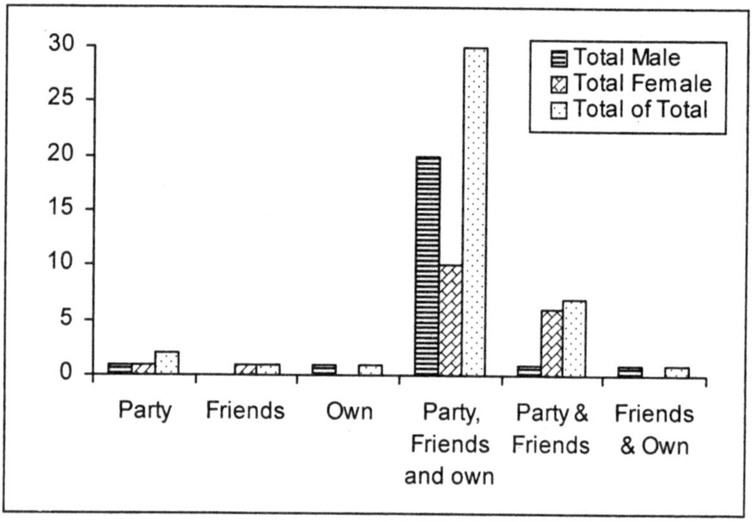

Fig. 25.3: Gram Panchayat Members as per the Source of Initiative (South Tripura)

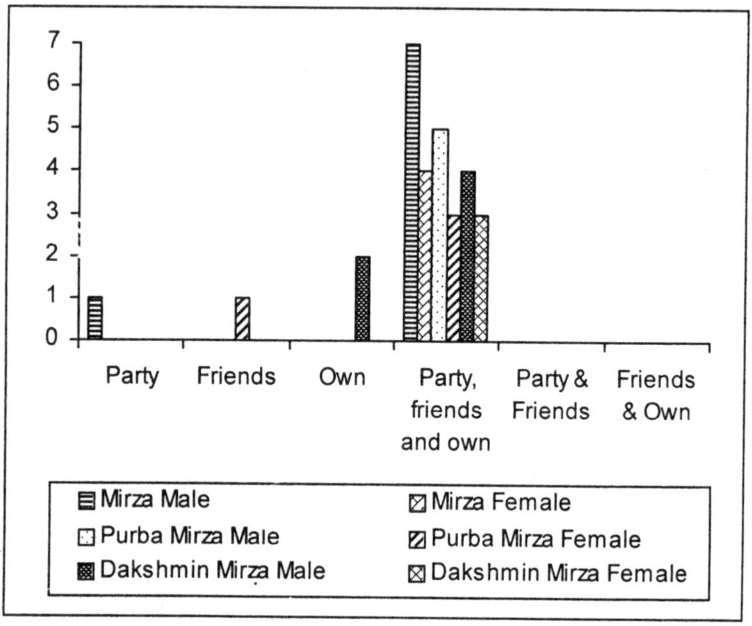

Fig. 25.4: Gram Panchayat Members as per the Source of Initiative (South Tripura Total)

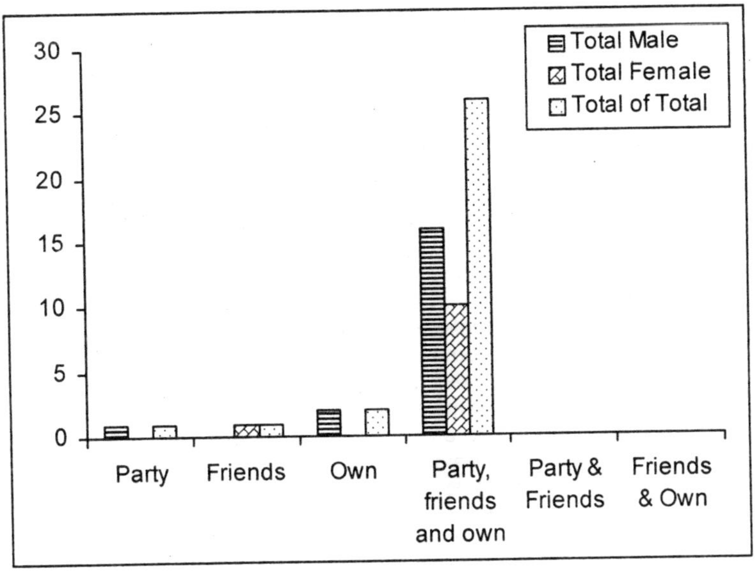

Fig. 25.5: Gram Panchayat Members as per the Source of Initiative (Grand Total West and South Tripura)

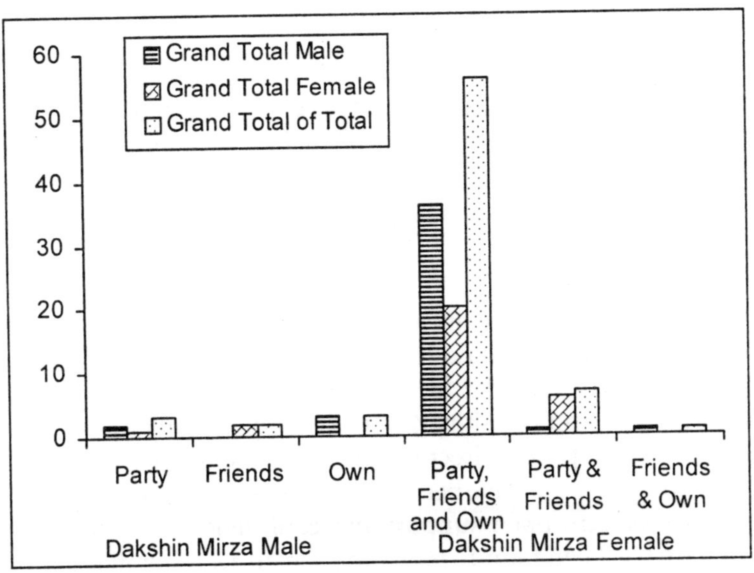

Individually, distributions of villages, in such ranking are interesting. Except in Paschim Pratappur, Dukli and Rajlakshminagar had equal representation in terms of male and female response to serve their respective political party directly. In Paschim Pratappur, 14.28 per cent female were not interested to serve directly.

Table 26: Distribution of Panchayat Members as per their Willingness to Serve the Party Directly

District	Gram Panchayat	Sex	Serve Party Directly		Sub-Total	Total
			Yes	No		
West Tripura	Dukli	Male	10	—	10	
		Female	5	—	5	15
	Raj Lakshminagar	Male	6	—	6	
		Female	6	—	6	12
	Paschim Pratappur	Male	8	—	8	
		Female	6	1	7	15
	Total	Male	24	—	24	
		Female	17(94.44)	1(55.56)	18(100%)	
		Total	41(97.62)	1(2.38)	42(100%)	42
South Tripura	Mirza	Male	8	—	8	
		Female	4	—	4	12
	Purba Mirza	Male	5	—	5	
		Female	4	—	4	9
	Dakshin Mirza	Male	6	—	6	
		Female	3	—	3	9
	Total	Male	19	—	19	
		Female	11(100.00)	—	11(100%)	
		Total	30(100.00)	—	30(100%)	30
	Grand Total	Male	43	—	43	
		Female	28(96.55)	1(3.45)	29(100%)	
		Total	71(98.61)	1(1.39)	72(100%)	72

Source: Survey 2001-02.

The Gram Panchayats in South Tripura, 100 per cent male and 100 per cent female expressed willingness to serve the political party directly. In all Gram Panchayats, viz. Mirza, Purba Mirza and Dakshin Mirza have been equally responsive to serve there partly directly. In total, 30 members out of total 30 in South Tripura have been in favour of serving party directly. So 100 per cent open support and confidence to serve party directly has been found among the constituent members.

Fig. 26. Distribution of Gram Panchayat Members as per their Willingness to Serve the Party (Political Affiliation) Directly

Fig. 26.1: Gram Panchayat Members as per their Willingness to Serve the Party (Political Affiliation) (West Tripura)

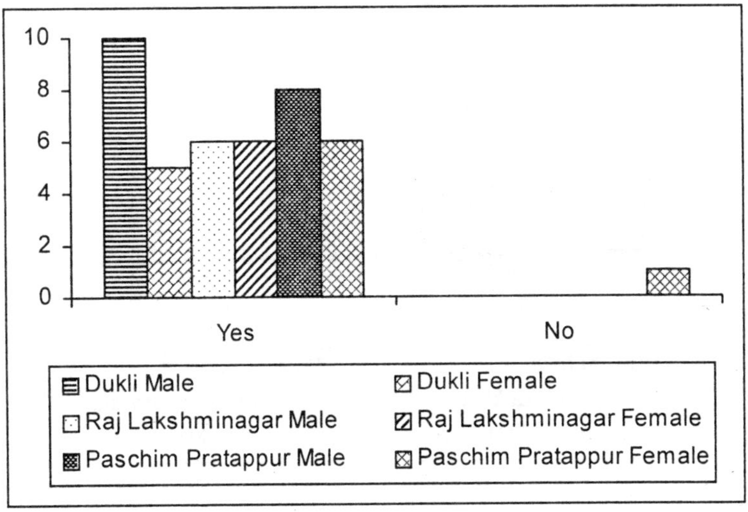

Fig. 26.2: Panchayat Members as per their Willingness to Serve the Party (Political Affiliation) (West Tripura Total)

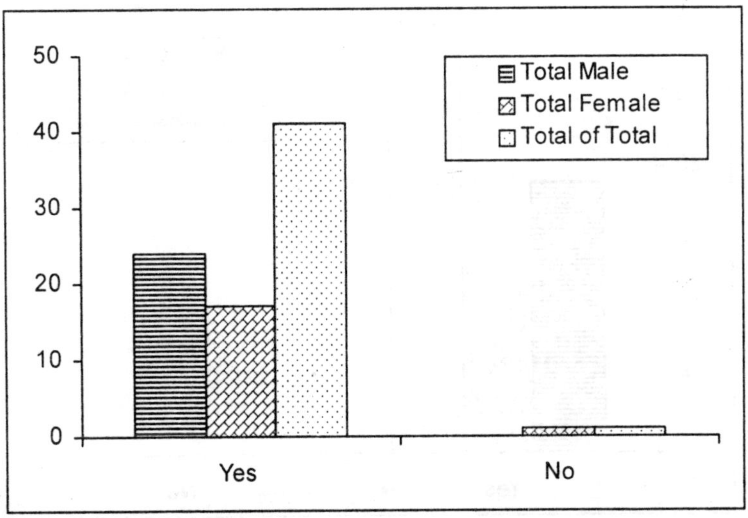

Fig. 26.3: Gram Panchayat Members as per their Willingness to Serve the Party (Political Affiliation) (South Tripura)

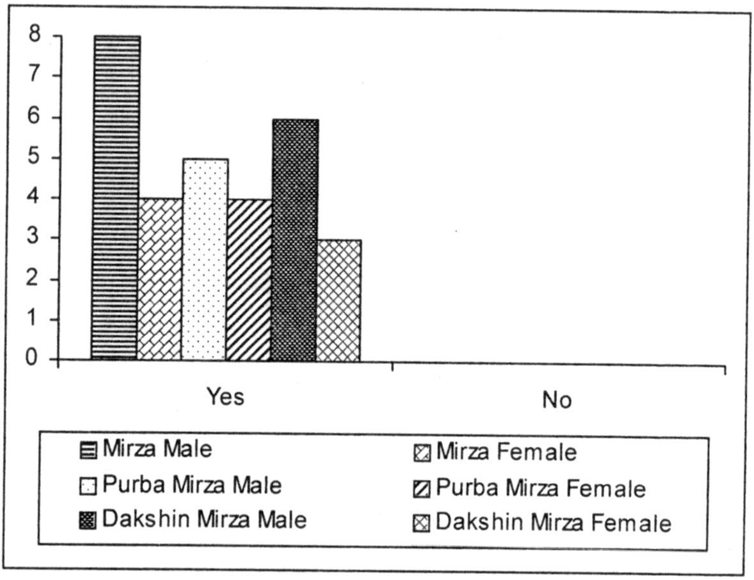

Fig. 26.4: Panchayat Members as per their Willingness to Serve the Party (Political Affiliation) (South Tripura Total)

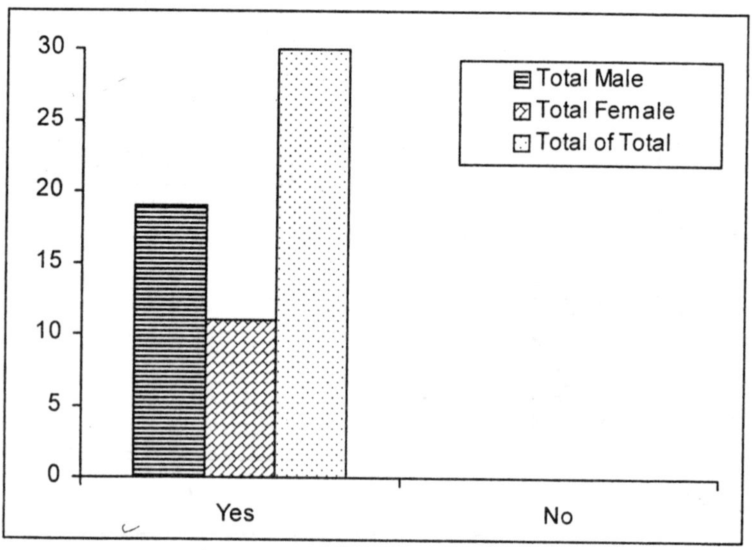

Fig. 26.5: Gram Panchayat Members as per their Willingness to Serve the Party (Political Affiliation) (Grand Total of South and West Tripura)

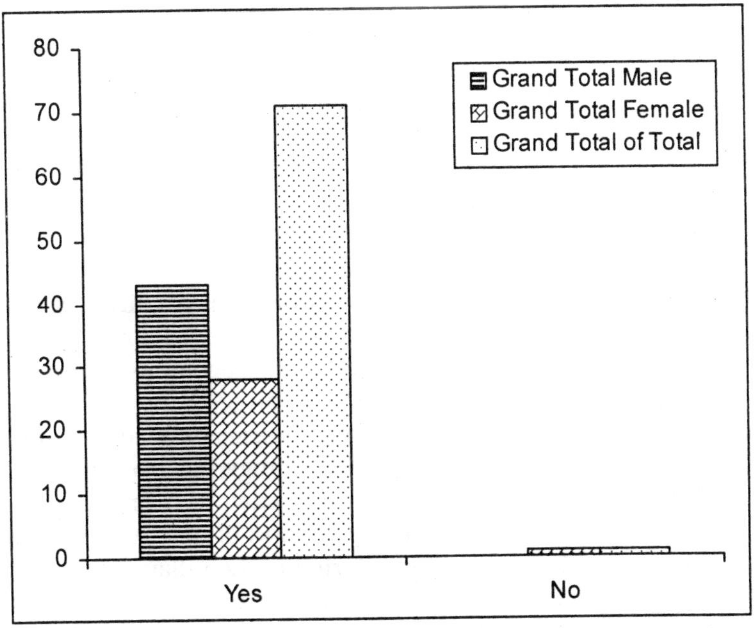

In total of two districts, 98.61 per cent have confided upon open service to party directly while 1.39 per cent did not want to serve party directly.

Involvement in Party According to Nature of Work

Involvement in the Panchayat through nature of service is one of the criteria to assess the members' commitment and attachment to the Panchayati Raj and its activities. As Panchayati Raj is an age-old institution its activities has an impressing impact upon the village life pattern. The workflow of the Panchayati Raj is very subtle and an enduring effect its activities may be felt in the village life. Since the very nature of Panchayati Raj has undergone transformation and a process of formalization of Panchayati Raj as structure emerged, far-reaching consequences may have come about by now. The manifestation of which may be gloss and glamorous in factual development with a pauperized population coming in and out of it. Is it the kind of Panchayati Raj that Gandhi had dreamt of? Is it the kind of self-sufficiency of the village what we know about Indian village characterized by village council? Has this Panchayat replaced the traditional village hegemony and instead it is giving an scale-neutrality service to all villagers irrespective of casts, creed or religion? If not, then what kind of new hegemony appearing and what forces in countering the corruption and alternative built in-check methods have been adopted to? A new process emerging should and must have its counter process. To check the corruption of existing process and its operator should be given occasional jerk and blow so that they can understand that absolute hegemony is not the lasting word in final assessment. Change is inevitable and lasting and ever-lasting concept may be a least concept in other day. What we perceive, a cosmetic change has been made in Panchayati Raj and a new kind of tax-collection has been introduced which was earlier absent and of new way of rural resource plundering has been started in the village life with a nominal service and lip service assurance. We have to think, whether we are reconstructing our village through Panchayats or making arrangement to plunder its resources again. Whether Panchayat is thinking in such a way that its constituent villagers have traditional mode of occupation and livelihood. Or it may be substituted by such economic activities, which they can adapt to very quickly as to their own benefit. The administrator's point of view should think over it before bringing about any planned occupational change. Some occupationally engaged people look nicer than some floating population with no specific occupation for a year or so. This cannot be conducive to smooth functioning of a state which claim civlized than barbaric. Rural development without considering rural cultural set up cannot be successful in proper way. Development and destruction, to some, is interrelated as someone argues that without destruction development or creation cannot take place. That is why, when a child is born, destruction of mother occurs? Child is also a development of many organic processes over a specific time in the mother's womb. Who will tell this to whom? Hunger for real estates and money will lead people where? Nobody knows? Rehabilitation is a process that any development programmer accompany. But rehabilitation does not occur systematically and the newly rehabilitated area may not be acceptable to the residents. These are the issues that come to the surface while such thing is on.

Table 27: Distribution of Gram Panchayat Members by their Involvement in Party according to Nature of Work

District	*Gram Panch-ayat*	*Sex*	*Nature of Service to the Party*				*Sub-Total*	*Total*
			1	*2*	*3*	*More than 3*		
West Tripura	Dukli	Male	—	—	1	9	10	
		Female	1	—	—	4	5	15
	Raj	Male	—	—	—	6	6	
	Lakshmi-nagar	Female	1	—	—	5	6	12
	Paschim	Male	—	—		8	8	
	Pratappur	Female	—	—	1	6	7	15
	Total	Male	—	—	1	23	24	
		Female	2(11.11)	—	1(5.56)	15(83.33)	18(100%)	
		Total	2(4.76)	—	2(2.76)	38(90.48)	42(100%)	42
South Tripura	Mirza	Male	—	—	—	8	8	
		Female	—	—	—	4	4	12
	Purba	Male	—	1	—	4	5	
	Mirza	Female	—	1	—	3	4	9
	Dakshin	Male	—	1	—	5	6	
	Mirza	Female	—	—	—	3	3	9
	Total	Male	—	2	—	17	19	
		Female	—	1(9.09)	—	10(90.91)	11(100%)	
		Total	—	3(10.00)	—	27(90.00)	30(100%)	30
Grand Total		Male	—	2	1	40	43	
		Female	2(6.89)	1(3.45)	1(3.45)	25(86.21)	29(100%)	
		Total	2(2.78)	3(4.16)	2(2.78)	65(90.28)	72(100%)	72

Source: Survey 2001-02.

Table 27 is a description of sex-wise variation in involvement in work a member performs. It has been noted in the table that 11.11 per cent female in West Tripura had 1 kind of work. 5.56 per cent female members have 3 kinds of work involvement and 83.33 per cent female members have more than 3 types of work involvement in the Panchayat. A minor variation can be observed in the inter-village and inter-sex distribution. In South Tripura, 9.09 per cent female members have got 2 types of work involvement and 90.91 per cent have more than three assignments in the Panchayats everyday.

Fig. 27. Distribution of Gram Panchayat Members by their Involvement in Panchayat according to Nature of Work

Fig. 27.1: Gram Panchayat Members by their Involvement in Panchayat according to Nature of Work (West Tripura)

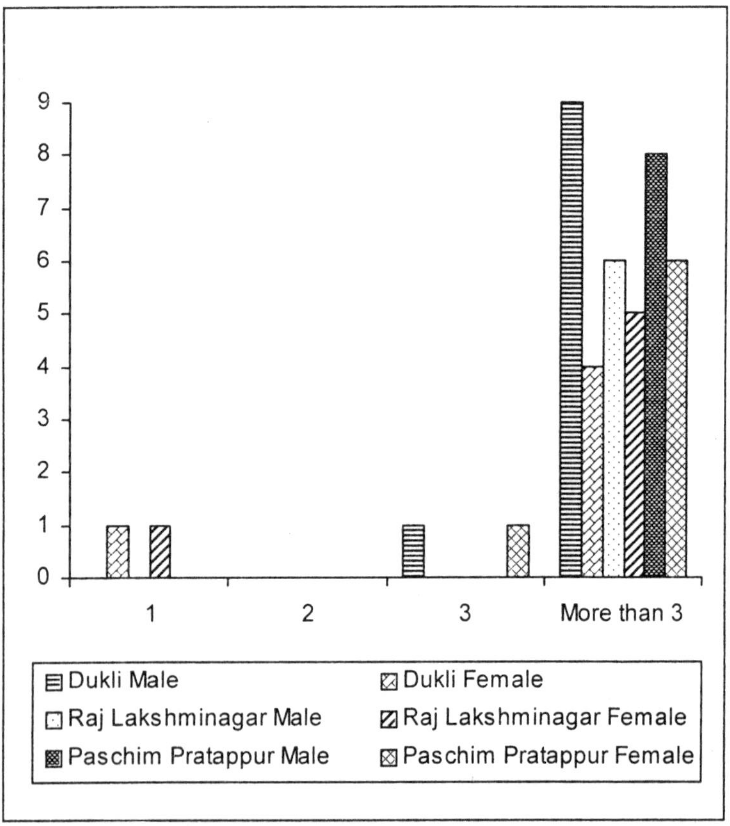

Fig. 27.2: Panchayat Members by their Involvement in Panchayat according to Nature of Work (West Tripura Total)

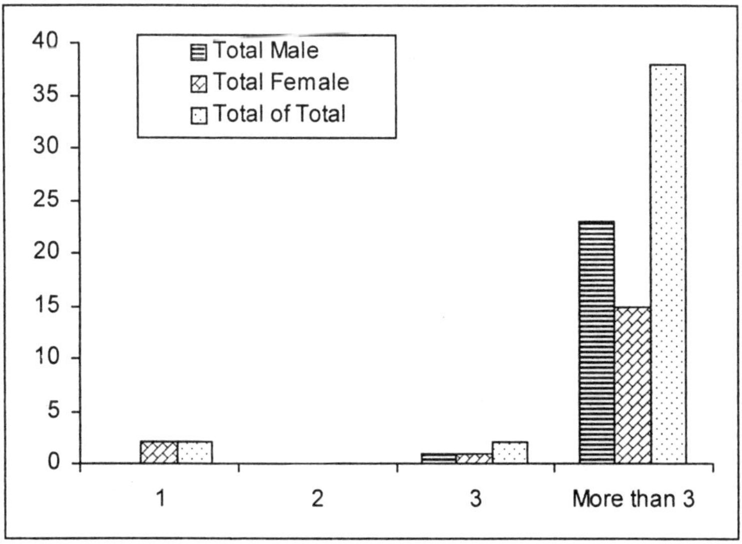

Fig. 27.3: Panchayat Members by their Involvement in Panchayat according to Nature of Work (South Tripura)

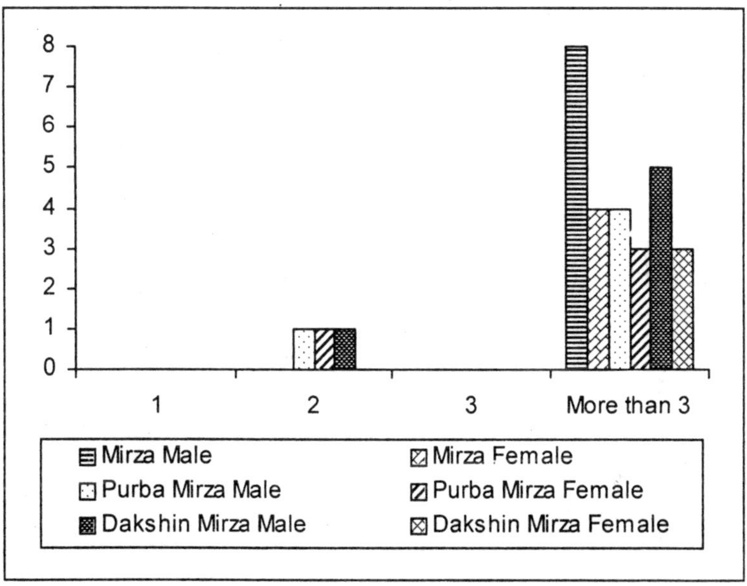

Fig. 27.4: Panchayat Members by their Involvement in Panchayat according to Nature of Work (South Tripura Total)

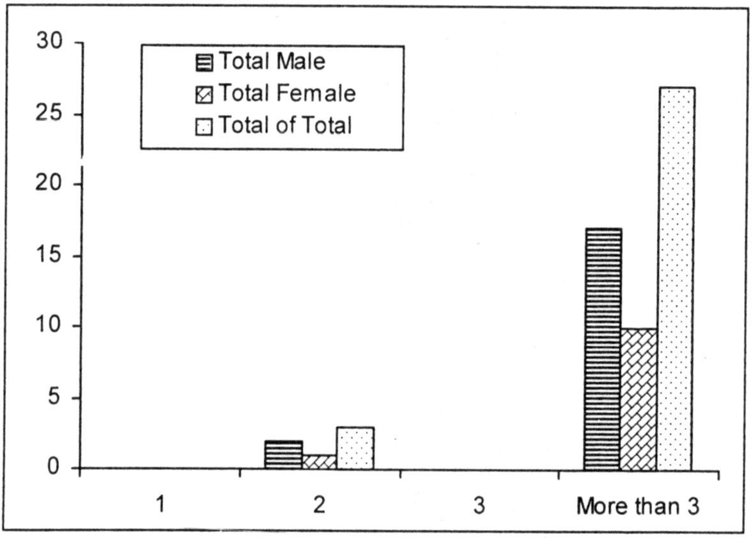

Fig. 27.5: Panchayat Members by their Involvement in Panchayat according to Nature of Work (Grand Total of South and West Tripura)

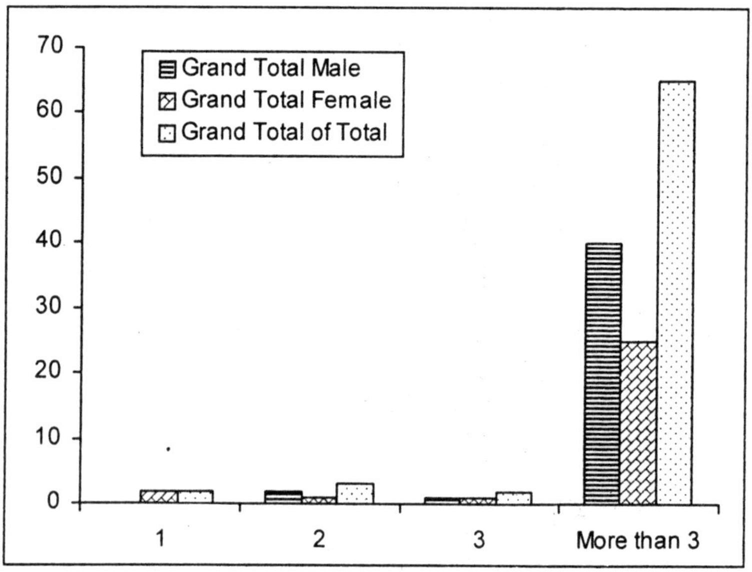

Male members have also a similar type of assignments. 2 members had 2 types of assignments per day and 17 male members have more than three assignments or working involvement.

Desire to Involve their Family Members in Political Party

West Tripura

Desire to involve their family members in the political body was investigated. Dukli, Raj Lakshminagar and Paschim Pratappur Gram Panchayats in West Tripura have shown their desire to involve their family members. Among the females

Table 28: Distribution of Panchayat Members as per their Desire to Involve their Family Members in Political Party

District	*Gram Panchayat*	*Sex*	*Desire to Participate their Family Members*		*Sub-Total*	*Total*
			Yes	*No*		
West Tripura	Dukli	Male	10		10	
		Female	5		5	15
	Raj Lakshminagar	Male	5	1	6	
		Female	5		6	12
	Paschim Pratappur	Male	8		8	
		Female	7		7	15
	Total	Male	23	1	24	
		Female	17(94.44)	1(5.56)	18(100%)	
		Total	40(95.24)	2(4.76)	42(100%)	42
South Tripura	Mirza	Male	8		8	
		Female	4		4	12
	Purba Mirza	Male	5		5	
		Female	4		4	9
	Dakshin Mirza	Male	6		6	
		Female	3		3	9
	Total	Male	19		19	
		Female	11(100.00)		11(100%)	
		Total	30(100.00)		30(100%)	30
	Grand Total	Male	42	1	43	
		Female	28(96.55)	1(3.45)	29(100%)	
		Total	70(97.22)	2(2.78)	72(100%)	72

Source: Survey 2001-02.

94.44 per cent saying 'yes' to involve their family members to Panchayat only, 5.56 per cent did not want their family members in Panchayats. Among the male 95.83 per cent male also wanted to involve their family members in the Panchayat. In Dukli and Paschim Pratappur 100 per cent male members and 100 per cent female members expressed such desire.

South Tripura

Respondents from South Tripura wanted to involve their family to participate in the political activities of the Panchayats. 100 per cent male and 100 per cent female members of Mirza, Purba Mirza and Dakshin Mirza Gram Panchayats are all keen to involve their family members in the Panchayat. This desires to participate their family members in the Panchayat is equally shown in intra Gram Panchayat and in total sample members also.

Fig. 28. Distribution of Panchayat Members as per their Desire to Involve their Family Members to Participate in Political Party

Fig. 28.1: Members as per their Desire to Involve their FamilyMembers to Participate in Political Party (West Tripura)

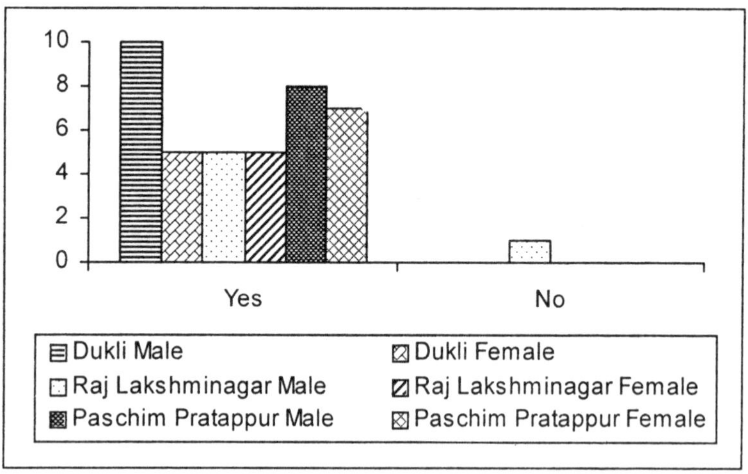

Fig. 28.2: Members as per their Desire to Involve their Family Members to Participate in Political Party (West Tripura Total)

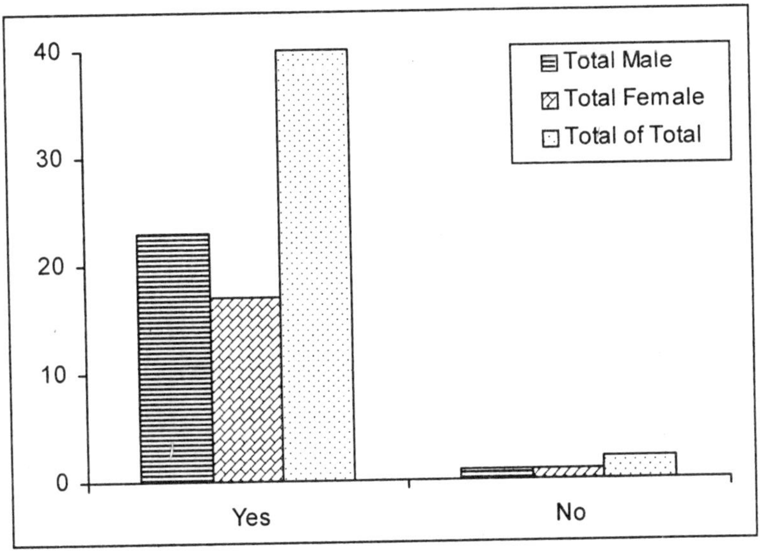

Fig. 28.3: Members as per their Desire to Involve their Family Members to Participate in Political Party (South Tripura)

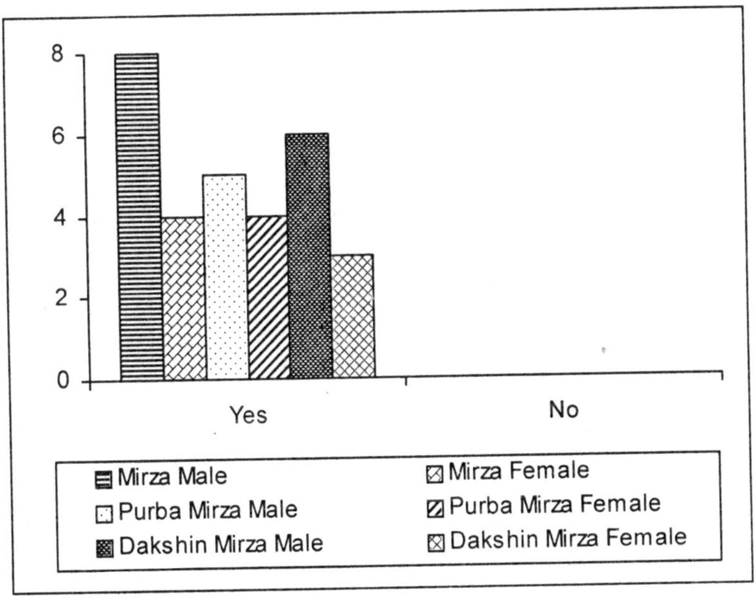

Fig. 28.4: Members as per their Desire to Involve their Family Members to Participate in Political Party (South Tripura Total)

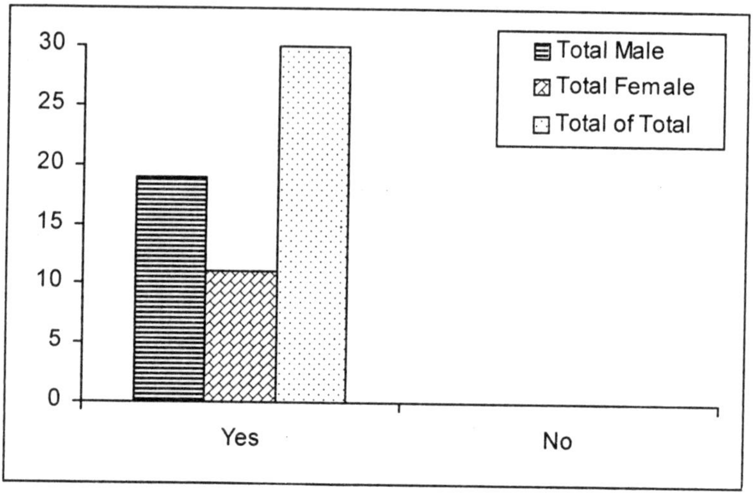

Fig. 28.5: Members as per their Desire to Involve their Family Members to Participate in Political Party (Grand Total of South and West Tripura)

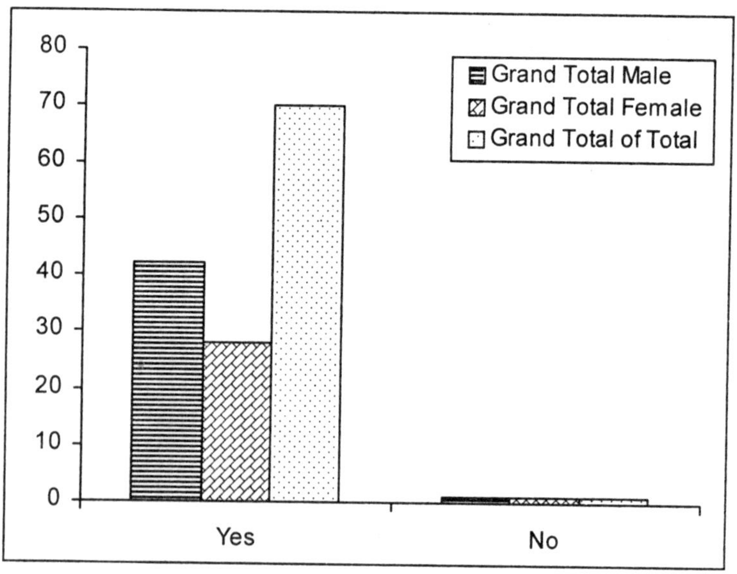

Interest in Reading Political Books/Journals

One of major indicators of the awareness of the members of Gram Panchayat is the habit of reading political books or journals. An inquiry was made to know the kind of books and journals related to political nature that they read.

Table 29: Distribution of Panchayat Members as per their Interest in Reading Political Books/Journals

District	*Gram Panchayat*	*Sex*	*Read any Political Books/Journals*		*Sub-Total*	*Total*
			Yes	*No*		
West Tripura	Dukli	Male	9	1	10	
		Female	4	1	5	15
	Raj	Male	5	1	6	
	Lakshminagar	Female	4	2	6	12
	Paschim	Male	7	1	8	
	Pratappur	Female	2	5	7	15
	Total	Male	21	3	24	
		Female	10(55.56)	8(44.44)	18(100%)	
		Total	31(73.81)	11(26.19)	42(100%)	42
South Tripura	Mirza	Male	7	1	8	
		Female	1	3	4	12
	Purba Mirza	Male	5		5	
		Female	2	2	4	9
	Dakshin	Male	4	2	6	
	Mirza	Female	3		3	9
	Total	Male	16	3	19	
		Female	6 (54.55)	5(45.45)	11(100%)	
		Total	22(73.33)	8(26.67)	30(100%)	30
	Grand Total	Male	37	6	43	
		Female	16(55.17)	13(44.83)	29(100%)	
		Total	53(73.61)	19(26.39)	72(100%)	72

Source: Survey 2001-02.

In West Tripura, 55.56 per cent female members and 44.44 per cent female members responded 'yes' and 'no' to question as to whether they read any political books or journals? 87.5 per cent male have read political books or journals while 12.5

per cent male members did not read any political book or journals before or while participating in the Panchayat activities. Such variation in reading habits of political books or journals in different Gram Panchayats is found among the male and females (see table—inner row and column).

Fig. 29. Distribution of Panchayat Members as per their Interest in Reading Political Books/Journals

Fig. 29.1: Members as per their Interest in Reading Political Books/ Journals (West Tripura)

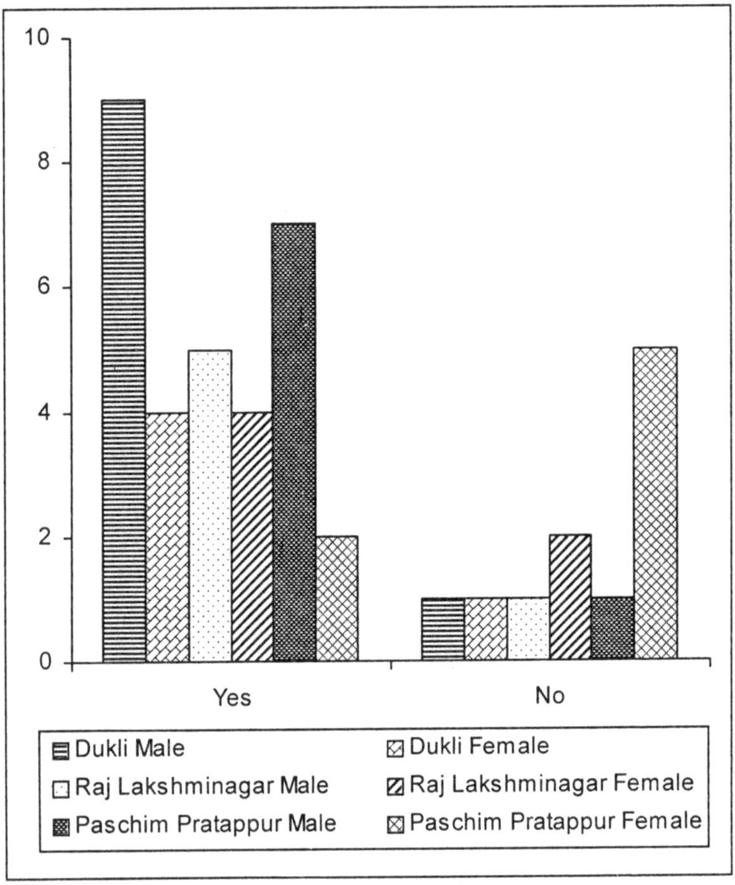

Fig. 29.2: Members as per their interest in reading Political Books/ Journals (West Tripura Total)

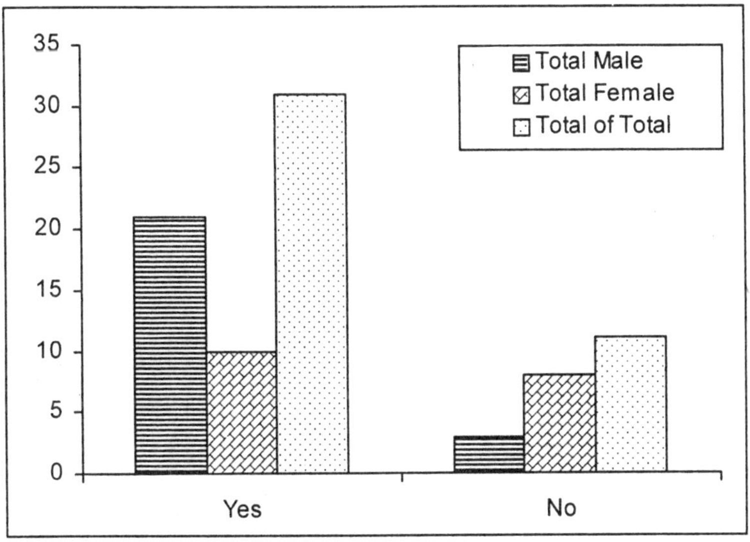

Fig. 29.3: Members as per their Interest in Reading Political Books/ Journals (South Tripura)

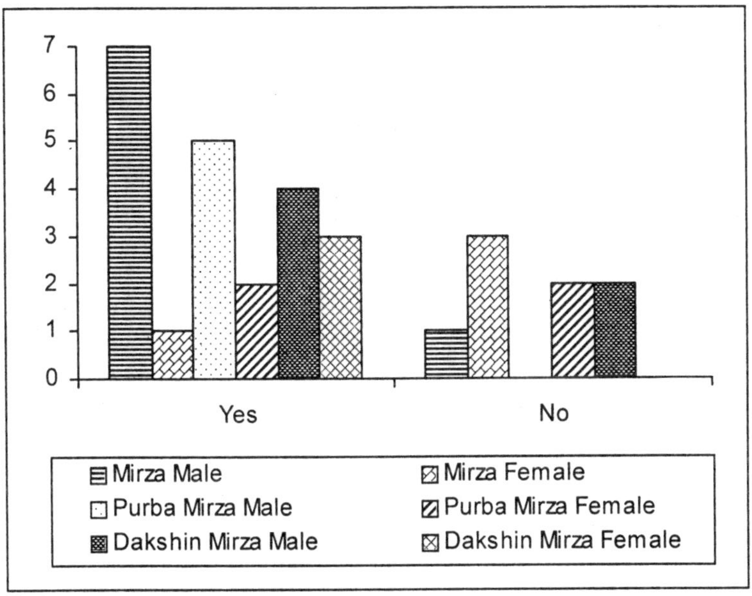

Fig. 29.4: Members as per their Interest in Reading Political Books/ Journals (South Tripura Total)

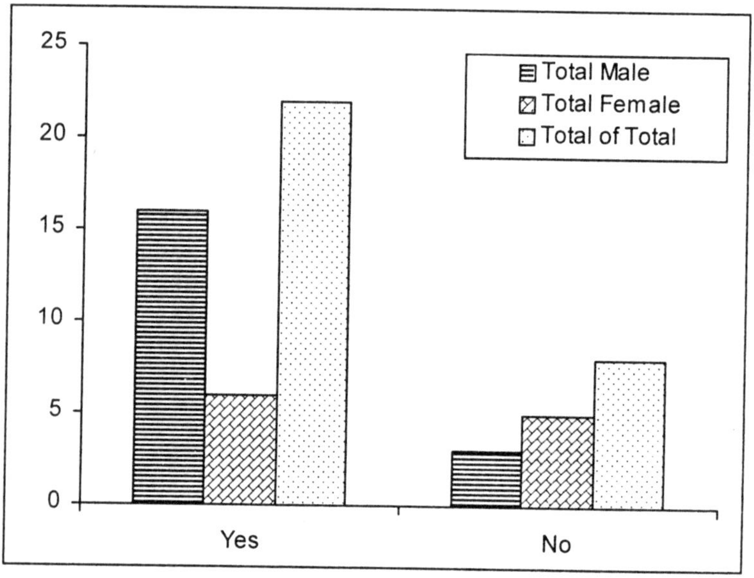

Fig. 29.5: Members as per their Interest in Reading Political Books/ Journals (Grand Total of West and South Tripura)

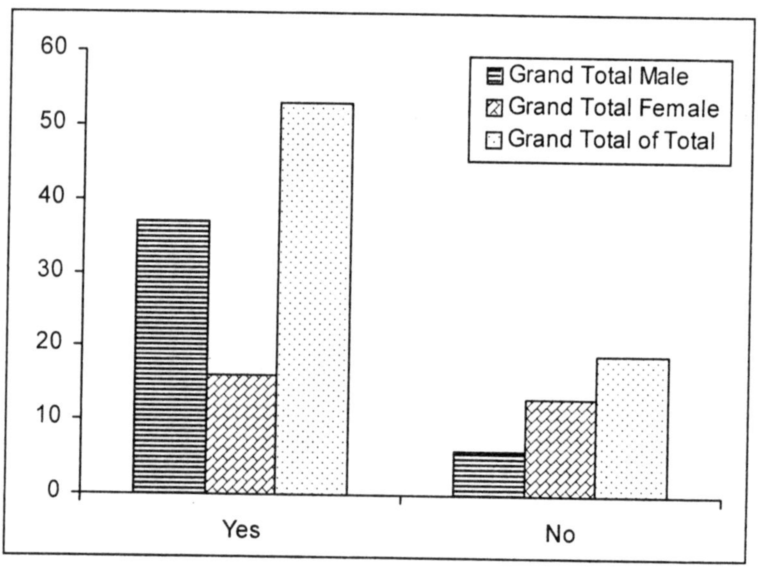

In South Tripura, female member's awareness is 55 per cent (54.55%). Among the male members, knowing of political books and journals is 84.21 per cent and not knowing of such books and journals is 15.79 per cent. Variations of knowledge can be obtained among the members of the smaller Gram Panchayat as well. Such as Mirza, 87.5 per cent male are in the reading of such books. In Dakshin Mirza, 66.66 per cent male are in the habit of reading of such awareness generating books. In Purba Mirza, 100 per cent male are aware of such books. Among the females in Dakshin Mirza 100 per cent female read those books and journals elating to political matter. So variation of knowledge is a phenomenon among the members.

Administrative Training

A preliminary administrative training and political training was imparted to the members of Gram Panchayats in order to make the Panchayat politically and administratively viable. In Table 30, we presented data as to how far the members of the Panchayats are trained in the administrative and political matters of the Panchayats.

It may be seen in the table that 33.33 per cent females in the Panchayats of West Tripura have received administrative training in the Panchayats and 66.67 per cent have not received any administrative training before being inducted into the Panchayat activities. 41.66 per cent male out of 24 male members in the Panchayats have received such training while 58.33 per cent did not have such training before being inducted into politico-administrative activities of the Panchayats. Interestingly in Raj Lakshminagar no female member had such training. In two other Gram Panchayats of West Tripura, both male and female members have undergone such politico-administrative training to some extent. Somewhere it is 50:50 and somewhere it is 40:60 even less among the female and male members.

In South Tripura, females have 72.73 per cent trained persons and 27.17 per cent did not have such training. Among the male members, 52.63 per cent have undergone administrative training at Panchayat while 47.36 per cent have not undergone such training at all. These administrative trainings were not equally imparted to even all members of the Gram Panchayats individually. As a result variation can be observed in receiving such training from Panchayat to Panchayat and gender to gender variation figures prominently. Such as, in Mirza Gram Panchayat, 75 per cent male received such training, 60 per cent male in Purba Mirza have received that training. 100 per cent female in Mirza have undergone such politico-administrative training. Similar variation in this regard can also be observed if one looks at it in detail (*vide* Table 30 and Figure 30).

Table 30: Distribution of Panchayat Members according to Administrative Training

District	*Gram Panchayat*	*Sex*	*Political/Administrative Training Status*		*Sub-Total*	*Total*
			Yes	*No*		
West Tripura	Dukli	Male	5	5	10	
		Female	3	2	5	15
	Raj Lakshminagar	Male	1	5	6	
		Female		6	6	12
	Paschim Pratappur	Male	4	4	8	
		Female	3	4	7	15
	Total	Male	10	14	24	
		Female	6 (33.33)	12(66.67)	18(100%)	
		Total	16(38.10)	26(61.90)	42(100%)	42
South Tripura	Mirza	Male	6	2	8	
		Female	4		4	12
	Purba Mirza	Male	3	2	5	
		Female	2	2	4	9
	Dakshin Mirza	Male	1	5	6	
		Female	2	1	3	9
	Total	Male	10	9	19	
		Female	8(72.73)	3(27.27)	11(100%)	
		Total	18(60.00)	12(40.00)	30(100%)	30
	Grand Total	Male	20	23	43	
		Female	14(48.28)	15(51.72)	29(100%)	
		Total	34(47.22)	38(52.78)	72(100%)	72

Source: Survey 2001-02.

Awareness of Laws

District-wise, panchayat-wise and sex-wise variation in awareness of the members in Tripura Gram Panchayats have been assessed in Table 31 with regard to laws. How far, the members of individual Panchayats are a ware of laws related to Panchayat functioning are of general concern. It has been seen in the Table 31, some members are aware of 1 law, some are aware of 2 laws and some are aware of 3 laws or more than 3 laws.

Fig. 30. Distribution of Panchayat Members according to their Status in Administrative Training

Fig. 30.1: Panchayat Members according to Status in Administrative Training (West Tripura)

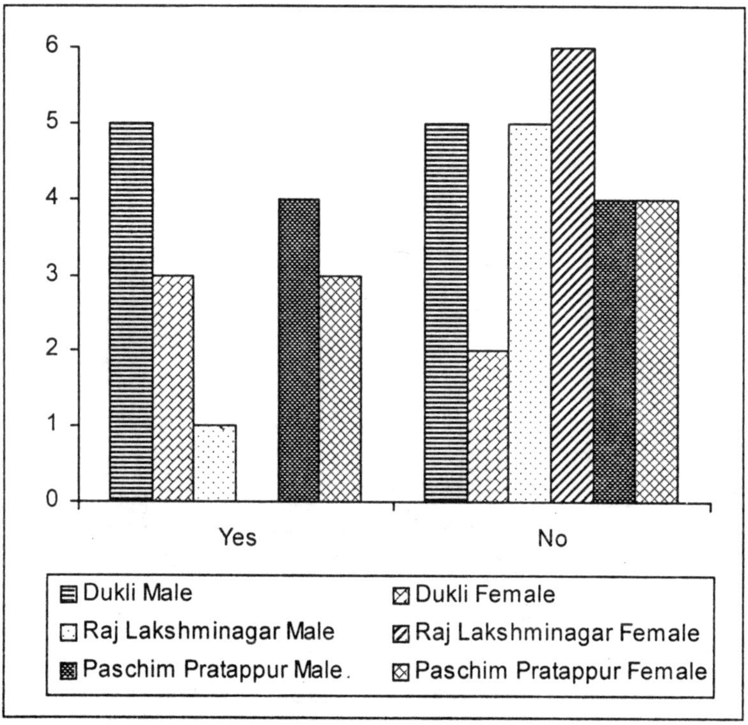

Fig. 30.2: Panchayat Members according to Status in Administrative Training (West Tripura Total)

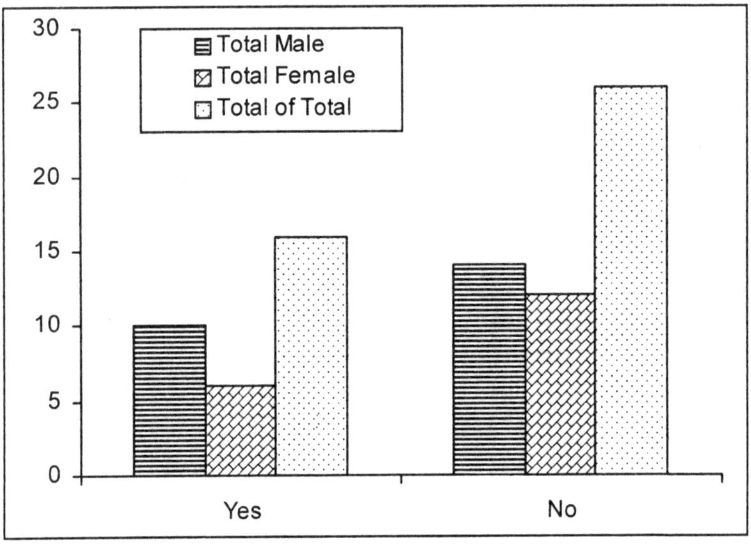

Fig. 30.3: Panchayat Members according to Status in Administrative Training (South Tripura)

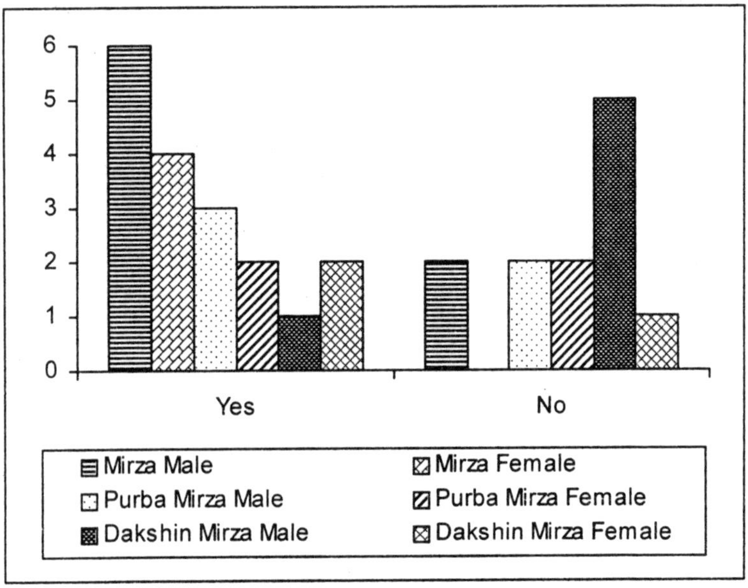

Fig. 30.4: Panchayat Members according to Status in Administrative Training (South Tripura Total)

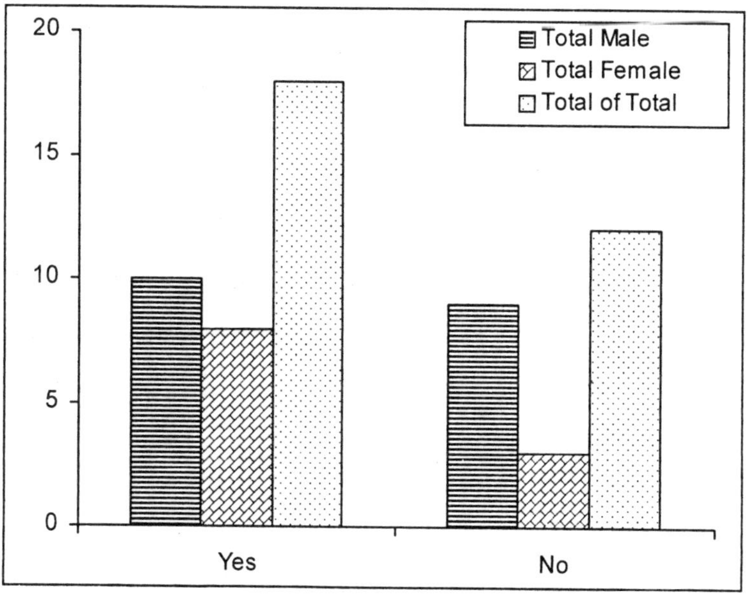

Fig. 30.5: Panchayat Members according to Status in Administrative Training (Grand Total of West and South Tripura)

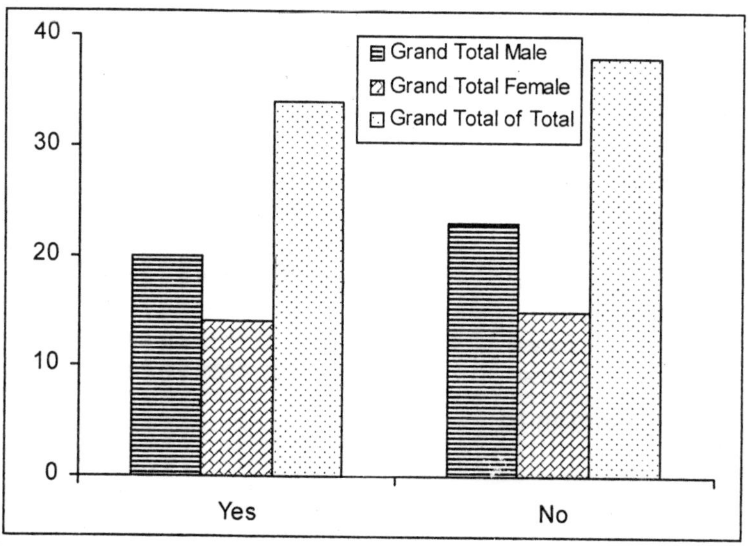

It may be seen in West Tripura that 5.56 per cent female members are aware of 1 law, 11.11 per cent female are aware of 2 laws and 5.55 per cent female members are aware of 3 laws. 77.78 per cent are aware of more than 3 laws.

In case of male members, 12.5 per cent are aware of 3 laws and 87.5 per cent male members are aware of more than 3 laws of the Panchayat affairs in West Tripura.

Table 31: Distribution of Panchayat Members as per their Awareness of Laws

District	*Gram Panchayat*	*Sex*	*Awareness of Legal Lows by Number*				*Sub-Total*	*Total*
			1	*2*	*3*	*More than 3*		
West Tripura	Dukli	Male	—	—	1	9	10	
		Female	—	1	—	4	5	15
	Raj Lakshmi-nagar	Male	—	—	2	4	6	
		Female	1	1	—	4	6	12
	Paschim Pratappur	Male	—	—	—	8	8	
		Female	—	—	1	6	7	15
	Total	Male	—	—	3	21	24	
		Female	1(5.56)	2(11.11)	1(5.55)	14(77.78)	18(100%)	
		Total	1(2.38)	2(4.76)	4(9.53)	35(83.33)	42(100%)	42
South Tripura	Mirza	Male	—	—	1	7	8	
		Female	—	1	2	1	4	12
	Purba Mirza	Male	—	1	—	4	5	
		Female	—	1	—	3	4	9
	Dakshin Mirza	Male	—	1	—	5	6	
		Female	—	—	—	3	3	9
	Total	Male	—	2	1	16	19	
		Female	—	2(18.18)	2(18.18)	7(63.64)	11(100%)	
		Total	—	4(13.33)	3(10.00)	23(76.67)	30(100%)	30
	Grand Total	Male	—	2	4	37	43	
		Female	1(3.45)	4(13.79)	3(10.35)	21(72.41)	29(100%)	
		Total	1(1.39)	6(8.33)	7(9.72)	58(80.56)	72(100%)	72

Source: Survey 2001-02.

Fig. 31. Distribution Panchayat Members as per their Awareness of Legal Laws

Fig. 31.1: Panchayat Members as per their Awareness of Legal Laws (West Tripura)

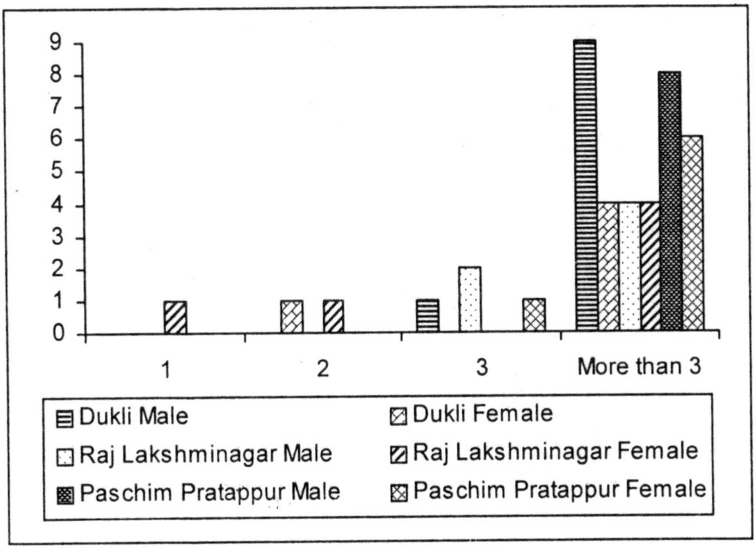

Fig. 31.2: Panchayat Members as per their awareness of Legal Laws (West Tripura Total)

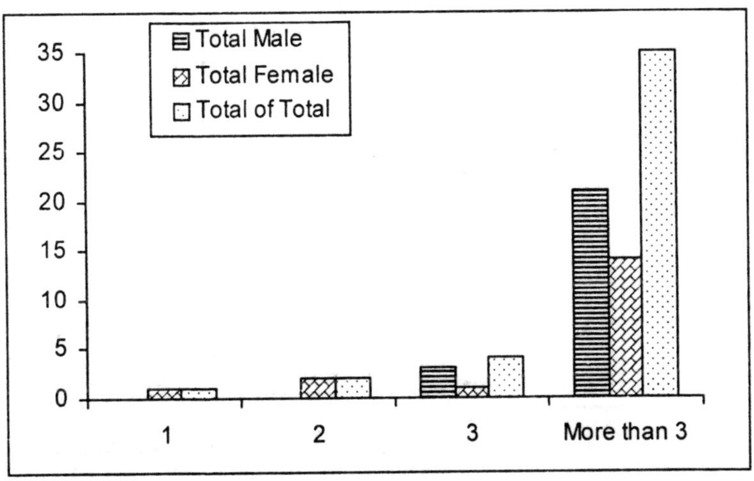

Fig. 31.3: Panchayat Members as per their awareness of Legal Laws (South Tripura)

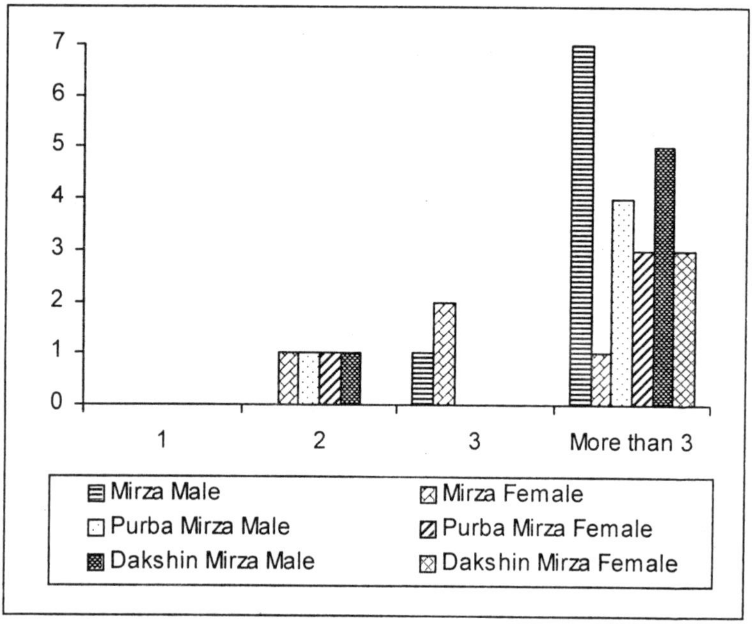

Fig. 31.4: Panchayat Members as per their awareness of Legal Laws (South Tripura Total)

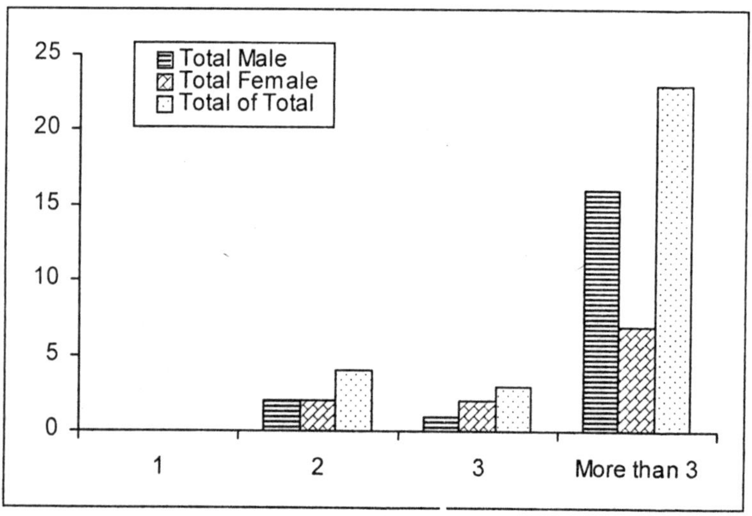

Fig. 31.5: Panchayat Members as per their awareness of Legal Laws (Grand Total of West and South Tripura)

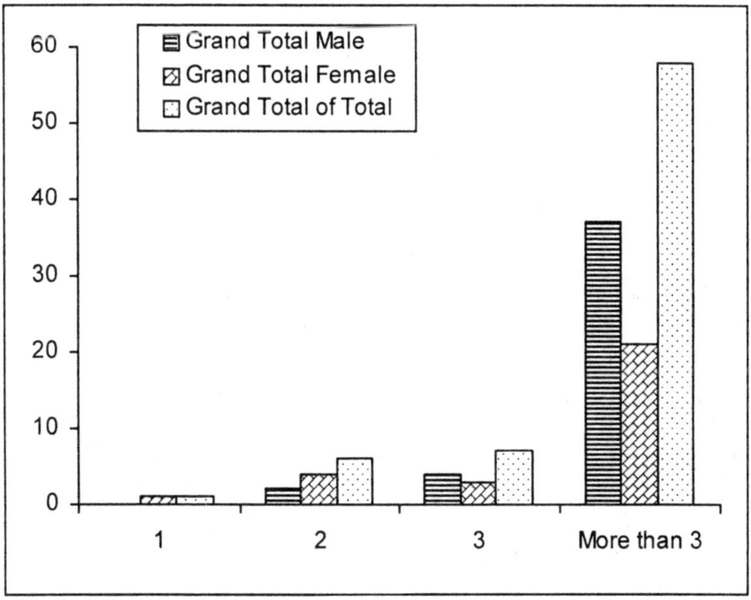

In case of South Tripura, 18.18 per cent females are aware of 2 laws, 18.18 per cent are aware of 3 laws and 63.64 per cent female members are well aware of more than 3 laws regarding Panchayats.

Among the male Panchayat member, 10.52 per cent are known of 2 laws, 5.26 per cent are known of 3 laws and 84.2 per cent are aware of more than 3 laws pertaining to Panchayats. In South Tripura, most of the members belonging to both male and females are aware of more than 3 laws. In Mirza Gram Panchayat, 25 per cent female are aware of 2 laws, 50 per cent are aware of 3 laws and 25 per cent are aware of more than 3 laws. 1 member each in Purba Mirza, Dakshin Mirza are aware of 2 laws of the Panchayats whereas most of the other members are quite aware of more than 3 laws.

Involvement and Type of Interaction with the Villagers

Visits of elected leaders to the village and people are made on different grounds. In Tripura, particularly, West and South Tripura leaders make occasional/regular visits to the village and the electorates. The reasons of the visits vary from place to place and on demand of the electorates somewhere. More or less, the nature of involvement and interaction was regular and based on voter's need or combination of voters' and party needs. The elected leaders with utmost care fulfil party needs. But this does not imply that leaders do not visit or make interaction with individual workers' need or felt need. So the visits and interactions are made in Tripura villages, are not only intended to voters' need but to monitor the work of rural development assigned to panchayat in the jurisdiction of the Gram Panchayat, is also one of them.

It may be observed from the data that in West Tripura, there are 17 out of 24 male members who have interacted regularly with the villagers whereas 14 female members (77.78 per cent) out of 18, who have interacted regularly with the villagers. Therefore, it is significant in West Tripura; female members were more interested than the male members regularly with the villagers. In addition to that, there are other types of interaction with the villagers like voters' need/in-between voters' need/party needs, regular voters of party needs etc. excluding voters needs categories are not too much important in terms of interactions with the villagers because data are to much few in number.

There are 14.29 per cent members of the panchayat who interacted with the villagers for the voters' need. So it can be said that those who have the right to vote get more importance by the Gram Panchayat members for their own existence and to hold the chair again. If we look into South Tripura district, these are 66.67 per cent members' were interacted among the villages regularly. If we break-up by gender-wise, there is marginal difference like 72.42 per cent and 27.58 per cent male and female Panchayat members respectively.

Nature of Involvement in Gram Panchayat Activities

The nature of involvement in Panchayat activities, has been levelled as much, average and not at all.

Table 32: Distribution of Panchayat Members as per their Involvement and Type of Interaction with the Villagers

District	Gram Panchayat	Sex	Type of Interaction						
			Regular	Voter's need	On Voter need in between	Voters/party need	Regular voters party need	Not regular	All
West Tripura	Dukli	Male	8	1	—	—	1	—	—
		Female	4	1	—	—	—	—	—
	Raj Lakshminagar	Male	3	2	—	—	—	—	1
		Female	5	—	—	—	—	—	1
	Paschim Pratappur	Male	6	1	—	—	—	1	—
		Female	5	1	—	—	—	—	1
	Total	Male	17	4	—	—	1	1	1
		Female	14(77.78)	2(11.11)	—	—	—	—	2(11.10)
		Total	31(73.81)	6(14.29)	—	—	1(2.38)	1(2.38)	3(7.14)
South Tripura	Mirza	Male	6	—	1	—	—	—	1
		Female	3	—	—	—	—	—	1
	Purba Mirza	Male	2	—	—	1	—	—	2
		Female	2	1	—	—	—	—	1
	Dakshin Mirza	Male	5	—	—	—	—	—	1
		Female	2	—	—	—	—	—	1
	Total	Male	13	—	1	1	—	—	4
		Female	7(63.64)	1(9.09)	—	—	—	—	3(27.27)
		Total	20(66.67)	1(3.33)	1(3.33)	1(3.33)	0	0	7(23.34)
	Grand Total	Male	30(27.58)	4	1	1	1	1	5
		Female	21(72.42)	3(10.34)	—	—	—	—	5(17.24)
		Total	51(7.83)	7(9.72)	1(1.39)	1(1.39)	1(1.39)	1(1.39)	10(13.89)

Source: Survey 2001-02.

Fig. 32: Distribution of Panchayat Members as per their Involvement and type of Interaction with the Villagers

Fig. 32.1: Panchayat Members as per their Involvement and type of Interaction with the Villagers (West Tripura and Total)

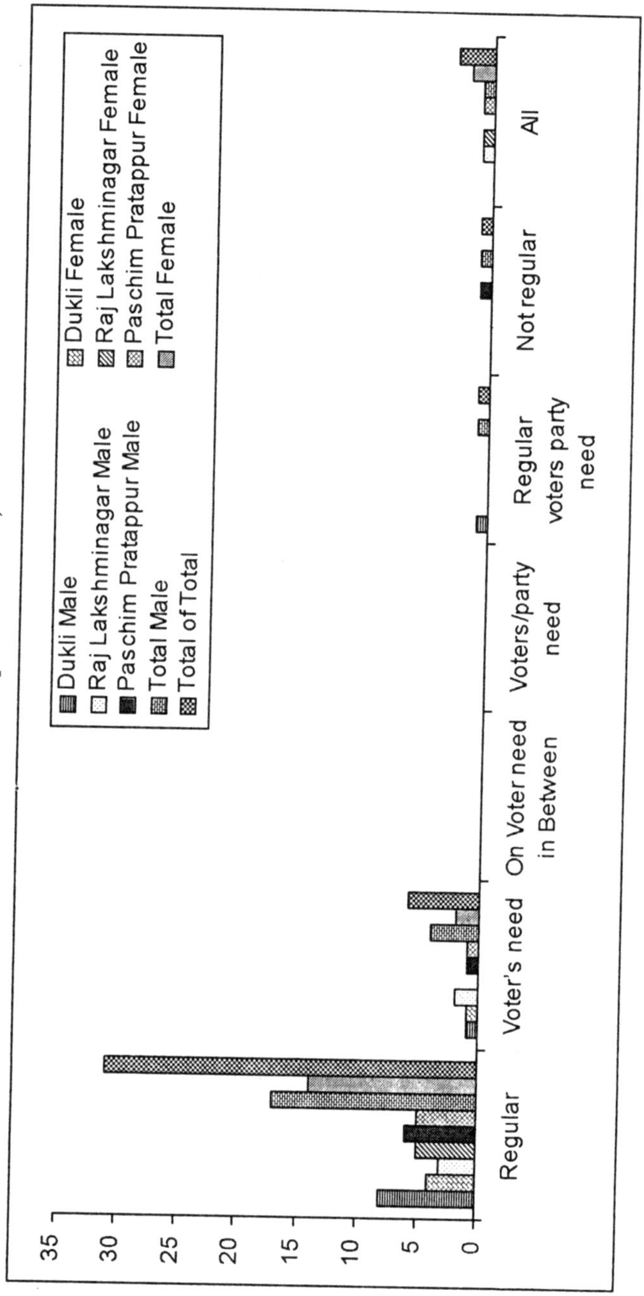

Fig. 32.2: Panchayat Members as per their Involvement and type of Interaction with the Villagers (South Tripura and Total)

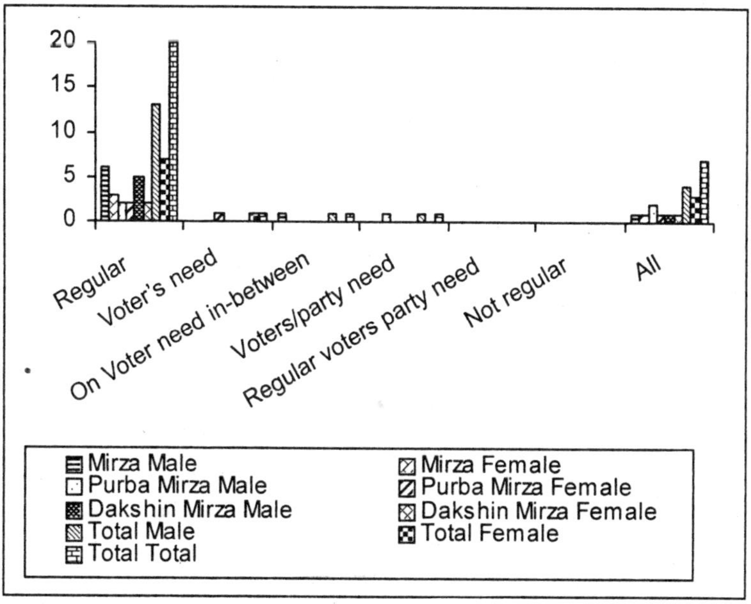

Fig. 32.3: Panchayat Members as per their Involvement and type of Interaction with the Villagers (Grand Total of West and South Tripura)

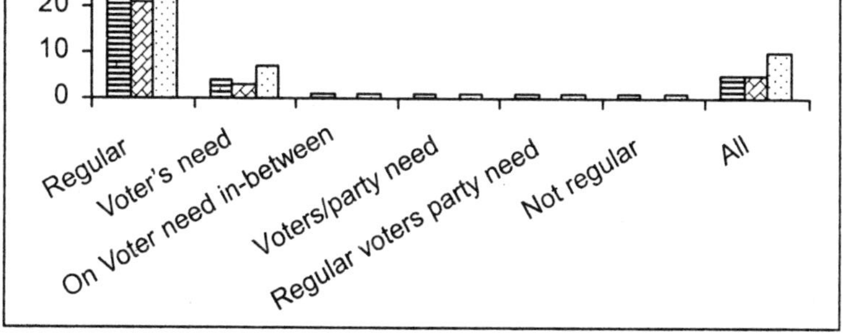

Individual villages, such as Dukli shows 70 per cent males' involvement as 'much' and 30 per cent had 'average' involvement. Female members of Dukli had 20 per cent with 'much' involvement, 60 per cent with 'average' involvement and another 20 per cent had no involvement. In Raj Lakshminagar, 50 per cent members had 'average' involvement while female members had 66.66 per cent with much involvement and 33.33 per cent females had average involvement. In Paschim Pratappur, 50 per cent male had 'much' involvement in the panchayat activities and another 50 per cent had average involvement in the same. 85.71 per cent female members in the same panchayat has an 'average' type of involvement and 14.28 per cent had no involvement.

Table 33: Distribution of Gram Panchayat Members as per their Nature of Involvement in Gram Panchayat Activities

District	*Gram Panchayat*	*Sex*	*Nature of Involvement in Panchayat Activities*		*Sub-Total*	*Total*
			More than average	*Average*		
West Tripura	Dukli	Male	7	3	10	
		Female	1	4	5	15
	Raj Lakshmi-nagar	Male	3	3	6	
		Female	4	2	6	12
	Paschim Pratappur	Male	4	4	8	
		Female		7	7	15
	Total	Male	14	10	24	
		Female	5(27.78)	13(72.22)	18(100%)	
		Total	*19(45.24)*	*23(54.76)*	*42(100%)*	*42*
South Tripura	Mirza	Male	7	1	8	
		Female	1	3	4	12
	Purba Mirza	Male	3	2	5	
		Female	1	3	4	9
	Dakshin Mirza	Male	2	4	6	
		Female	2	1	3	9
	Total	Male	12	7	19	
		Female	4(36.36)	7(63.64)	11(100%)	
		Total	*16(53.34)*	*14(46.66)*	*30(100%)*	*30*
	Grand Total	Male	26	17	43	
		Female	9(31.04)	20(68.96)	29(100%)	
		Total	*35(48.61)*	*37(51.39)*	*72(100%)*	*72*

Source: Survey 2001-02.

Fig. 33: Panchayat Members as per their Nature of Involvement in Gram Panchayat Activities

Fig. 33.1: Members as per their Nature of Involvement in Panchayat Activities (West Tripura)

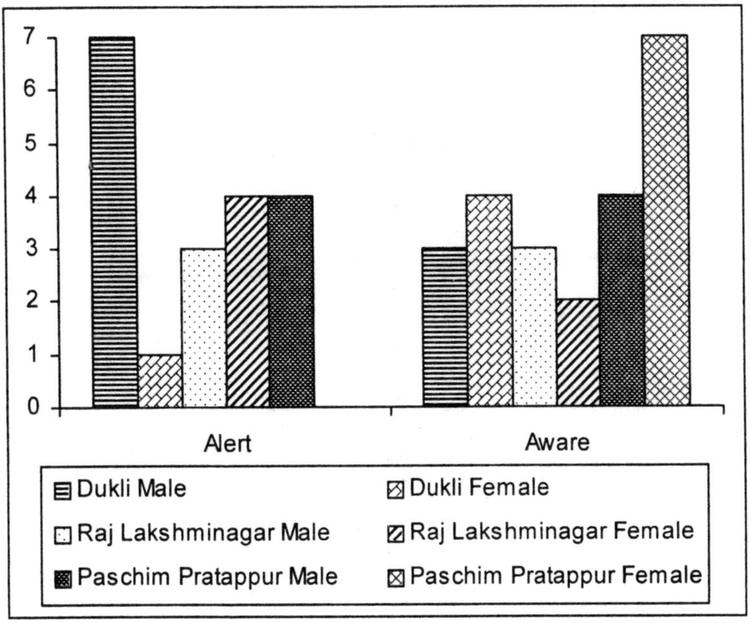

Fig. 33.2: Members as per their Nature of Involvement in Panchayat Activities (West Tripura Total)

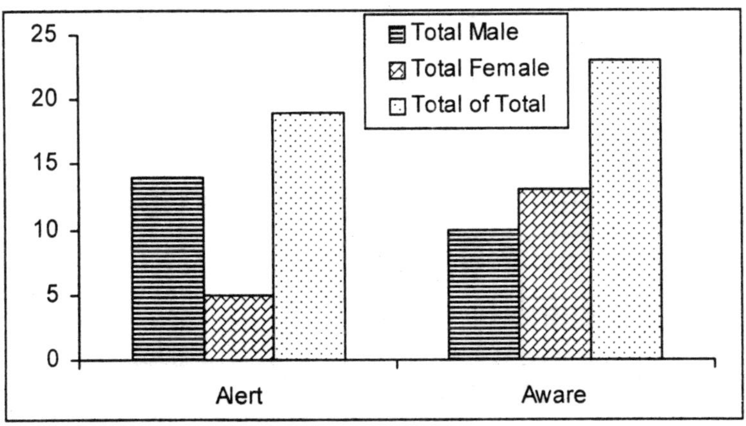

Fig. 33.3: Members as per their Nature of Involvement in Panchayat Activities (South Tripura)

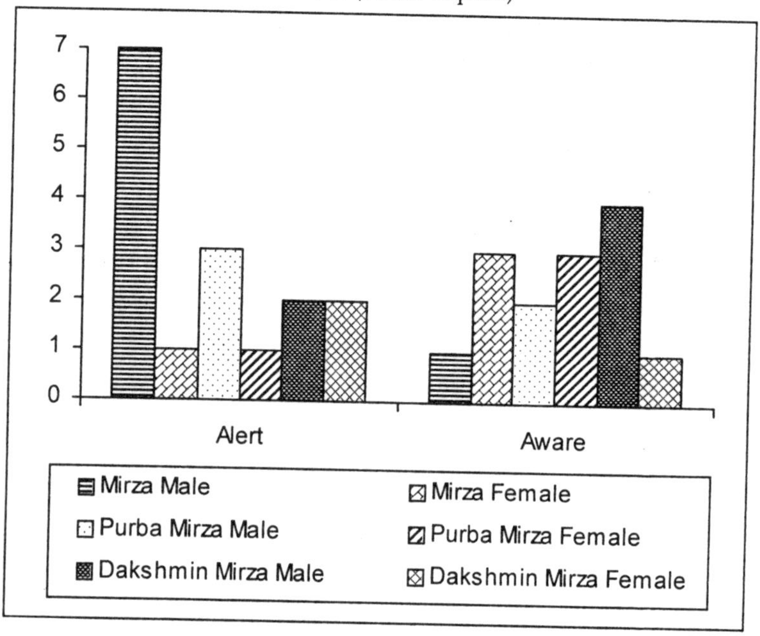

Fig. 33.4: Members as per their Nature of Involvement in Panchayat Activities (South Tripura Total)

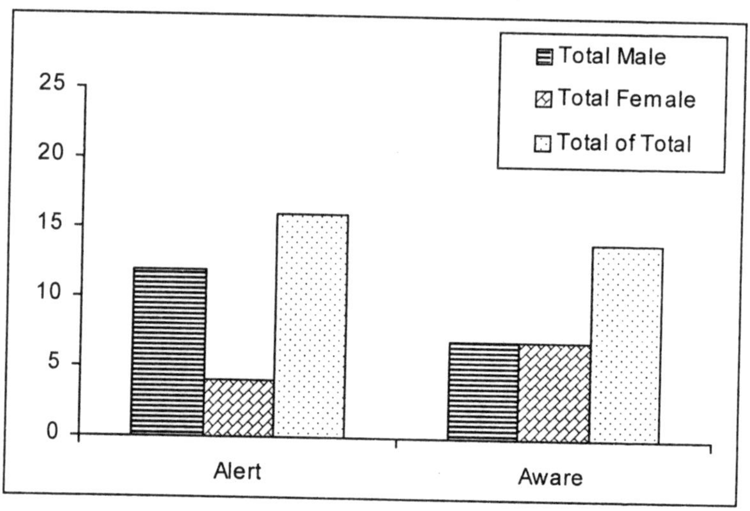

Fig. 33.5: Members as per their Nature of Involvement in Panchayat Activities (Grand Total of West and South Tripura)

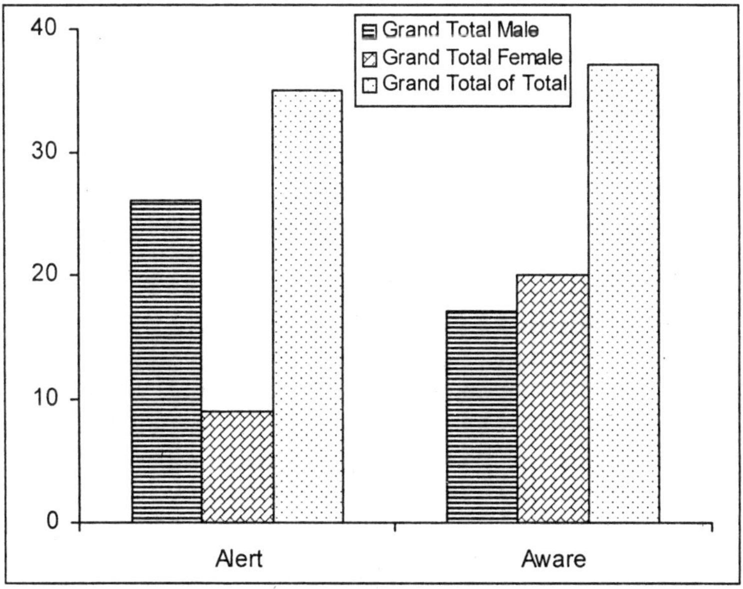

In South Tripura Gram Panchayat, 87.5 per cent male members have 'much' involvement while 12.5 per cent had average type of involvement in Mirza Gram Panchayat 25 per cent female members had 'much' involvement and 75 per cent female had 'average' type of involvement in Mirza Gram Panchayat activities. In Purba Mirza 60 per cent male had involvement what we call 'much' and 40 per cent male had involvement what we call 'average' type of involvement in Panchayat. Among the females, 25 per cent in Purba Mirza, had 'much' involvement and 50 per cent female had 'average' type of involvement. Another 25 per cent had no involvement to mention. In Dakshin Mirza, 33.33 per cent male members had 'much' involvement and 66.66 per cent male had 'average' involvement. 66.66 per cent female in Dakshin Mirza, had 'much' involvement and 33.33 per cent had 'average' involvement. Hence, there are various types of involvement of Panchayat members as to the panchayati activities.

Awareness of Local Problem

Awareness has been defined as great/intense and Average Categories. A greater depth is required to define 'much' and average in this regard. But for our purpose, we have restricted to 'much' and 'average' on the basis of some indicators.

Table 34 shows that 83.33 per cent female members in West Tripura Gram Panchayats have got what are call; 'great' awareness and 16.67 per cent female have average type of awareness. 91.66 per cent male in the same district have got 'much' awareness with regard to local problems. 8.33 per cent male members in the panchayats of the same district have possessed 'average' type of awareness. In Dukli, Gram Panchayat 80 per cent members belonging to male have 'much' awareness. About the local problems, 20 per cent male members in Dukli, possesses average type of awareness. Among the females, 80 per cent belong to category having 'much' awareness while 20 per cent having average awareness. In this way, most of the Gram Panchayat members belonging to both male and female sex have 'much' awareness about the local problems. 100 per cent male members in Raj Lakshminagar and Paschim Pratappur have 'much' awareness about the local problems.

In South Tripura, 81.82 per cent female members in the gram panchayats have 'much' awareness and 18.18 per cent have 'average' type of awareness with regard to local problems. 89.47 per cent belong to 'much' aware male members and 10.53 per cent belong to members with average kind of awareness about the local problems in three gram panchayats individually. We can notice, 87.5 per cent male have much awareness and 12.5 per cent have average awareness in Mirza Gram Panchayat and 100 per cent female have much awareness and more of them had average awareness about the problems.

In Purba Mirza, 80 per cent male members have 'much' and 20 per cent male members have average awareness. Female members have 50:50 much and average awareness respectively. In Dakshin Mirza, 100:100 male and female have 'much' awareness about the local problems.

Table 34: Distribution of Gran Panchayat Members as per their Awareness in Local Problem

District	*Gram Panchayat*	*Sex*	*Type of Awareness*		*Sub-Total*	*Total*
			More than average	*Average*		
West Tripura	Dukli	Male	8	2	10	
		Female	4	1	5	15
	Raj Lakshminagar	Male	6		6	
		Female	5	1	6	12
	Paschim Pratappur	Male	8		8	
		Female	6	1	7	15
	Total	Male	22	2	24	
		Female	15(83.33)	3(16.67)	18(100%)	
		Total	*37(88.10)*	*5(11.90)*	*42(100%)*	*42*
South Tripura	Mirza	Male	7	1	8	
		Female	4		4	12
	Purba Mirza	Male	4	1	5	
		Female	2	2	4	9
	Dakshin Mirza	Male	6		6	
		Female	3		3	9
	Total	Male	17	2	19	
		Female	9(81.82)	2(18.18)	11(100%)	
		Total	*26(86.67)*	*4(13.33)*	*30(100%)*	*30*
	Grand Total	Male	39	4	43	
		Female	24(82.76)	5(17.24)	29(100%)	
		Total	*63(87.50)*	*9(12.50)*	*72(100%)*	*72*

Source: Survey 2001-02.

Fig. 34: Panchayat Members as per their Awareness in Local Problem

Fig. 34.1: Members by Level of their Awareness of Local Problems (West Tripura)

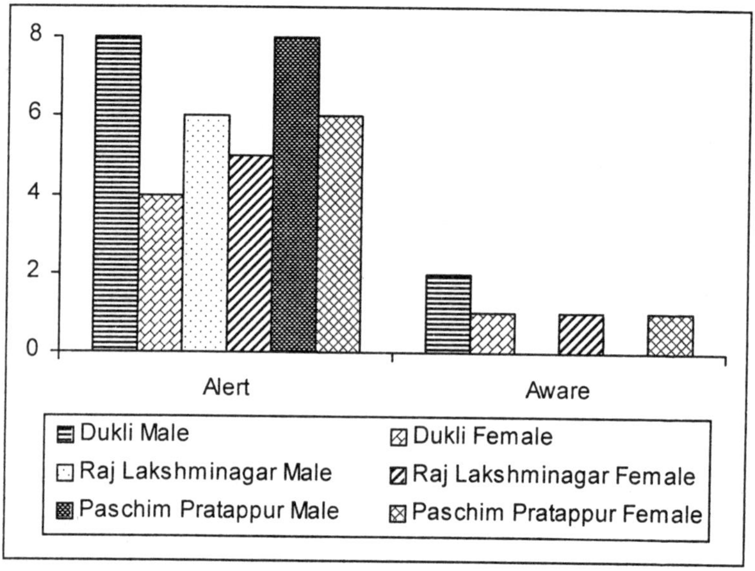

Fig. 34.2: Members by Level of their Awareness of Local Problems (West Tripura Total)

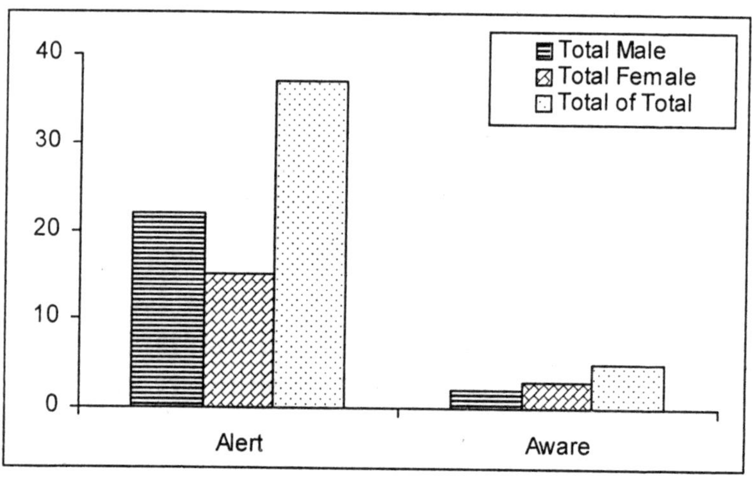

Fig. 34.3: Members by level of their Awareness of Local Problems (South Tripura)

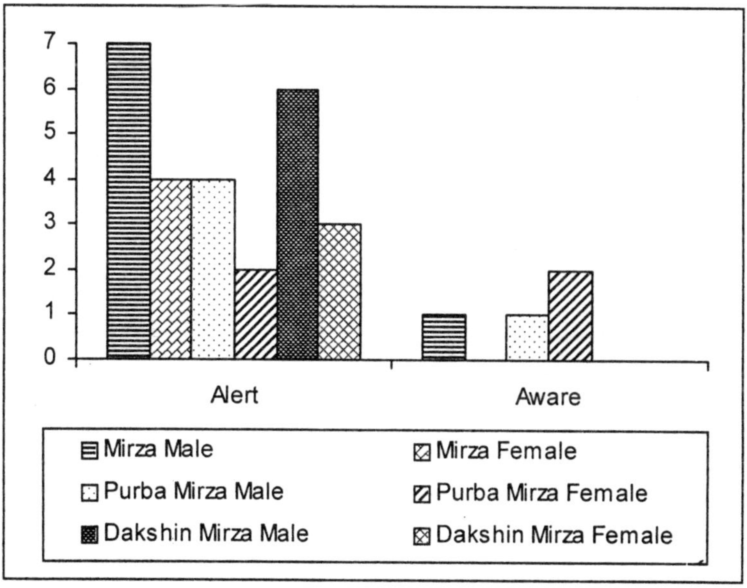

Fig. 34.4: Members by level of their Awareness of Local Problems (South Tripura Total)

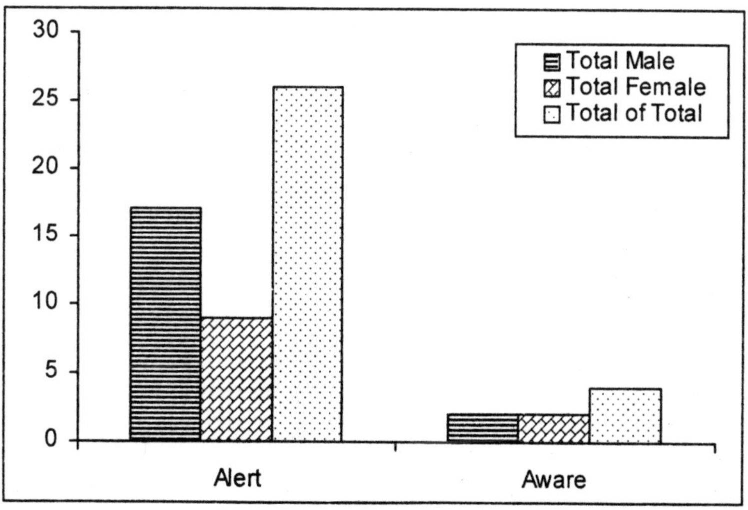

Fig. 34.5: Members by level of their Awareness of Local Problems (Grand Total of West and South Tripura)

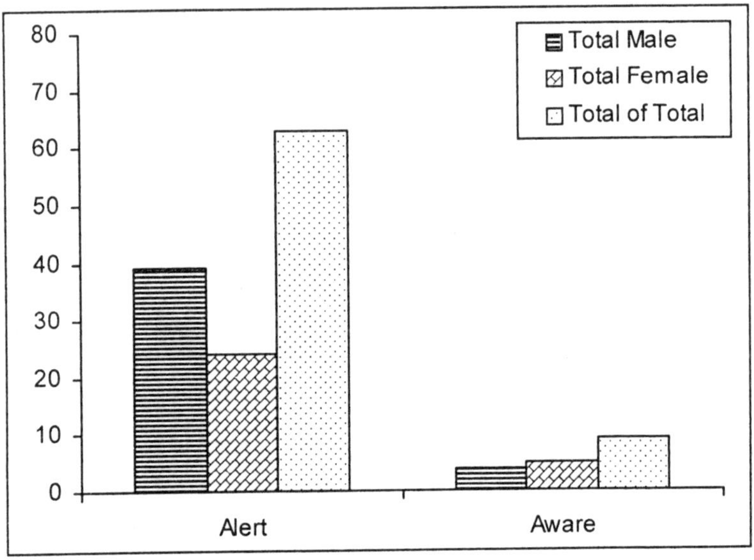

The following questions were asked to the Female Panchayat Members:

Assistance in Functioning of Gram Panchayat from their Male Colleagues

This small table relates to the help received from the males by the female members. In West Tripura district, all female members in Dukli, Raj Lakshminagar and Paschim Pratappur said 'yes' which means they have received assistance from the male folks while performing panchayat duties.

Similarly, in South Tripura, all female members of Mirza, Purba Mirza and Dakshin Mirza Gram Panchayats said that they had received all kinds of assistance from their male folks while dealing with panchayat activities. 100 per cent females each in Gram Panchayats said that they had received all kinds of assistance from their male folks while dealing with panchayat activities. 100 per cent females each in Gram Panchayats said that they received all assistance from the male folks.

Table 35: Distribution of female Panchayat members with regard to the assistance in functioning of gram panchayat from their male colleagues

District	*Gram Panchayat*	*Get help from their Male Folks*		*Total*
		Yes	*No*	
West Tripura	Dukli	5	—	5
	Raj Lakshminagar	6	—	6
	Paschim Pratappur	7	—	7
	Total	18	—	18
South Tripura	Mirza	4	—	4
	Purba Mirza	4	—	4
	Dakshin Mirza	3	—	3
	Total	11	—	11
	Grand Total	29	—	29

Source: Survey 2001-02.

Fig. 35: Female Panchayat Members with Regard to the Assistance from their Male Colleagues in Functioning of Gram Panchayat

Fig. 35.1: Female Members with Regard to the Assistance from their Male Colleagues in Functioning of Panchayat (West Tripura and Total)

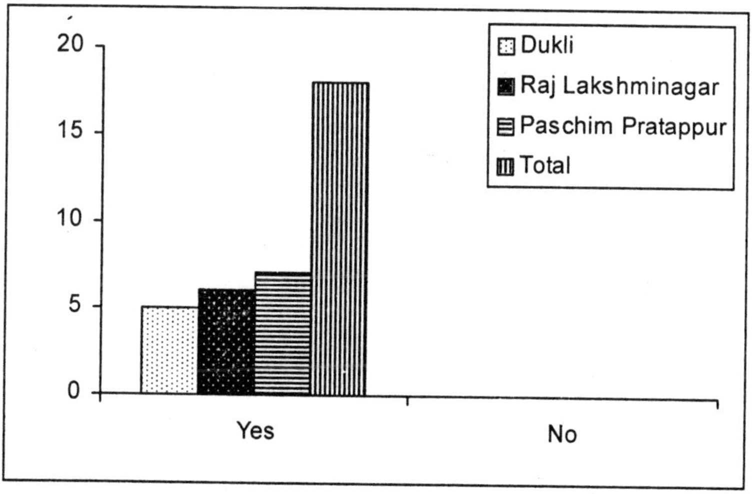

Fig. 35.2: Female Members with Regard to the Assistance from their Male Colleagues in Functioning of Panchayat (South Tripura and Total)

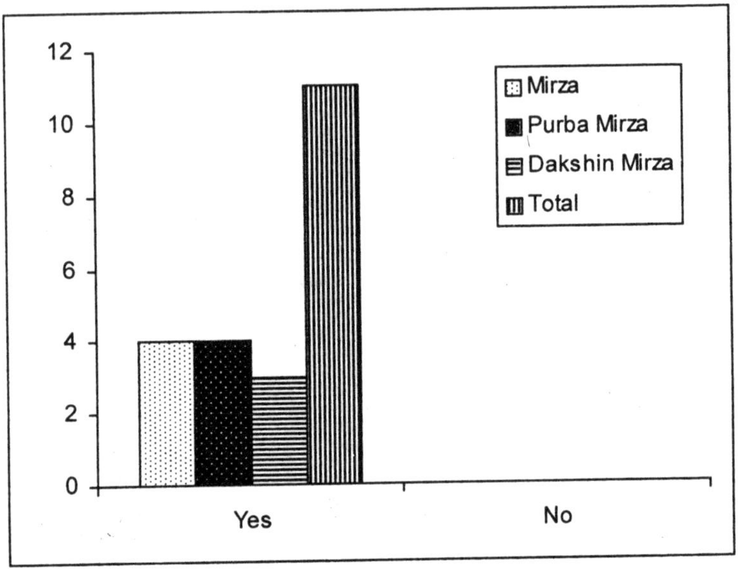

Fig. 35.3: Female Members with Regard to the Assistance from their Male Colleagues in Functioning of Panchayat (Grand Total of West and South Tripura)

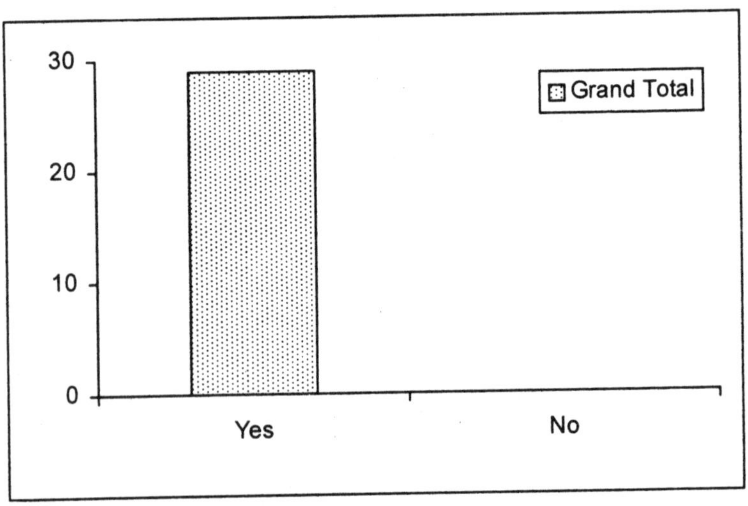

Discussing Problems with Male Gram Panchayat Members

The following table gives an account of female members having discussion with male Gram Panchayat Members or not.

Table 36: Distribution of Female Gram Panchayat Members According to their Discussing Problems with Male Gram Panchayat Members

District	*Gram Panchayat*	*Discussion with Male Members*		*Total*
		Yes	*No*	
West Tripura	Dukli	5	—	5
	Raj Lakshminagar	6	—	6
	Paschim Pratappur	6	1	7
	Total	17	1	18
South Tripura	Mirza	4	—	4
	Purba Mirza	4	—	4
	Dakshin Mirza	3	—	3
	Total	11	—	11
	Grand Total	28	1	29

Source: Survey 2001-02.

In West Tripura, except in Paschim Pratappur where one woman member did not have discussion with male members to solve the local problems of the panchayat. Remaining Gram Panchayats, i.e. Dukli and Raj Lakshminagar had 5 and 6 female members who held discussion with the male folks. To say, i.e. 100 per cent female in these GPs have held discussion with the male members.

In South Tripura, in all Gram Panchayats, viz. Mirza, Purba Mirza and Dakshin Mirza had 100 per cent females each who held discussion with their male members in order to discuss any local problems affecting Panchayats activities.

Fig. 36: Female Gram Panchayat Members according to their Involvement in Discussing Problems with Male Gram Panchayat Members

Fig. 36.1: Female Members according to their Involvement in Discussing Problems with Male Gram Panchayat Members (West Tripura and Total)

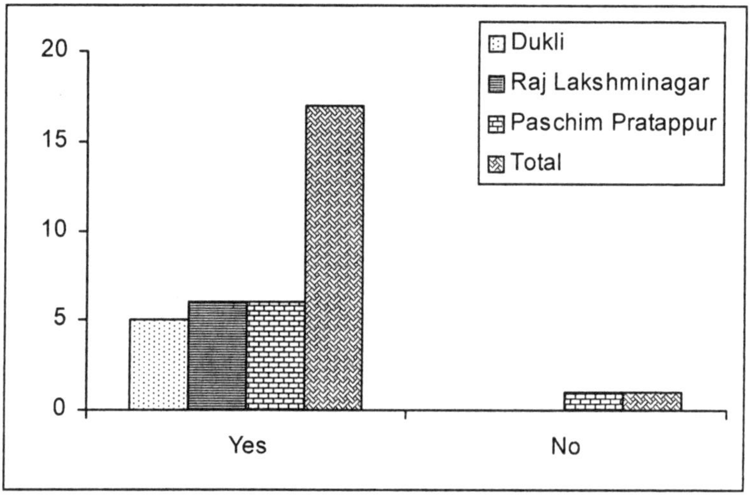

Fig. 36.2: Female Members according to their Involvement in Discussing Problems with Male Panchayat Members (South Tripura and Total)

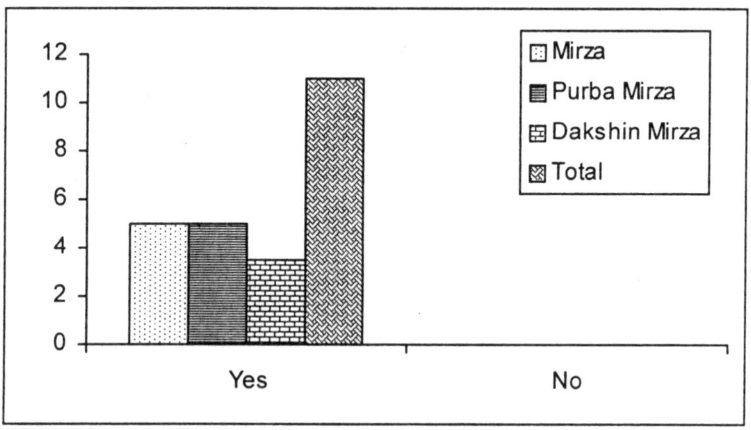

Fig. 36.3: Female Members according to their Involvement in Discussing Problems with Male Panchayat Members (Grand Total of West and South Tripura)

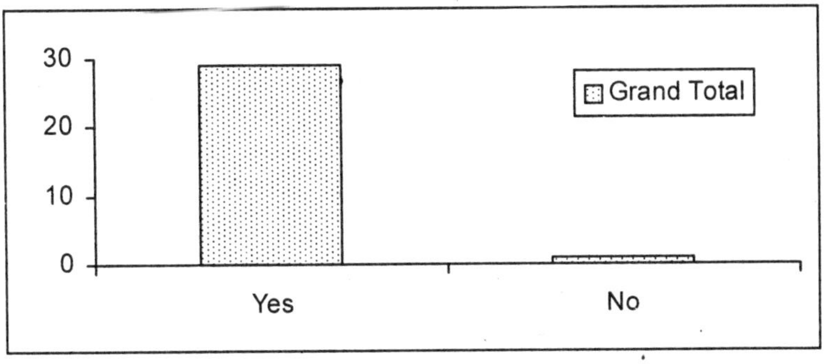

Taking Independent Decisions in Gram Panchayat

Another table containing data regarding the independence of the decision-making in Gram Panchayats by the female has been presented.

We present the data Panchayat-wise by districts. The West Tripura district has total 18 female members. Of which 44.44 per cent female members take independent decisions in Gram Panchayat. So, 55.55 per cent female did not take independent decisions in Gram Panchayat.

Table 37: Distribution of Female Gram Panchayat Members according to their taking Independent Decisions in Gram Panchayat

District	*Gram Panchayat*	*Take Independent Decisions*		*Total*
		Yes	*No*	
West Tripura	Dukli	1	4	5
	Raj Lakshminagar	4	2	6
	Paschim Pratappur	3	4	7
	Total	8	10	18
South Tripura	Mirza	3	1	4
	Purba Mirza	1	3	4
	Dakshin Mirza	1	2	3
	Total	5	6	11
	Grand Total	13	16	29

Source: Survey 2001-02.

In South Tripura, 45.45 per cent female did take decisions of panchayat independently while 54.55 per cent female did not take decisions independently in the Gram Panchayats.

Individual Gram Panchayats have different pictures in this regard. In West Tripura district Dukli Gram Panchayat has 20 per cent female who took independent decisions. 66.66 per cent female members in Raj Lakshminagar had taken decisions independently and 42.85 per cent female members in Paschim Pratappur had taken decisions independently.

Fig. 37: Distribution of Female Gram Panchayat Members according to their taking Independent Decisions in Gram Panchayat

Fig. 37.1: Female Members according to their taking Independent Decisions in Panchayat (West Tripura and Total)

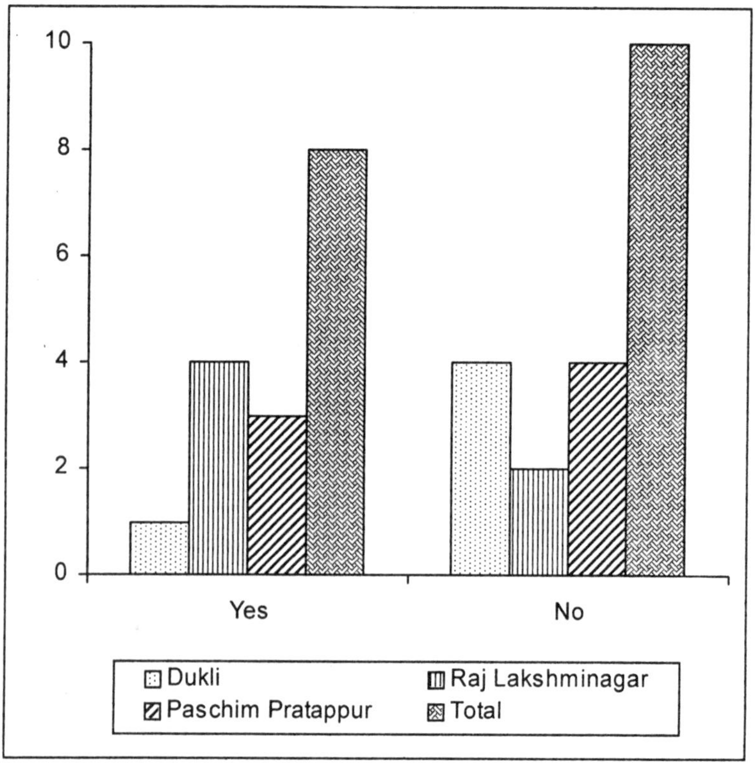

Fig. 37.2: Female Members according to their taking Independent Decisions in Panchayat (South Tripura and Total)

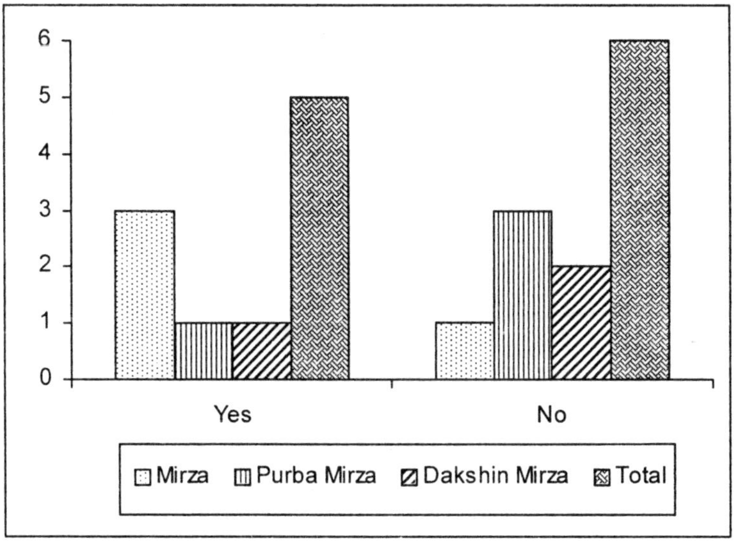

Fig. 37.3: Female Members according to their taking Independent Decisions in Panchayat (Grand Total of West and South Tripura)

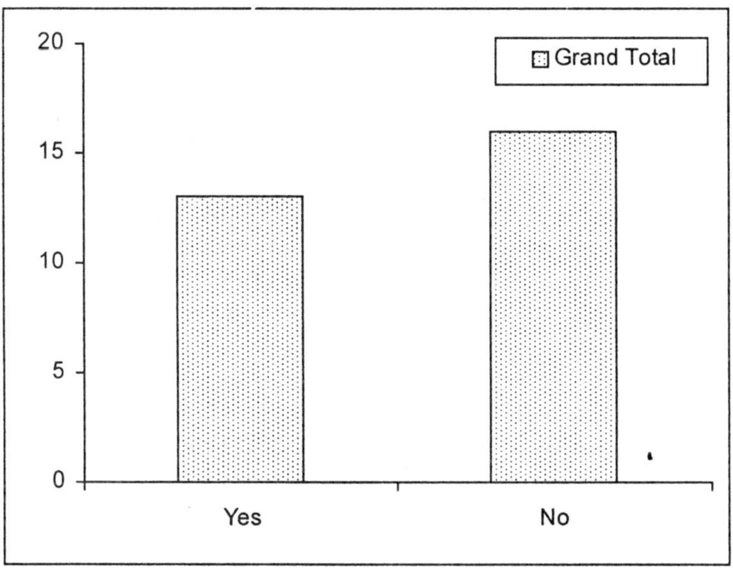

In South Tripura, 75 per cent female members in Mirza Gram Panchayat took decisions independently, 25 per cent female members in Purba Mirza had taken independent decisions and 3.33 per cent female members took such decisions independently.

So differential degree of independent decision-making has occurred in Gram Panchayats of Tripura.

Awareness of the Rules of Gram Panchayat Functioning

Awareness of Gram Panchayat rules and regulations has been the parameters used here to know the level of awareness of two districts have been under discussion, as they constituted the sample. Total number of women members in West and South Tripura is 29 of which 18 came from West Tripura and 11 came from South Tripura. In West Tripura, 88.8 per cent women are conversant with rules and regulation of the Gram Panchayats. 5.55 per cent women are aware of the rules and regulations and another 5.55 per cent women stated that they know about rules and regulations of the same.

Table 38: Distribution of Female Gram Panchayat Members as per their Awareness of the Rules of Gram Panchayat Functioning

District	*Gram Panchayat*	*Awareness of Gram Panchayat rules and regulations*		*Total*
		Alert	*Aware*	
West Tripura	Dukli	1	4	5
	Raj Lakshminagar	—	6	6
	Paschim Pratappur	—	7	7
	Total	1	17	18
South Tripura	Mirza	1	3	4
	Purba Mirza	—	4	4
	Dakshin Mirza	1	2	3
	Total	2	9	11
	Grand Total	5	26	29

Source: Survey 2001-02.

South Tripura had 11 women members in the Gram Panchayats. Of them 18.18 per cent are aware of the rules and regulations of the Panchayat. 54.54 per cent are known to the rules and regulations of the panchayats and 27.27 per cent women members are well known about the Gram Panchayat rules and regulations.

Fig. 38: Distribution of Female Gram Panchayat Members as per their Awareness of the Rules of Gram Panchayat Functioning

Fig. 38.1: Female Members as per their Awareness of the Rules of Panchayat Functioning (West Tripura and Total)

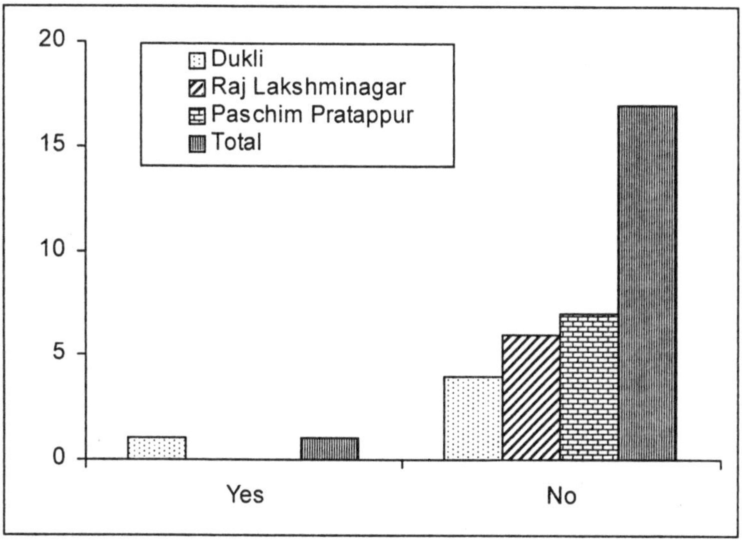

Fig. 38.2: Female Members as per their Awareness of the Rules of Panchayat Functioning (South Tripura and Total)

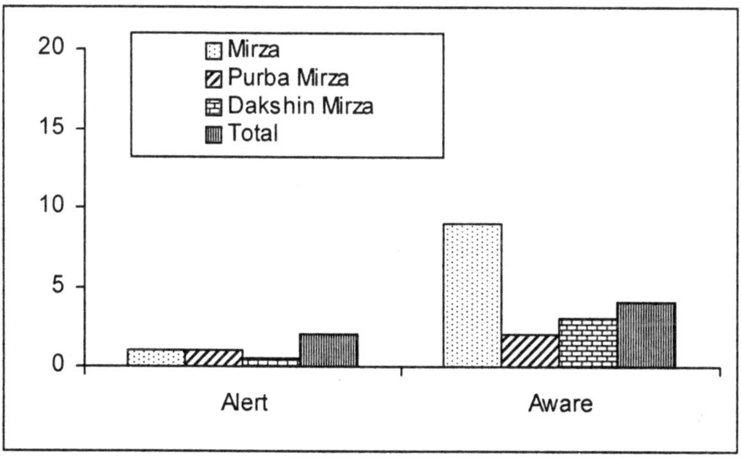

Fig. 38.3: Female Members as per their Awareness of the Rules of Panchayat Functioning (Grand Total of West and South Total)

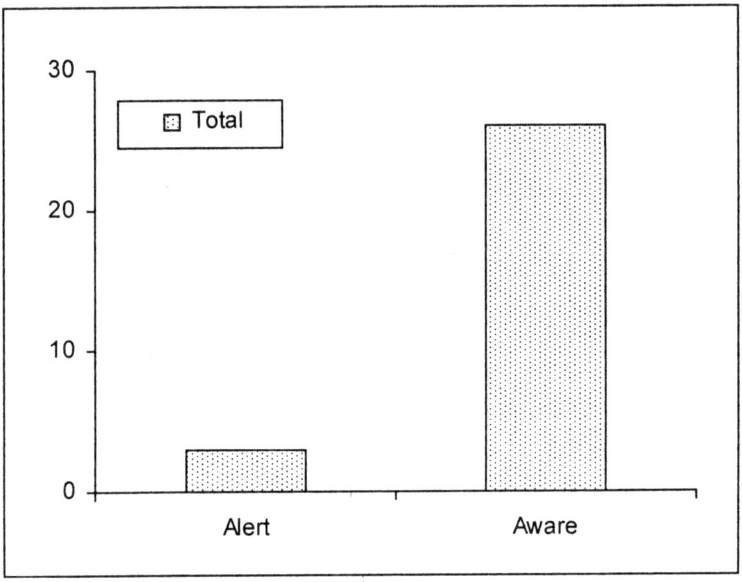

8

Credit for Poverty Eradication

Getting assistance in time of need is problematic in society. Informal loan in time of need is quite common in rural areas.

Our concern here is basically, to see how far the loan and assistance of Government bodies has been able to reach the needy in particular.

What are the types of loan available to ameliorate the poverty of the people at village societies? This loan or assistance giving took place from Panchayats in Dukli, Raj Lakshminagar and Paschim Pratappur in West Tripura district and this took place in Mirza, Purba Mirza and Dakshin Mirza Panchayats in South Tripura.

Heads of Loans

Loans are sanctioned for 17 activities. A long list of 17 items of loan is presented in Table 39 (loan obtain 94-95 to 97-98). Schemes on which loans were given are stated here. They are—(1) Puffed rice, (2) Selling of rice, (3) Selling of vegetable, (4) Duckery, (5) Goatery, (6) Piggery, (7) Sal-leaf plate manufacturing, (8) Rope-making, (9) Patta on land (male and female), (10) Agriculture land, (11) House building, (12) Poultry, (13) Fishery, (14) Selling readymade garments, (15) Wheel of bullock cart making, (16) Rice making from paddy, and (17) Mat making.

Cottage industry playas an important role in rural areas in Tripura. Cottage industries include smith works such as iron-smithy for household consumption and for cultivation.

Cottage industry loan are next important to poultry. This is important that cottage industry is taking it root despite its slightly complicated set up. It is assumed that cottage industry at rural level requires some expertise and a minimum technical knowledge. It is more likely that type of cottage industry differs to a great extent in rural context. This may be said that the cottage industry-based loan is encouraging as it basically aimed to promote production. Following are the figures in incidence of cottage industries over the seven years.

Table 40, states that there are five broad categories of loan given by gram panchayat to rural women. These categories are selling articles, poultry, land related cottage industries and house building. Number of beneficiaries has been increased both in West and South Tripura under different heads of categories between 1994 and 2001.

In South Tripura, poultry have been the area of loan receiving effectively. Cottage industries occupy important role, as the percentage (25.71) is higher among all items loan.

In West Tripura, figures for loan are as follows, 18, 19, 20, 22, 21, 24, and 25 obtaining 1994-94 to 2000-2001. In south Tripura, figures for such loan are 19, 21, 26, 28, 31, 32, and 35. Figures are shown as 37, 39, 46, 49, 52, 55, and 60 during 1994-95 to 2000-01 together of selling articles in both the districts.

Table 41, involves an analysis of loan receiving. In this regard, cottage industries find the prominent place in South Tripura district. With 25.71 per cent of all loans, cottage industries place is noteworthy. It is followed by poultry with a 24.54 per cent incidence.

West Tripura is a district where loanee takes loan for poultry purpose much. The percentage of which is 28.25 per cent. After poultry, next loan receiving is in cottage industries with 26.89 per cent. Similar trends can also be observed in grand total percentage of both districts. The type of cottage industries which are told here are very minor-works such as rope-making, husking paddy, mat making and wheel of bullock cart etc. are some of them.

Table 39: Total number of Women Beneficiaries for 1994-2001 by District, Schemes and Year-wise in Tripura

Sl. No.	Items of Loan	District														Total						
		West Tripura							South Tripura													
		94-95	95-96	96-97	97-98	98-99	99-00	00-01	94-95	95-96	96-97	97-98	98-99	99-00	00-01	94-95	95-96	96-97	97-98	98-99	99-00	00-01
1.	Puffed rice	3	4	4	5	6	5	5	4	6	7	8	8	10	10	7	10	12	14	14	15	15
2.	Selling of rice	3	3	3	5	6	5	5	2	6	7	8	10	8	10	5	9	12	14	16	13	15
3.	Selling of vegetables	6	4	7	6	5	7	7	4	5	6	6	6	7	5	10	9	12	11	11	14	12
4.	Selling of Ready-made garments	6	7	6	5	4	7	8	9	4	6	6	7	6	10	15	11	10	10	11	13	18
	Total	*18*	*18*	*20*	*21*	*21*	*24*	*25*	*19*	*21*	*26*	*28*	*31*	*31*	*35*	*37*	*39*	*46*	*49*	*52*	*55*	*60*
5.	Duckery	7	7	8	8	9	10	12	7	7	7	8	10	11	12	14	14	15	16	19	21	24
6.	Goatery	7	8	7	8	9	10	12	7	7	8	8	12	12	12	14	15	15	16	21	22	24
7.	Piggery	4	5	6	7	9	12	10	5	7	10	8	8	11	10	9	12	16	15	17	23	20
8.	Poultry	10	10	11	12	9	12	11	10	9	6	8	5	5	12	20	19	17	20	14	17	23
	Total	*28*	*30*	*32*	*35*	*36*	*44*	*45*	*29*	*30*	*31*	*32*	*35*	*39*	*46*	*57*	*60*	*63*	*67*	*71*	*83*	*91*
9.	Patta (male + female)	4	2	9	10	15	13	12	5	9	10	10	14	14	18	9	11	19	20	29	27	30
10.	Agricultural land	2	5	9	19	15	13	20	5	7	10	13	16	18	22	7	12	19	32	31	31	42
	Total	*6*	*7*	*18*	*29*	*30*	*26*	*32*	*10*	*16*	*20*	*26*	*30*	*32*	*40*	*16*	*23*	*38*	*55*	*60*	*58*	*72*

(*Contd.*)

(*Contd.*)

Sl. No. Items of Loan	District														Total						
	West Tripura							South Tripura													
	94-95	*95-96*	*96-97*	*97-98*	*98-99*	*99-00*	*00-01*	*94-95*	*95-96*	*96-97*	*97-98*	*98-99*	*99-00*	*00-01*	*94-95*	*95-96*	*96-97*	*97-98*	*98-99*	*99-00*	*00-01*
11. Sal-leaf plate manufacturing	—	—	4	8	10	10	10	—	—	—	6	6	6	6	—	—	4	14	16	16	16
12. Rope making	—	1	2	2	3	4	5	2	6	8	8	8	10	10	2	7	10	10	11	14	15
13. Fishery	—	—	—	—	—	—	—	—	—	—	—	—	—	—	—	—	—	—	—	—	—
14. Wheel of Bullock cart	—	—	—	—	—	—	2	—	—	—	—	—	2	2	—	—	—	—	—	2	4
15. Rice making from paddy	10	12	10	10	8	8	10	—	—	10	10	8	8	8	10	12	20	20	16	16	18
16. Mat making	15	21	15	16	22	10	10	16	17	22	10	20	22	22	31	38	37	26	42	32	32
Total	*25*	*34*	*31*	*36*	*43*	*32*	*37*	*18*	*23*	*40*	*34*	*42*	*48*	*48*	*43*	*57*	*71*	*70*	*85*	*80*	85
17. House building loan	10	10	12	14	16	20	20	10	12	12	16	20	22	32	20	22	24	30	36	42	52
Total	10	10	12	14	16	20	20	10	12	12	16	20	22	32	20	22	24	40	36	42	52
Grand Total	*87*	*99*	*113*	*135*	*146*	*146*	*159*	*86*	*102*	*129*	*136*	*158*	*172*	*201*	*173*	*201*	*242*	*271*	*304*	318	360

Source: Survey 2001-02.

Table 40: Number of Women Beneficiaries obtained Loan for Different Socio-welfare

District	Year	Items of Loan					
		Selling Articles	*Poultry*	*Land*	*Cottage*	*House*	*Total*
West Tripura	94-95	19	29	10	18	10	86
	95-96	21	30	16	23	12	102
	96-97	26	31	20	40	12	129
	97-98	28	32	26	34	16	136
	98-99	31	35	30	42	20	158
	99-00	31	39	32	48	22	172
	00-01	35	46	40	48	32	201
	Total	*191 (19.41)*	*242 (24.59)*	*174 (17.68)*	*253 (25.71)*	*124 (12.60)*	*984 (100%)*
South Tripura	94-95	18	28	6	25	10	87
	95-96	18	30	7	34	10	99
	96-97	20	32	18	31	12	113
	97-98	21	35	29	36	14	135
	98-99	21	36	30	43	16	146
	99-00	24	44	26	32	20	146
	00-01	25	45	32	37	20	159
	Total	*147 (16.61)*	*250 (28.25)*	*148 (16.72)*	*238 (26.89)*	*102 (11.52)*	*885 (100%)*
Total	94-95	37	57	16	43	20	150
	95-96	39	60	23	57	22	166
	96-97	46	63	38	71	24	195
	97-98	49	67	55	70	30	241
	98-99	52	71	60	85	36	255
	99-00	55	83	58	80	42	280
	00-01	60	91	72	85	52	327
	Grand Total	*338 (18.09)*	*492 (26.32)*	*322 (17.23)*	*491 (26.27)*	*226 (12.09)*	*1869 (100%)*

Source: Survey 2001-02.

Selling Articles: Puffed rice, Rice, Vegetables and Garment
Poultry: Duckery, Goatery, Piggery and Poultry
Land: Patta (male+female) and Agricultural land
Cottage: Sal-leaf plate manufacturing, Rope making, Fishery, Wheel of Bullock cart, Rice making from paddy and mat making
House: House Building

9

Problems of Women Members

1. My previous study on Scope and Constraints of Rural Women Leadership with Special Reference to Experimentation in Self-government Bodies revealed that most of the Panchayat members did not attend the meetings in the Panchayat regularly. They never visited Zilla Parishad offices except when the meetings were held.
2. Occasionally men escorted then and accompanied them to the meeting hall and promoted to speak.
3. If any woman wished to raise any issue, she was not able to do so. But things began to change after completion of one block year. Now most women were found expressing themselves in the meetings. Still there are constraints of patriarchal psycho-social conditioning of socialization of officials.
4. The males in their work also observe. Sometimes a few more members had non-cooperative role in the meeting. Therefore, many problems were raised in the meetings without which it was not possible to continue the meeting of the Panchayats very effectively. Most women members' feel frustrated when they interact with the officials. According to their statement "we feel uneasy when we want to know anything from officials (male) of the Panchayat Samiti. Most of the time they ignored us and wanted to talk male members in lieu of us."
5. In Mirza Gram Panchayat in Tripura, two women members had blamed the government for not devolving

more powers and resources on Panchayat and significantly, this had happened in presence of Government personnel, B.D.O. of Kankraban in South Tripura district in Tripura.

6. Meeting of the Gram Panchayats is not held regularly. In many cases, meeting take place only on paper.
7. The year 2000 was celebrated as the Gram Sabha year. Gram Sabha was sought to be the soul of Panchayat. It consists of all adults (voters) of the village who should collectively discuss their problems and take decision on problems facing the village. It was thought that it would bring accountability and transparency in administration and development apart from enhancing people's participation in various developments programmes in democratic way. And if it does meet, it is mainly to solve social problem or feuds among the villagers. According to Panchayat rule, it meets twice every year. But in most of the Panchayats, it meets once in a year.
8. The constitution of village development group for each village appears to be another attempt to keep on watch the functioning of the Panchayat. The idea behind the group is to check the Panchayat from misutilization of Panchayat funds. However, in many cases, it is seen that Panchayat members succeeded in putting their own man as members in the village development group.
9. A few of women members are irrelevant to the village level responsibilities. A long list of functions appears to have been given to the Panchayat. Further, most of the women Panchayat members have not been imparted any orientation course that can acquaint them with their power and responsibilities. Lack of awareness of powers and functions on the part of the Panchayat members, does come in the way of active participation in the Panchayati Raj affairs and confidence building to shoulder leadership responsibilities.

10. In Panchayat, new act has reserved 1/3rd of the elected position to women in all Panchayati Raj institutions. A few cases, during the election at the Gram Panchayat, photograph of the husband was on the positions of the contesting female candidates along with the candidates herself. Names of the husband and wife were there. The situation should be treated as transitory, because this scenery was seen at the first time of the election.
11. It is seen that nearly half of the women representatives had contested election on their own and all the women Panchayat members received family support. But few of them of the studied sample were faced with family problem after election was over.
12. Initially many women were unwilling entrants in the Gram Panchayat election. But family, party and friends took initiative in inducting them in the Gram Panchayat for them. Many faced the wrath of their families for being late in the family and neglecting the domestic work. Sometimes, of course, interpersonal tension prevails within the family, as women are going out at any time for working outside which creates tension.

Despite the above constraints, it can be said that the upsurge of women's participation is Panchayat in noticeable. Women have started asserting themselves leading to new kind of situation in the society. Reservation of seats has given them an opportunity and has created condition for a sort of social revolution. Things are changing, but slowly. We can say this is still a lack of consensus on the issue of political empowerment of women at par with men. In our society there is a patriarchal value, political as well as social empowerment of women is too much difficult. We observe most of the Panchayat women members are not aware of the Rules and Regulations. Therefore, women Panchayat members sometimes depend on male members for functioning in the Panchayat. But things are fast changing.

At present many of them has delivered lectures in the meeting, participated in house to house election campaigns.

The reservation policy for women has opened a new chapter for the female participation in the Gram Panchayat. Many politicians and Government Personnel are of the view that it would be stepping-stone for women to get into National Politics and their number might increase in subsequent years.

10

Some Observations & Conclusion

During 1993-98 the women's participation in Gram Panchayat has substantially increased but there is no point of being complacent. It was observed that mere reservation would not solve thé problem unless women members are given due power to function effectively. Some steps may be suggested below:

(i) All women panchayat members should be trained by suitable resource persons dealing with Self-government activities. It is necessary for training to be periodic in order to update them to the situation.

(ii) The training should include the philosophy as well as administration of Panchayati Raj, the political and social essence of democracy and the attitude towards the people.

(iii) The training courses should address such general work and programmes, which are specific to women's welfare. Group discussion as well as the classroom work may be necessary.

(iv) Particular attention must be paid to the development of inter-personal communication skills amongst the trainees.

(v) Training programmes should be for small group of persons so that there is sufficient interaction between trainers and trainees.

(vi) Lastly, a system of appreciating the contribution made by women members especially new ones should be introduced in the Gram Panchayat. By this way, they will try to understand the different problems and increase different activities, honestly and effectively.

Women need to learn to cope with stress, combine and organize family-work with office work efficiently. A good women member in Gram Panchayat has to win friends and influence people. It is not enough to do only a good job but make her successes known in a humble manner so that people take her as their own.

Existing difficulties, such as lack of self-confidence, support from the family, society and the stress of outdoor work can be overcome if they cultivate their capabilities and intelligence in a consistent way.

The decentralization of democracy is the essence of self-government. There is scope to strengthen the different tiers of the Panchayati Raj Institutions so that they can function autonomously at their respective levels.

The newly elected representatives cannot be expected to acquire overnight, the capability needed in different fields. Till they achieve such competence, they should be assisted by elderly and experienced Panchayat personals. They should be involved in planning process formulating of rules and regulations in administration. They should also have lesson on legal rights and constitutional provisions.

It may be recommended that there should be separate training programmes for women, at least in the initial stages.

The women's dual responsibilities should be appreciated and shared by male members. The women panchayat members need to work with anganwadi, creche, pre-primary schools etc. so that the quality of life of village women may be improved. These structures should be sustained through community resources. Older women can look after the younger children and in return provided status and honorarium.

Unfortunately, women panchayat members still face male dominance not only in the family but also in the official work. It is often observed that the women Pradhan only is given recognition by the development administration but not other women members.

If women's scope of participation in public work is to be strengthened and sustained, there should be a campaign for women's education on a war footing. This education should include issue rights of women, their legal and constitutional rights, and their responsibilities in social and political life, economic autonomy, among other things. Women's education will enable them to see the society without prejudices. An educated, aware and politically motivated woman can transform the political process and give it a more democratic, realistic and human face.

Women Panchayat Members were also found to encourage other women in joining different training. A group was given vocational training even in masonry work, which at least promoted one woman from a worker to a contractor.

The reservation of seats for women in Gram Panchayat, resulted in a new wave of awareness and empowerment amongst women at the grassroots level. Since 1993, we have seen ample examples of the newly elected first timers among the Women Panchayat Members who were very effective in implementing different schemes of female literacy, rural development, water and land conservation and prohibition etc. It has also been observed that most of the time women were allowed to take decisions in different aspects in the Gram Panchayat functioning. From these it can be said that women proved their capability of sharing political power as ably as the men folks. The need is to empower the women and free them from the clutch of the male domination both socially and politically. They should manage their own affairs and organization without interference from any corner. Their voice should be allowed to be aired.

Conclusion

A crucial indicator of women's empowerment is the extent of women's political participation (UNDP 1995). Political participation occurs in many ways; it includes participation in political mobilization, in the electoral process and in decision-making at different levels in political system.

Political participation plays a significant role in survival of an ongoing political system. Political consciousness and political awareness which brings the sense of interest articulation among the general masses. When the masses are mobilized, the outcome is effective participation of the masses in the affairs of the political system. In this framework the significance of political participation acquires a paramount importance. Political participation implies participation by the various people in the politics of the country. Political participation may imply participation by the non-politicized people as well as political ones. It goes without saying that goals are numerous as there are persons engaged in political participation.

We find that it is difficult to come across the society which is far from politics, whether politics is taken in the good sense or bad sense. Politics, as capture or pursuit of power and public ends, has always characterized all human societies in one way or another to a greater or lesser extent. The need for politicization of the people arises only in those societies where politics of pursuit of power for public ends does not figure prominently. In various societies, non-political factors, such as, economic, religious, cultural etc., may dominate the thinking and activity of the people.

Political participation is a complex phenomenon and essentially an outcome of social, economic, political and psychological preconditions and circumstances. Despite their numerical strength women have the rudimentary position in political process simply because everything is conducive to be so. Mythology, religion, social and cultural taboos, behaviour training, physical mobility restriction, mode of work, provision for reward and punishment all are used to socialize girls to internalize the notion that their activities should be confined only to some preordained and constricted circles. The ingrained discrimination is manifested in personal, political, systematic and structural differentiation between men and women and it is one of the cardinal causes of invisibility of women in politics. In the face of their passable position and inexperience penetration right up to the political decision-making process is certainly one uphill proposition for women members in general.

It is also true that political participation equally depends on a number of preconditions like understanding of process, information of the problems, skilful deliberative skill, dominant position in the party hierarchy in the party based process and more importantly the organizational position or modicum of power a group possesses in a given order. Suffice it to say that women are clearly disadvantaged in all these fronts. Thus women members in panchayat institutions not only should have gestation period but also should require to be emancipated from various structural and situational constraints. The study, nevertheless, has indicated that participation of women in panchayat decision-making process in terms of attendance, opinion expressed, and issue raised in the PR meetings, confidence reposed and satisfaction for effective participation was noteworthy. They were not *meek* or *mute* spectators or ornaments in decision-making process, rather a likely force to reckon with. They maintained contact with villagers, took villager's demand into cognizance and tried to deliver whatever possible for them.

In our study, we find that, most of women members had no previous political exposure and experience. Most of them did not hold any type of political post and even they were not primary members of any parties.

In 1993, after the reservation of seats for women in gram panchayat, they ultimately stood for election and were sponsored by the parties. It is also observed that, at the beginning, local level party leaders searched for required number of women candidates from the inner circle of their family women, because of compulsion of reserved seats. Duverger (1955 : 129) is still convincing arguing that men are the medium between women and political world.

But at present, women have joined various socio-economic and political activities. It is also true that, almost everywhere they are caught in a dilemma of role adjustment. Bias against women is likely to slow down only gradually.

The question is whether women should concentrate only on their exclusive problems. Women's issues like drinking water, health, fuel and fodder, childcare etc. should preoccupy the attention and activities of women members.

Women may have some exclusive problems such as maternity and childcare but all development issues almost equally concern both women and men. Their interests cannot be isolated from the economic, social and political interests of other groups.

But it is observed that women members unanimously asserted that they were not favour of exclusive women's issue, they rather tried to work for collective interests of village also.

Appendices

Appendix I

Female Panchayat Members at a Glance in Our Study Area in Tripura (South and West Tripura Districts)

Sl. No.			*Female*	*Percentage*
1.	Caste/Tribe/Religion	SC	14	48.27
		ST	2	6.89
		OBC	5	17.24
		General	7	24.14
		Muslim	1	3.44
			29	**100**
2.	Economic Class	Landless	22	75.86
		Marginal (<7.5)	7	24.14
		Small (7.5—15)	—	—
			29	**100**
3.	Annual income of the female leader	No Income	22	75.86
		Below 6000	3	10.34
		6001—15000	2	6.89
		15001—25000	1	3.45
		25001—36000	—	—
		36001—55000	1	3.45
		More than 55000	—	—
			29	**100**
4.	Age Group	26—35	7	24.14
		36—50	18	62.07
		51—60	2	6.89
		More than 60	2	6.89
			29	**100**
5.	Household Annual Income	6001—15000	1	3.45
		15001—25000	5	17.24
		25001—36000	9	31.04
		36001—55000	3	10.34
		More than 55000	11	37.93
			29	**100**

(*Contd.*)

(*Contd.*)

Sl. No.			Female	Percentage
6.	Household Annual Expenditure	Below 6000	1	3.45
		6001—15000	1	3.45
		15001—25000	7	24.14
		25001—36000	7	24.14
		36001—55000	3	10.1
		More than 55000	10	34.48
			29	**100**
7.	Family Size	1—2	—	—
		3—4	8	27.55
		5—7	19	65.52
		8—9	1	3.45
		10—11	1	3.45
			29	**100**
8.	Family Type	Nuclear	14	48.28
		Extended	15	51.72
			29	**100**
9.	Education	Upto V	1	3.45
		VI—X	20	68.96
		XI—XII	2	6.9
		Graduate	2	6.9
		Above Graduate	—	—
		Just Literate	4	13.8
			29	**100**
10.	Marital Status	Never married	2	6.9
		Married	26	89.65
		Widow	1	3.45
		Divorced/Separated	—	—
			29	**100**
11.	Adult Male	1	5	17.24
		2	8	27.59
		3	9	31.03
		More than 3	7	24.14
			29	**100**
12.	Adult Female	0	—	—
		1	15	51.72
		2	7	24.14
		3	7	24.14
		More than 3	—	—
			29	**100**
13.	Male Child	0	18	62.07
		1	7	24.14
		2	3	10.34
		3	1	3.45
			29	**100**

(*Contd.*)

(*Contd.*)

Sl. No.			*Female*	*Percentage*
14.	Female Child	0	22	75.86
		1	5	17.24
		2	2	6.9
		3	—	—
			29	**100**
15.	Party Affiliation	C.P.I.(M)	28	96.55
		Congress	—	—
		F.B.	1	3.45
			29	**100**
16.	Affiliation to Mass Front	No Affiliation	—	—
		Krishak Sava	1	3.45
		DYFI	2	6.9
		Women Front	26	89.65
		SC, ST, OBC Front	—	—
		Social Welfare	—	—
		CITU	—	—
		Labour Union	—	—
			29	**100**
17.	Main Earner	Yes	2	6.90
		No	27	93.10
			29	**100**

Appendix II

Male and Female Punchayat Members at a glance in our Study Area in Tripura (South and West Tripura District)

Sl. No.			*Male*	*Female*	*Total*
		Total	*43 (59.72)*	*29(40.28)*	*72 (100.00)*
1.	Caste/Tribe/ Religion	SC	21	14(48.27)	35
		ST	2	2(6.90)	4
		OBC	7	5(17.24)	12
		General	11	7(24.14)	18
		Muslim	2	1(3.45)	3
2.	Economic Class	Landless	30	22(78.86)	52
		Marginal (<7.5)	11	7(24.14)	18
		Small (7.5—15)	2	—	2
3.	Annual Income of the Leader	No. Income	6	22(75.86)	28
		Below 6000	5	3(10.34)	8
		6001—15000	4	2(6.90)	6
		15001—25000	12	1(3.45)	13
		25001—36000	3	—	3
		36001—55000	9	1(3.45)	10
		More than 55000	4	—	4
4.	Age Group	26—35	11	7(24.13)	18
		36—50	20	18(62.07)	38
		51—60	4	2(6.90)	6
		More than 60	8	2(6.90)	10
5.	Household Annual Income	6001—15000	4	1(3.45)	5
		15001—25000	11	5(17.24)	16
		25001—36000	2	9(31.04)	11
		36001—55000	12	3(10.34)	15
		More than 55000	14	11(37.93)	25

(Contd.)

(*Contd.*)

Sl. No.			Male	Female	Total
6.	Household Annual Expenditure	Below 6000	1	1(3.45)	2
		6001—15000	4	1(3.45)	5
		15001—25000	12	7(24.14)	19
		25001—36000	7	7(24.14)	14
		36001—55000	7	3(10.10)	10
		More than 55000	12	10(34.48)	22
7.	Family Size	1—2	1	—	1
		3—4	15	8(27.55)	23
		5—7	22	19(65.52)	41
		8—9	3	1(3.45)	4
		10—11	2	1(3.45)	3
8.	Family Type	Nuclear	19	14(48.28)	33
		Extended	24	15(51.72)	39
9.	Education	Upto V	3	1(3.45)	4
		VI—X	29	20(68.96)	49
		XI—XII	2	2(6.90)	4
		Graduate	4	2(6.90)	4
		Above Graduate	2	—	2
		Just Literate	3	4(13.80)	7
10.	Marital Status	Never married	9	2(6.90)	11
		Married	33	26(89.65)	59
		Widow	—	1(3.45)	1
		Divorced/ Separated	1	—	1
11.	Adult Male	1	10	5(17.24)	15
		2	14	8(27.59)	22
		3	11	9(31.03)	20
		More than 3	8	7(24.14)	15
12.	Adult Female	0	1	—	1
		1	17	15(51.72)	32
		2	20	7(24.14)	27
		3	1	7(24.14)	8
		More than 3	4	—	4
13.	Male Child	0	22	18(62.07)	40
		1	18	7(24.14)	45
		2	2	3(10.34)	5
		3	1	1(3.45)	2
14.	Female Child	0	24	22(75.86)	46
		1	14	5(17.24)	19
		2	3	2(6.90)	5
		3	2	—	2

(*Contd.*)

(Contd.)

Sl. No.			*Male*	*Female*	*Total*
15.	Party Affiliation	C.P.I.(M)	41	28(96.55)	69
		Congress	1	—	1
		F.B.	1	1(3.45)	2
16.	Affiliation to Mass Front	No Affiliation	3	—	3
		Krishak Sava	17	1(3.45)	18
		DYFI	9	2(6.90)	11
		Women Front	1	26(89.65)	27
		SC, ST, OBC Front	3	—	3
		Social Welfare	2	—	2
		CITU	4	—	4
		Labour Union	4	—	4
17.	Main Earner	Yes	33	2(6.90)	35
		No	10	27(93.10)	37

APPENDIX III

Number of All-Women Panchayats at State Level

Sl. No.	*States*	*Numbers*
1.	Tripura	1
2.	West Bengal	4
3.	Madhya Pradesh	7
4.	Maharashtra	13

APPENDIX IV

Women Elected Members in the Panchayat as on 1.1.1996

Sl. No.	States	Gram Panchayats	Panchayat Smitis	Zilla Parishads	Overall Percentage
1.	Gujarat	21351 (64052) [33.3]	1275 (3765) [33.9]	254 (764) [33.2]	33.36
2.	Haryana	17928 (54159) [33.1]	807 (2418) [33.4]	101 (303) [33.3]	33.12
3.	Himachal Pradesh	NA	NA	NA	37.8
4.	Karnataka	27689 (80627) [46.7]	1343 (3340) [40.2]	335 (919) [36.5]	46.38
5.	Kerla	3954 (10685) [37.0]	564 (1543) [36.6]	105 (300) [35.0]	36.9
6.	Madhya Pradesh	184000 (484394) [38.0]	2991 (9097) [32.9]	315(942) [32.4]	37.88
7.	Punjab	23832 (78983) [30.2]	326 (2441) [13.4]	89 (274) [32.6]	29.68
8.	Rajasthan	33566 (103712) [32.4]	1740 (5257) [33.0]	331 (997) [33.1]	32.41
9.	Tripura	1809 (5427) [33.3]	67(196) [34.2]	24 (70) [34.3]	33.37

Bibliography

Ahmed, Imtiaz: "Women in Politics" in Devaki Jain's (ed), *Indian Women*, Chapter 22, New Delhi: Publications Divisions, Ministry of Information and Broadcasting, Government of India, chapter 22, 1975.

Atul Kohli: 'Parliamentary Communism and Agrarian Reform Evidence from India's West Bengal' in *Asian Survey*, 1989.

Bandyopadhyay, D.: 'Fourth General Election of Panchayats in West Bengal' in *Mainstream*, June 26, 1993.

Basab Chattopadhyay and Prantosh Sen: 'Who Controls Rural West Bengal? A Case Study of Gram Panchayat Members of Murshidabad District', in *Socialist Perspective*, Vol. 19, No. 4, 1999.

Basu, A.K.: 'State Panchayat relations in West Bengal' in *Quarterly Journal of the Local Self-government Institute*, 51(14), April-June 1981.

Basu, Aparna: 'The Role of Women in the India Struggle for Freedom', in B.R. Nanda (ed.), *Indian Women: From Purdha to Modernity*, New Delhi, Vikas Publications, 1976.

Basu, Asok: 'Rural Development Strategy in West Bengal', in *Quarterly Journal of the Local Self-government Institute*, 51(4), April-June, 1981.

Baus, Biman: Choukidari Panchayat theke Nirbachita Panchayat (From Choukidari Panchayat to Elected Panchayat) in *Nandan* (In Bengali), August 1995.

Baus, Jyoti: 'Panchayati Raj: Two alternative approaches' in *Yojana*, 33 (1&2), January 26, 1989.

Baus, Kalipada: 'Are the villagers satisfied with Panchayats?' in *Commerce, 156* (4000), January 16-22, 1988.

Beteille, A.: *Caste, Class and Power,* Berkeley: University of California Press, 1966.

Beteille, A.: *Studies in Agrarian Social Structure,* Delhi, Oxford University Press, 1974.

Board of Revenue, Government of West Bengal: *Dynamics of Rural Situation in West Bengal,* 1978.

Cain, Mcad, Sycda Rokeya Khanam and Shamsun Nahar: Class, Patriarchy, and Women's Work in Bangladesh, in *Population and Development Review,* 5 September, pp. 405-438, 1979.

Caldwell, John C.: The Mechanisms of Demography Change in Historical Perspective, in *Population Study,* 35(March): pp. 5-27, 1981.

Chaudhury, R.: 'Patterns of Leadership in a West Bengal Village' in *Economic and Political Weekly,* Vol. 14, 1965.

Cohn, B.S.: *The Changing Status of a Depressed Caste in Village India,* (ed.), Mckim Mariott. Bomleary: Asia Publishing House, 1961.

Conway, M. Magaret *et al.*: The News Media in Children's Political Socialization in *Public Opinion Quarterly*, 45(2) Summer 81, pp. 164-178, 1996.

Dasgupta, Biplab: Gram Banglar Sreni Binyas (Class relation in Bengal) in *Deshhitaishee, Annual Puja Issue,* 1980.

Dasgupta, S.: *Adivasi Politics in Paschim Midnapore in Subaltern Studies* (ed.). R. Guha, Delhi: Oxford University Press, 1985.

Datta, Prabhat: 'The Panchayat Experiment in West Bengal', in *Administrative Change,* Vol. XI, No. 1, July-December 1983.

David C. Schwartz & Sandra Kenyon Schwerty: *New Directions in Political Socialization.* The Free Press, 1975.

David C. Schwartz: *New Directions in Political Socialization.* The Free Press, pp. 335, 1975.

David Ziblati: High School Extra-curricular Activities and Political Socialization, 361, 1965, pp. 30-32. in *The Annals of American Academy of Political and Social Sciences,* pp. 30-32, 1965.

Dennis Jack: *Socialization to Politics,* p. 503, 1973.

Dixon, Ruth B.: *Rural Women at Work: Strategies for Development in South Asia,* Bettomore: John Hopkins University Press, 1978.

Dixon, Ruth. B: 'Women's Rights and Fertility'. *Reports on Population/Family Planning*. No.17 (January), 1975.

Dyson, Tim and Mick Moore: On kinship structure, female autonomy and demographic behaviour in India, in *Population and Development Review,* 9(March), pp. 35-60, 1983.

Easton, David, 1964: *A System Analysis of Political Life*, New York: John Wiley and Sons, 1964.

Franda, M.F.: Intra-regional factionalism and coalition-building in West Bengal, in the *Journal of Common Wealth and Political Studies,* 1970.

Ghosh, B.N. & De, Utpal: "Leadership and the Performances of Panchayat in Rural Development: An Experience from Tripura", in *Man & Development,* pp. 135-148, Vol. XXXV, No. 4, Chandigarh, December, 2003.

Ghosh, Anjali: *Peaceful Transition in Power,* Firma K.L., Calcutta, 1981.

Ghosh, B.N., De Utpal (ed): *Issues on Empowerment of Women,* Mohit Publication, New Delhi, 2004.

Ghosh, B.N., De, Utpal: Women and Development in Rural India, in edited volume on *Dimensions of Rural Development in North-East India,* edited by B. Datta Roy & Gurudas Das, pp. 244-259, Akansha Publishing House, New Delhi, 2003.

Ghosh, B.N.: "Biswayan O Bharatiya Nari" (in Bengali), in *Biswayan, Ganatantra O Tritiya Biswaya,* published by Jadavpur University and Indian Academy of Social Sciences, West Bengal Branch, Vol. 2, pp. 236-248, Kolkata, December, 2001.

Ghosh, B.N.: "Gram Panchayater Karma Kande Mahilader Anshagrayan: Bharate Panchayate Nirbachita Sadasyader Rajyawari Talika", (in Bengali) p. 5, *Tripura Darpan,* Agartala, Tripura, 5th May, 2001.

Ghosh, B.N.: "Panchayat: Gram Banglar Rupantar O Mahilader Anshagrayan", (in Bengali) in *Arthaniti-Rajniti,* pp. 29-32, Third-Fourth issue, Calcutta, July/December, 1999.

Ghosh, B.N.: "Position of Tribal Women in their Society: A few cases". in *Vanyajati,* pp. 4-8, Vol. XLVIII, No. 4, New Delhi, October 2000.

Ghosh, B.N.: "The Way the Santal Women Live", in *Science Courier,* 8th Year, No. 2, pp. 30-32, Calcutta, April-May-June 1997.

Ghosh, B.N.: "Women Leadership in Gram Panchayat: Prospect and Constraints", in *Socialist Perspective,* Vol. 27, No. 1-2, pp. 35-45, Calcutta, June-September 1999.

Ghosh, B.N.: *A note on Panchayati Raj in Tripura in Vanyajati,* pp. 2-10, January, New Delhi, 2006.

Ghosh, B.N.: "Emergence of Rural Leadership: Some Observations", in *Socio-Economic Development in India* (Ed.) B. Roy, Vol. 1, pp. 219-242, Mohit Publications, New Delhi, 2001.

Ghosh, B.N.: Human Resource Development in North Eastern States with special reference to women, in *Education in North East India: Experiment and Challenge,* edited by Bilons Lyndem & Utpal Kumar De, pp. 41-62, Concept Publishing Company, New Delhi, 2004.

Ghosh, B.N.: Paschimbanga Panchayate Mahilader Jogdon: Sakshamatar Pathe, (in Bengali) in *Arthaniti Rajniti,* pp. 20-25, 1st issue, 1999, Calcutta.

Ghosh, B.N.: Pleasure of Fieldwork. Some of our experiences in "*Socialist Perspective*", Vol. 22, No. 3-4, pp. 176-184, Calcutta, 1995.

Ghosh, B.N.: *Rural Leadership & Development,* Mohit Publication, New Delhi, 1996.

Ghosh, B.N.: Social Outlook of the Aspirants for Rural Leadership: Case Study in Gram Panchayat, in *Man and Life,* Vol. 21, No. 3& 4, pp. 155-168, Calcutta, 1995.

Ghosh, B.N.: *Tribal Farmers and New Agricultural Technology,* Akansha Publishing House, New Delhi, 2005.

Ghosh, B.N.: "Women and Development in Rural India" with De, Utpal in edited volume on *Dimensions of Rural Development in North-East India,* edited by B. Datta Ray and Gurudas Das, pp. 244-259, Akansha Publishing House, New Delhi, 2003.

Ghosh, B.N.: "Status and Empowerment of Women vis-à-vis Development and Welfare" in *Issues on Empowerment of Women,* edited by Utpal Kumar De and Bhola Nath Ghosh, pp. 1-16, Mohit Publications, New Delhi, 2004.

Ghosh, B.N.: "Empowerment of Women" with De, Utpal in *Issues on Empowerment of Women,* edited by Utpal Kumar De and Bhola Nath Ghosh, pp. 109-122, Mohit Publications, New Delhi, 2004.

Ghosh, B.N.: Witchcraft: A Critical Approach", in *Dimentions in Indian Anthropology,* Vol. 11, edited by S. Sahay, Pradip Kumar Sahay & Gautam Kumar Bera, pp. 336-343. Serial Publications, New Delhi, 2005.

Ghosh, B.N.: "Process of Empowerment of Women: A Comparative Study of Tripura and Meghalaya" with De, Utpal, in *Women Emancipation: Focus North-East,* edited by Asok Kumar Roy and B. Datta Roy, pp. 265-287, North-east India Council for Social Science Research, Shillong, Om Sons Publications, New Delhi, 2008.

Ghosh, B.N.: "Women in decision making: experiences from two states in north east India", in *Women Empowerment Movements in North-East India,* edited by L.S. Gassah, pp. 198-215, Om Sons Publications, New Delhi, 2008.

Ghosh, B.N.: "Some aspects of gender differences in two states of north east India" in *Women's Speak,* edited by Bhola Nath Ghosh & Subhabrata Dutta, pp. 99-114, Mittal Publications, New Delhi, 2008.

Ghosh, B.N.: "Witch-hunting and status of Tribal women" in *Women's Speak,* edited by Bhola Nath Ghosh & Subhabrata Dutta, pp. 69-88, Mittal Publications, New Delhi, 2008.

Ghosh, B.N.: *Issues on Empowerment of Women,* edited jointly with De, Utpal, Mohit Publications. New Delhi. pp. 407 + XIX, 2004.

Ghosh, B.N.: *Women's Speak,* Edited jointly with Subhabrata Dutta, Mittal Publications, New Delhi, 2008.

Ghosh, B.N.: Women's Participation in Gram Panchayat: State-wise distribution of elected Panchayat members in India, in *Social Transformation in Rural Sector,* (Ed) S.D. Mukhopadhyay & S. Chowdhury, Visva-Bharati, Dept. of Agricultural Extention, pp. 175-179, 2000.

Ghosh, B.N.: Words and Actions: Leadership and Development in the Dusty Rear, in *Welfare, Choice and Development (Essays in Honour of Professor Amartya Sen),*

(Ed) B. Roy, pp. 113-128, Kanishka Publishers, Distributors, New Delhi, 2000.

Ghosh, B.N.: "Role and Status of Santal Women", in *Vanyajati*, Bharatiya Adimjati Sevak Sangh, Vol. XLIII, No. 3, pp. 5-8, New Delhi, 2000.

Ghosh. B.N.: *Rural Women Leadership*, Mohit Publication, New Delhi, 2002.

Greenstein F.I.: Personality and Political Socialization: the Theories of Authoritarian and Democratic Character, in *The Annals of American Academy of Political and Social Sciences*, 361, 1965, p. 295.

Heridwar Singh: *Democratic Orientation of Students in India: A Study of Political Socialization*, Concept Publishing Company. 1983.

Howell Martinez: The Influence of Gender Role on Political Socialization: An Experimental Study of American Children, in *Women & Politics*, pp. 33-46, 1982.

Kaur, Inderjeet: *Status of Hindu Women*, Allahabad: Chugh Publication: 1963.

Khan, Mumtaz Ali: *Status of Rural Women in India*, New Delhi: Utpal Publishing House, 1982.

Kholi, A.: Communist Reforms in West Bengal: Origins, features and relations with New Delhi, in *State Politics in Contemporary India: Crisis and Continuity* (ed.). J.R. Wood, Colorado: West-view Press, 1984.

Liten, G.K.: 'Caste, Gender and Class in Panchayats Case of Burdhaman', in *Economic and Political Weekly*, July 8, 1992.

Liten, G.K.: 'Panchayat Leaders in East Bengal District', in *Economic and Political Weekly*, October 1980.

Lieten, G.K.: 'Panchayat Leaders in West Bengal District', in *Economic and Political Weekly*, October 1, p. 2075, 1988.

Madhura Swaminathan: Village Level Implementation of IRDP: Comparison of West Bengal and Tamil Nadu, in *Economics and Political Weekly*, Vol. XXX, No. 13, pp. 17-27, 1992.

Mishra, S.N.: *Political Socialization in Rural India*, Inter-India Publications, p.153, 1980.

Mukherjee, Apratim: 'West Bengal: Marxist Panchayat?' in *Hindustan Times,* August 14, 1979.

Mukherjee, N. and Bandyopadhyay, D.: *New Horizons for West Bengal's Panchayats: A Report for the Government of West Bengal,* 1993.

Mukherjee, Subrata Kumar: 'Panchayat in West Bengal' in *Mainstream,* 27(44), July 29, 1989.

Mukhopadhyay, Rajat Subhra: 'Resource Distribution and Power Structure: A Case Study of a West Bengal Village' in *Eastern Anthropologist,* Vol. 35, No. 1, 1985.

Nanda, B.R.: *Indian Women: From Purdha to Modernity.* New Delhi: Vikas Publications: 1976.

Neil Webster: *Panchayati Raj and Decentralization of Development Planning in West Bengal,* Calcutta, K.P. Bagchi, p. 131, 1992.

Nicholas, R.: 'Factions: a comparative analysis', in *Political System and the Distribution of Power.* (ASA2), (ED.), M. Banton, London: Tavistock Publication. 1965.

Nicholas, R.: 'Rules, Resources and Political Activity', in *Local Level Politics* (ed.). M.J. Swartz, London: University of London Press, 1969.

Nicholas, R.: 'Village Factions and Political Parties in Rural West Bengal', in *Journal of Common Wealth Political Studies.* 2: 17-32, 1963.

Orenstein, H.: *Gaon: Conflict and Cohesion in an Indian Village.* New Jersey: Princeton University Press, 1965.

Prewitt Kenneth: Political Socialization and Leadership Selection, in *The Annals of American Academy of Political and Social Sciences,* 361. pp. 96-111, 1965.

Prodosh Nath: 'Panchayat and Rural Development' in *Society and Change,* October-December 1982.

Rama Reddy, G. (Ed): *Patterns of Panchayati Raj in India.* Madras: Macmillan Company of India. 1977.

Rao, N.J. Usha: *Women in Developing Society,* New Delhi: Ashis Publications, 1983.

Ray, R. and Rattan Ray: 'Zamindars and Jotdars: A Study of Rural Politics in Bengal. *Modern Asian Studies,* 9, 81-102. 1975.

Safilos-Rothschild, Constantine: Female Power, Autonomy and Demographic change in the Third World, in R. Anker, M. Buvinic and N.H. Youssef, (eds.) *Women's Roles and Population Trends in the Third World,* pp. 117-132 London: Crom Helm, 1982.

Sengupta, Sunil: 'West Bengal Rural Scene: A Review;' in *Science and People,* August 1989.

Swaminathan, M.: Village level implementation of IRDP: Comparison of West Bengal and Tamil Nadu, in *Economic and Political Weekly,* 25:13.

Tripura Human Development Report, 2007.

Webster, Neil: Panchayati Raj in West Bengal: Popular Participation for the People or the Party? in *Development and Change* 23(4), 1992.

Westergaard Kirsten: *People's Participation, Local Government and Rural Development in West Bengal.* Centre for Development Research, 1986.

Index